THE

SACRED CITY OF THE HINDUS

Owing to the antiquity and rarity of this book, certain pages are regrettably absent, and readability is compromised due to the blurring of the original text. If you possess any insights regarding the availability of these missing sections, kindly inform us. Your assistance is crucial in ensuring the completion of this significant work for the benefit of future generations.

THE

SACRED CITY OF THE HINDUS

AN ACCOUNT OF BENARES

IN

ANCIENT AND MODERN TIMES.

BY THE

REV. M. A. SHERRING,

M.A., LL.B., LOND.

GYAN

Published by

GYAN

Gyan Publishing House
5, Ansari Road
Daryaganj, New Delhi-110002
Phone: 011-47034999, 9811692060
E-mail: books@gyanbooks.com

Distribution Network
gyanbooks.com
India, USA, Canada, UK, Australia

ISBN: 978-93-6208-226-8 (HB)
First Published, 1868

2nd Impression 2024

Printed at: Gyan Press, Delhi.

THE SACRED CITY OF THE HINDUS
Author: M. A. SHERRING

THE SACRED CITY OF THE HINDUS.

Photographed by D. Tresham, Esq.

RAJA OF AHMETY'S TEMPLE.

THE

SACRED CITY OF THE HINDUS:

AN ACCOUNT OF BENARES

IN

ANCIENT AND MODERN TIMES.

BY THE

REV. M. A. SHERRING,

M.A., LL.B., Lond.,

MISSIONARY OF THE LONDON MISSIONARY SOCIETY; AUTHOR OF THE "THE INDIAN CHURCH DURING THE REBELLION," "INVESTIGATION OF THE CAUSES OF THE INDIAN MUTINY," ETC.

WITH AN

INTRODUCTION

BY

FITZEDWARD HALL, ESQ.,

M.A., D.C.L. OXON.

1868.

PREFACE.

The history of a country is sometimes epitomized in the history of one of its principal cities. The city of Benares represents India, religiously and intellectually, just as Paris represents the political sentiments of France. There are few cities in the world of greater antiquity, and none that have so uninterruptedly maintained their ancient celebrity and distinction. In Benares, Buddhism was first promulgated; in Benares, Hinduism has had her home in the bosom of her most impassioned votaries. This city, therefore, has given impulse and vigour to the two religions which to this day govern half the world.

An account of a city of such remarkable associations, which has occupied such a prominent place in the annals of the human race, is not without its importance, and ought not to be devoid of interest. Having resided in it for several years, I have enjoyed peculiarly favourable opportunities for becoming acquainted with its inner life and character. The task I have set myself is not that of discussing the religious systems existing there,—which would be an unnecessary undertaking, it having been so frequently accomplished by abler hands,—but of giving a representation of Benares as she was in the past, and as she is in the present. Her early condition—her connexion with ancient Buddhism—her architectural remains—her famous temples, holy wells and tanks, and numerous ghâts or stairs leading down to the Ganges—the legends concerning them—the peculiar customs at the temples—the ceremonies of the idolater—the modes of worship—the religious festivals, and other topics, illustrative of the character which Benares maintains as the sacred city of India, are dwelt upon, with some amount of detail, in this volume. I have deemed it of moment, also, in a book of this nature, to make some observations on the influence which education, European civilization, and, above all, Christianity, are now exerting upon the city. As Benares has held a foremost place in the history of India for two thousand five hundred years, at the least, so, in all likelihood, she is destined to retain that position in the new era of enlightenment which has already dawned upon the land.

Portions of this work have, at various times, appeared in print, in contributions to the Calcutta Review and the Journal of the Asiatic Society of Bengal, and in a

Lecture delivered before the Benares Institute, published in the Transactions of that Society.

I would express my warmest thanks to CHARLES HORNE, Esq., C.S., late Judge of Benares, for his very valuable assistance in the archæological researches described in this book, especially in Chapters xix. and xx. My thanks are also due to J. H. B. IRONSIDE, Esq., C.B., Magistrate of Benares, for his kindness in placing at my disposal a paper on the *Melas* or Festivals of Benares, drawn up by Babu Sítal Prasád, Deputy Inspector of Schools. I would likewise acknowledge my great obligations to D. TRESHAM, Esq., Head Master of the Government Normal School, Benares, for his excellent photographs of the city, from which the illustrations of this volume have been taken.

M. A. SHERRING.

July 2nd, 1868.

CONTENTS.

Preface v
Introduction—By FITZEDWARD HALL, Esq., D.C.L. xvii

CHAPTER I.

Early history of Benares.—Sanctity of the city.—Mythic character of Indian history.—Ancient Buddhist records respecting Benares.—Śákya Muni, or Buddha, preached the doctrine of Buddhism first in Benares.—Antiquity of Benares.—Hiouen Thsang's account of his visit to the city in the seventh century of the Christian era.—Macaulay's description of Benares.—Connexion of Benares with the religious history of half the human race.—Its connexion with Buddhism.—Life and labours of Buddha.—Benares subsequent to the fall of Buddhism in India.—The Brahman.—Sons of the Ganges.—Devotees and pilgrims.—Benares, the religious centre of India 1

CHAPTER II.

No Architectural remains dating prior to the third century before Christ yet found in India.—Ancient Hindu Edifices of the primitive period, not of a rude character.—Did the Hindus borrow from the Assyrian and Persian Sculptors?—Ancient remains found chiefly in the northern quarter of the city.—Mohammedan lust for Hindu edifices.—Shifting tendency of the modern city.—Origin of the appellation "Benares." 19

CHAPTER III.

Puranic form of Modern Hinduism.—Increase of Temples in Northern India.—Number of Temples in Benares.—Temple of Bisheśwar, the idol-king of Benares.—Ancient Temple of

Bisheśwar, now a Mohammedan Mosque.—The Well Gyán Bápí.—Temple of A'd-Bisheśwar.—The Well Káśí Karwaṭ.—Temple of Saníchar.—The goddess Annpúrṇá and her temple.—Temples of Gaṇeś and S'ukreśwar 37

CHAPTER IV.

Temple of Bhaironáth, the god-magistrate of Benares.—Daṇḍpán, or the Deified Staff.—Temple of the Planet.—Kál-kúp, or Well of Fate.—Image of Mahákál, or Great Fate.—The Maṇikarṇiká Well and Ghát.—Legends respecting the Well.—Temple of Tárakeśwar.—Sindhia Ghát, and the Raja of Nagpore's Ghát.—Temple of Bṛiddhkál.—Shrines of Márkaṇḍeśwar and Daksheśwar. — Legend of Raja Daksh. — Temples of Alpmṛiteśwar and Ratneśwar 61

CHAPTER V.

Legend respecting Divodás. — Temple of Divodáseśwar. — The Well Dharm-kúp.—Rádhá-Kṛishṇa.—The Nág-Kúáṅ, or Serpent's Well.—Old Images.—Temples of Bágeśwarí, Jwarahareśwar, and Siddheśwar 82

CHAPTER VI.

Benares, Káśí, and Kedár, the three Grand Divisions of the city.—No old Hindu Temples in Benares.—Puranic character of the Káśí Division of the City.—No trustworthy information concerning Ancient Buildings to be obtained either from Hindus or from their sacred writings.—Preference of the Old Fanes by Pilgrims.—Trilochan Temple.—Legends respecting Trilochan.—The Idolater's idea of the benefit resulting from Worshipping in this Temple.—Koṭ Lingeśwar.—Nának Sháh, the Sikh Guru.—Painting in the Trilochan Temple, depicting the Punishments of Hell.—Trilochan Ghát.—Gáe Ghát.—Temples of Nirbuddheśwar and A'd Mahádeva.—Gor Jí, the Gujarati Brahman. . 93

CHAPTER VII.

Panchgangá Ghát.—Legends respecting it.—Lakshmaṇbálá Temple.—The Minarets.—Temple of Kámeśwar.—The Machaudarí Tírth or Place of Pilgrimage 107

CHAPTER VIII.

Temple of Jágeśwar, a Resort of the Native Aristocracy of Benares.—Káśí-Deví, Goddess of the City of Benares.—Karṇghaṇṭa Táláo or Tank.—Temple of the Demon Bhút-Bhairo.—Temple of Bará Gaṇeś.—Jagannáth.—Satís 116

CHAPTER IX.

The Piśách-Mochan Tank.—Legend of the Goblin Piśách.—The Festival of Loṭá-Bhaṇṭa, or the Egg-plant.—The Gháts and Temple of Piśách-Mochan.—Súraj-Kuṇḍ or Tank of the Sun.—The Hom or Burnt Sacrifice.—The god Ashṭáng-Bhairo.—Temple of Dhruveśwar or the Pole Star 123

CHAPTER X.

The Mán-Mandil Ghát.—Temple of Dálbhyeśwar.—Temple of the Moon or Someśwar.—The Mán-Mandil Observatory, erected by Raja Jay Sinh.—Description of its Instruments.—The Nepalese Temple 129

CHAPTER XI.

Daśáśamedh Ghát and Temple.—Legend of Daśáśamedh.—Siddheśwarí Temple.—Chandra Kúp, or Well of the Moon.—Temple of the goddess S'ankaṭá Deví.—S'ankaṭá Ghát.—Rám Ghát 139

CHAPTER XII.

The Bengali population of Benares.—The popular Temple of Kedáreśwar.—Legend of Kedár.—Mánsarwar Tank and surrounding Temples.—Bál-Kṛishṇa and Chaturbhuj Idols.—Máneśwar Temple.—The great Image of Tilubhaṇḍeśwar.—Ancient mutilated Statue.—Temple of Duláreśwar.—Peepul tree at Chaukí Ghát.—Swinging gods 146

CHAPTER XIII.

Durgá Kuṇḍ Temple.—Bloody Sacrifices; their meaning.—Sacred Monkeys.—Legend of Durg and Durgá.—Durgá Kuṇḍ or Tank.—Kurukshetr Táláo or Tank.—The Lolárik Kúáṅ or Well.—Ancient Sculptures 157

CHAPTER XIV.

Temple of the Maharaja of Benares at Rámnagar.—Raja Cheit Singh's Tank.—Virtue of Pilgrimage to the Rámnagar side of Benares.—Temple of Vedavyás.—Panch-kosí Road, or Sacred Boundary of Benares.—Pilgrimage of the Panch-kosí.—Sanitary condition of Benares.—Improvements suggested . . 169

CHAPTER XV.

Barna Sangam, or Confluence of the Barna and Ganges.—A'd-keśav Temple.—Barna Ghát.—Ráj Ghat Fort; its use in 1857.—Remains of Buddhist Monastery.—Tank of Bhairo.—Láṭ or Pillar of S'iva.—Ancient Pillar.—Account of Disturbance in Benares when the Pillar was thrown down.—The Ghazeepore Road.—Ancient Bridge over the Barna 184

CHAPTER XVI.

S'ivála Ghát.—The Old Fort.—Raja Cheit Singh; History of his Insurrection and of the proceedings of Warren Hastings in connexion therewith 197

CHAPTER XVII.

Hindu and Mohammedan Melás or Religious Festivals, held periodically, in Benares 213

CHAPTER XVIII.

The Buddhist Ruins at Sárnáth—Their Antiquity.—Summary of the Narratives of Fa Hian and Hiouen Thsang, respecting the buildings formerly existing at Sárnáth and in its neighbourhood.—Points of agreement in the Narratives.—Modern Explorers of the Ruins.—Extent and Nature of the Remains.—The Great Tower: Description of it by Major-General Cunningham, and account of his Excavations.—Age of Buddhist Topes or Towers.—Remains of a Buddhist Monastery—Mr. Thomas's Account of them.—Discovery of large numbers of Statues and Bass-reliefs.—Excavated Chamber.—Foundation of an Ancient Tower—Major-General Cunningham's Description of it.—The Chaukandí Tower.—The I'śipattana Hall, or abode of Buddhist Devotees.—Remains of Vihára or Temple-monastery.—Small Building, containing Sixty Sculptures.—The Seal Chaityas.—The Buddhist Formula.—Śákya Muni, the historical Buddha—His visit to Benares.—Spread of Buddhism from Benares.—Decline of Buddhism in India.—Destruction of Buddhist Structures at Sárnáth, by fire.—Fall of Buddhism 230

CHAPTER XIX.

Ancient Buddhist Ruins at Bakaríyá Kuṇḍ.—Remains of old Wall.—Carved Stones and Ancient Pillars.—Remains of small Buddhist Temple.—Remains of larger Temple.—Traces of Buddhist Monastery 271

CHAPTER XX.

Further Account of Ancient Remains recently discovered in Benares and its vicinity.—Meaning of the epithets 'ancient' and 'old' in relation to Benares.—Ancient Remains, No. I., in Ráj Ghát Fort.—Ancient Remains, No. II., near Ráj Ghát Fort.—Ancient Remains, No. III., Small Mosque in the Budáoṅ Mahalla.—Ancient Mound or Ridge.—Ancient Remains, No. IV., Tiliyá Nálá and Maqdam Sáhib.—Ancient Remains, No. V., Láṭ Bhairo.—Ancient Remains, No. VI., Battís Khambhá.—Ancient Remains, No. VII., Arhái Kangura Mosque; Hindu Temple of Kírtti Bisheśwar.—Ancient Remains, No. VIII., Chaukhambhá Mosque.—Ancient Remains, No. IX., Aurungzeb's Mosque, near Bisheśwar Temple.—Ancient Remains, No. X., Ád-Bisheśwar Temple and neighbouring Mosque.—Ancient Remains, No. XI., Stone Pillar standing in Sone ká Táláo.—Note 288

CHAPTER XXI.

Source of the great wealth of Benares—Its chief Articles of Commerce—Its Native Bankers—Its Poor—Increased desire for Education.—The Government or Queen's College.—Monolith in the College Grounds.—The Normal School.—The Church of England Mission.—The London Society's Mission.—The Baptist Society's Mission.—Native Schools of various classes.—The Benares Institute.—Public Buildings in the suburbs.—Monument to Mr. Cherry.—Influential Native Gentlemen of Benares. 328

CHAPTER XXII.

Sentiments engendered by the contemplation of the city of Benares—Its history, the history of India.—Principles of progress at work in the city.—Changes visible in native society.—The Brahmo Samáj.—Diminished study of Sanskrit. —Diminished faith in Idolatry in Benares and Northern India generally.—Influence of education on Hindu youths.—A Martin Luther for India.—Influence and spread of Christianity.—Gungá-putras, or sons of the Ganges.—Literary and Religious Societies amongst the natives.—The Benares Institute—Nature of its discussions.—Lecture of Pandit Lakshmají—His account of the consequences of Hinduism.—Effect of Missions and Education on Benares and on India.—Religious agitation in India.—What is the destiny of Idolatry and of Christianity in India?—The Future in respect of Benares.—Remarks of the Rev. Dr. Thomson, a Bishop of the Methodist Episcopal Church of the United States, on the religious and social condition and future prospects of India 341

APPENDIX A.

Narrative of Fă Hian, concerning his visit to Benares and Sárnáth. Extracted from the Foĕ Kouĕ Ki by MM. Rémusat, Klaproth, and Landresse 364

APPENDIX B.

Narrative of Hiouen Thsang. Translated by the author from the "Mémoires sur les Contrées Occidentales de Hiouen Thsang," of M. Stanislas Julien, translator of the original Chinese work 366

APPENDIX C.

Further information concerning Divodás 381

Index 382

LIST OF ILLUSTRATIONS.

	PAGE
Raja of Ahmety's Temple	Frontispiece
Temple at Maṇikarṇiká Ghát	70
Raja of Nagpore's Ghát	72
The Minarets	110
The Nepalese Temple	137
Rám Ghát	145
Great Buddhist Tower at Sárnáth	236
Carving on the Buddhist Tower, No. I.	240
,, ,, ,, No. II.	241
Ancient Buddhist Temple at Bakaríyá Kuṇḍ	283

INTRODUCTION.

Alike as to limits and as to influence, the Indian kingdoms of former times were, with few exceptions, inconsiderable; such of them as lay conterminous were often at open feud; and their cities, or fortified towns, constituted, in fact, their only stable boundaries. It was, probably, with the dominion of the Kâśis as it was with other seats of Hindu power. Deriving its origin from some city, as Pratishṭhâna,[1] or Vârâṇasî,[2] it must have acquired extent and consideration by very gradual development.

At least since a hundred and twenty years before our era, Vârâṇasî, as denoting a city, has been a name

[1] *Vide infra*, p. xxv., note 1.

[2] Also called Varâṇasî and Varaṇasî, according to the *Haima-kośa* and the *Śabdaratnâvalî*, respectively. The latter of these vocabularies is of small authority.

A rational system of Romanized spelling would give us, instead of Benares, Banâras. The form बनारस was the work, perhaps, of the Muhammadans. It should appear that the metathesis of *r* and *ṇ*, in the original word, must be later than the times of Fă Hian and Hiouen Thsang. *Vide infra*, p. xxviii., notes 1 and 2.

In the ordinary belief of the vulgar of Benares, the name of their city is connected with Raja Banâr,—a mythical magnate, of whom mention is associated with that of the reformer Kabîr, of the beginning of the fifteenth century. *Asiatic Researches*, Vol. XVI., p. 57. "According to some of the Muhammadan accounts," says Mr. James familiar to Brahmanical literature.[1] The word is crudely referred, by modern inventiveness, to a combination of Varaṇâ and Asi;[2] and all the other explanations that we have of its source are equally questionable.

Prinsep, but without naming his voucher for the statement, Benares "was governed by a Raja Banâr, at the time of one of Mahmûd's invasions, or in A.D. 1017, when one of his generals penetrated to the province, and defeated the Raja."—*Benares Illustrated*, p. 9. General Cunningham states that Raja Banâr is traditionally believed to have rebuilt Benares about eight hundred years ago. *Journal of the Asiatic Society of Bengal*, for 1863, Supplementary Number, p. xcvi.

[1] Vârâṇasî is specified more than once in Patanjali's *Mahábháshya*. On the age of that work, see my edition of Professor Wilson's translation of the *Vishṇu-purâṇa*, Vol. II., p. 189, *ad calcem*.

[2] So allege the Pandits of the present day; repeating, no doubt, a long-current conceit of their predecessors: see the *Asiatic Researches*, Vol. III., pp. 409, 410. This notion, though it has found expression in the *Araish-i-mahfil* and other recent Muhammadan books, is, I believe, only implied in the Purâṇas. It is said, for instance, in the third chapter of the *Vâmana-purâṇa*, that Vârâṇasî lies between the Varaṇâ and the Asi:

हरिरुवाच ।

महेश्वर शृणुष्वेमां मम वाचं कलस्वनाम् ।
ब्रह्महत्याक्षयकरीं शुभदां पुण्यवर्धिनीम् ॥
योऽसौ ब्रह्माण्डके पुण्ये मदंशप्रभवोऽव्ययः ।
प्रयागे वसते नित्यं योगशायीति विश्रुतः ॥
चरणाद्दक्षिणात्तस्य विनिर्गता सरिद्वरा ।
विश्रुता वरणेत्येव सर्वपापहरा शुभा ॥
सव्यादन्या द्वितीया च असिरित्येव विश्रुता ।
ते उभे च सरिच्छ्रेष्ठे लोकपूज्ये बभूवतुः ॥
तयोर्मध्ये तु यो देशस्तत्क्षेत्रं योगशायिनः ।
त्रैलोक्यप्रवरतीर्थं सर्वपापप्रमोचनम् ॥
न तादृशं हि गगने न भूम्यां न रसातले ।
तत्रास्ति नगरी पुण्या ख्याता वाराणसी शुभा ॥
यस्यां हि भोगिनो नाशं प्रयान्ति भवतो लयम् ॥

Convertible, in later usage, with Vârâṇasî is the de-

There is a statement to the like effect in a section of the *Padma-purâṇa*, the *Kâśî-mâhâtmya*, V., 58:

वाराणसीति यत्ख्यातं तन्मानं निगदामि वः ।
दक्षिणोत्तरयोर्नद्यौ वरणासिश्च पूर्वतः ॥

The same idea occurs more than once in a putative appendage to the *Skanda-purâṇa*, the *Kâśî-khaṇḍa*. It will suffice to quote XXX., 20, 21:

दक्षिणोत्तरदिग्भागे कृत्वासिं वरणां सुराः ॥
क्षेत्रस्य मोक्षनिक्षेपरक्षारिवृतिमाययुः ।

Particular reference may, also, be made to stanzas 69 and 70 of the same chapter; and similar passages might be extracted from other Purâṇas.

The Asi—now known as the Asî, and still trickling during the rainy season, despite Father Vivien de Saint-Martin's scepticism as to its existence,—has a niche in the *Haima-kośa*, a work of the twelfth century. The Varuṇâ (*sic*) and Asî are named in the Calcutta edition of the *Mahâbhârata, Bhîshma-parvan, śl.* 338. But, in my annotations on the English translation of the *Vishṇu-purâṇa*, Vol. II., p. 152, it is surmised that this stanza is an interpolation; and it may be added that is omitted from the text of the *Mahâbhârata* as accepted by the commentator Nîlakaṇṭha; while the scholiast Arjunamiśra reads, at least in my manuscript, Charuṇâ and Asi.

Dr. Schwanbeck—*Megasthenis Indica*, p. 36, note,—is reminded, by Arrian's Ἐρέννεσις, of Varâṇasî. Hereupon, Professor Lassen—*Indische Alterthumskunde*, Vol. I., Appendix, p. LIV.,—precipitately took the two for one; and he still holds to this opinion; for, in the second edition of his great work, Vol. I., p. 161, note 1, (1867), he writes: "Des Megasthenes Erennesis ist die vereinigte Varâṇasî." This "conjunct Varâṇasî"—or, rather, what he unwarrantably calls its modern name, Barâṇaśî,—he compounds, incautiously, after Mr. Walter Hamilton, of two unknown streams, the Varâ and the Naśî.

The *Jâbâla-upanishad* places Avimukta—which is a Paurâṇik title of Benares,—between the Varaṇâ and the Nâśî or Nâsî; and the commentator, Śankarânanda, disciple of Ânandâtman, etymologizes the words. An anonymous expositor of the same Upanishad, whose work I consulted in India, reads *varaṇâ* and *asî*, explains them by *pingalâ* and *iḍâ*, and makes the result of their conjunction, *vârâṇasî*, in some acceptation or other, to be equivalent to *sushumṇâ*. One need not stop to expatiate on such trifling.

signation Kâśi[1] or Kâśî.[2] Whence it arose history has

Something of the same sort is to be seen in the fifth chapter of the *Káśí-khaṇḍa.*

Father Vivien de Saint-Martin—the genesis of whose fictitious river I trace in note 2 to p. xxviii.,—began with being disposed to make the Asî an affluent to the Varâṇâ, with a Varâṇasî below their confluence, and the city Varâṇasî therefrom denominated. *Mémoires sur les Contrées Occidentales,* Vol. II., p. 361. Here "il serait très-possible que l'un de ces ruisseaux se fût nommé Asî, et qu'après sa réunion à la Varâṇâ, la petite rivière eût pris le nom composé de Varâṇasî qu'elle aurait communiqué à la ville." This, as speculation, will pass; but, to this writer, with his bias in favour of the theological or mythopeic method of geographizing, what are, at first, only suggestions, very soon ripen into indubitable certainties: "Cette rivière [the 'Ερέννεσις], la dernière de la liste d'Arrien, se reconnaît sans difficulté dans la Varânasî, petite rivière qui se jette dans la gauche du Gange à Bénarès, qui en a pris son nom (en sanscrit Vârânâsî)." *Etude sur la Géographie Grecque et Latine de l'Inde,* p. 286.

This author more than inclines to see Vârânâsî in the words Erarasa (or Cragausa) metropolis, foisted into the Latin translation of Ptolemy. *Ibid.,* pp. 227, 351. Here, very much as just above, having to do with a Latin interpolation, he sets out with describing it as such, and as offering "un reste de ressemblance qu'on entrevoit encore à travers la corruption du mot;" and, a little while afterwards, as if process of time necessarily stood for an accession of facts and reasons, persuades himself that he may speak of "une ville que Ptolémée énumère sous le nom altéré d' Erarasa," and that he finds, therein, "la trace bien reconnaissable de Vârânâsî, forme sanscrite de notre Bénarès."

I have everywhere scrupulously reproduced the varieties of spelling indulged in by the writer just cited.

The final *á* and the initial *a* of two words coalescing into a compound might, possibly, yield *a*; and Varaṇâ and Asî would, therefore, combine into Varaṇasî. But this form seems to be the peculiar property of a single recent and very indifferent lexicographer; and, moreover, the name of the second stream is, correctly, Asi, not Asî. In the *Káśí-khaṇḍa,* XXX., 18, it is the subject of a pun, in connexion with *asi,* "a sword."

[1] This is the oldest form, and that recognized in the *Haima-kośa* and by Ujjwaladatta's commentary on the *Uṇṇádi-sûtra.*

[2] Kâśi is not so markedly feminine as the more usual Kâśî, its derivative. Most Indian cities have feminine appellations.

long forgotten;[1] but conjecture may, possibly, unravel its etymology.[2]

Among the descendants of Âyus[3] was Kâśa, whose son is noticed under the patronyms[4] of Kâśeya,[5] Kâśîya,[6] and Kâśi.[7] The regal successors of Kâśi, and

---

Kâśikâ is found in the *Kâśî-khaṇḍa,* XXX., 70, and elsewhere. Compare Avantikâ for Avantî, as in note 1 to p. xxxiii., *infra.*

[1] The vocabularists refer the word to *kâś,* "to shine." And herewith agrees the *Kâśî-khaṇḍa,* XXVI., 67:

काशते च यतो ज्योतिस्तदनाख्येयमीश्वर ।
अतो नामापरं चास्तु काशीति प्रथितं विभो ॥

In the stanza immediately preceding this, the city is called Muktikshetra. Kṛishṇa is speaking; and he says that the radiance of Kâśî emanates from S'iva.

If, where they interpret Kâśî by "splendid," Colonel Wilford and his numerous followers intend to take the word from the adjective *kâśin,* they have forgotten that the feminine is not *kâśî,* but *kâśinî.* See the *Asiatic Researches,* Vol. III., p. 409.

[2] Professor Wilson has already written: "It seems probable that the city [of Kâśî] was founded, not by him [Kshattravṛiddha], but by his grandson or great-grandson, denominated Kâśa and Kâśirâja." Mr. James Prinsep's *Benares Illustrated,* p. 8. It is meant, here, I suppose, to hint a derivative connexion of Kâśî with Kâśa or Kâśirâja. The latter name Professor Wilson everywhere puts, erroneously, for "King Kâśi." See note 7 in the present page.

[3] See the English *Vishṇu-purâṇa,* Vol. IV., pp. 30-32.

[4] Compare Mâṇḍûkeya, from Mâṇḍûka; and S'wâphalki, from S'waphalka.

[5] So reads the *Harivaṁśa, śl.* 1734, in the best MSS. accessible to me.

[6] *Gaṇa* on Pâṇini, IV., II., 90; and the *Brahma-purâṇa.*

[7] *Bhâgavata-purâṇa,* IX., XVII., 4. In the *Vishṇu-purâṇa,* he is called *Kâśirâja;* but the term, a compound, is there to be explained "Raja Kâśi." Differently, *Kâśirâja, Kâśipati,* etc., descriptive of Ajâtaśatru, Divodâsa, Pratardana, and others, signify "Raja of the Kâśis." That काशिराजः may be the same as काशिषु नृपः is clear from the *Mahâbhârata, Anuśâsana-parvan, śl.* 1949 and 1952.

equally their subjects, were called Kâśis.[1] Though at first a masculine appellation, Kâśi, as applied to the city so styled, is feminine.[2] An exact parallel to this hypothetical evolution is not far to seek. The name of King Champa, femininized, became that of the metropolis of Anga, Champâ.[3]

The term Kâśi, denominating, if not a city,[4] a people

[1] Kâśi's successors were likewise known as Kâśyas and as Kâśikas. These terms are, all, actually employed. The last is, also, applied to persons or things pertaining to Kâśi.

[2] Kuntî, a woman, was so called from Kunti, a man.

Kâśî, according to the *Vishṇu-purâṇa*,—see the English translation, Vol. IV., p. 159,—was the name of the wife of Bhîmasena. The reading is, however, erroneous, most probably. I find, as a variant, Kâśeyî. This, like the corresponding Kâśyâ of the *Mahâbhârata*, *Âdi-parvan*, *śl.* 3829, is a derivative of Kâśi.

[3] See the English *Vishṇu-purâṇa*, Vol. IV., p. 125.

I am not unaware of the *gaṇa* on Pâṇini, IV., II., 82.

[4] "In the *Mahâbhârata*, frequent mention of Kâśî occurs," according to Professor Wilson, as quoted in *Benares Illustrated*, p. 8. I should be much surprised to find Kâśî mentioned even once in the *Mahâbhârata*.

Not till medieval times, it seems, do we read of the city of Kâśî. To the authority, on this behalf, of the Purâṇas may be added that of an inscription which I have deciphered and published in the *Journal of the Asiatic Society of Bengal*, for 1862, pp. 14, 15. The document in question, a land-grant, was issued by Vinâyakapâla, Raja of Mahodaya or Kanauj, about the middle of the eleventh century, it may be. Kâśî is there indirectly described as in the *vishaya* of Vârâṇasî, in the *bhukti* of Pratishṭhâna. For Pratishṭhâna, *vide infra*, p. xxv., note 1.

It is, in my judgment, very doubtful indeed that Ptolemy's *Κασσίδα* metamorphoses Kâśi, as has been confidently asserted by Colonel Wilford and very many others. See the *Asiatic Researches*, Vol. III., p. 410; Vol. IX., p. 73.

Fă Hian may have intended to reproduce *Kâśirâjya*, "kingdom of the Kâśis," in his words rendered by "le royaume de *Kia chi*." *Vide infra*, p. xxviii., note 1.

and its chieftains, occurs repeatedly in Sanskrit works of all but the highest antiquity.[1] Of Kâśi, in whatever sense of the word, we cannot, however, collect, from indigenous records, materials from which to con-

The expression काशिपुरीं वाराणसीं, in the *Daśa-kumâra-charita*, means "Vârâṇasî, a city of the Kâśis." In the subjoined verse, from the *Râmâyaṇa*, *Uttara-kâṇḍa*, XXXVIII., VI., 17, Vârâṇasî is qualified by an expression meaning, the commentator says, "a city in the country of the Kâśis:"

तद्भवानद्य काशेयपुरीं वाराणसीं व्रज।

Finally, in the *Mahâbhârata*, *Âdi-parvan*, *śl.* 4083, 4084, we read of the king of the Kâśis as dwelling in the city of Vârâṇasî.

[1] The oldest among them, probably, is Pâṇini, IV., II., 116; with which compare IV., II., 113. Then come the *Śatapatha-brâhmaṇa*, the *Bṛihad-âraṇyaka* and *Kaushîtaki-brâhmaṇa Upanishads*, etc., etc. In some of these works, the substantive is involved in the adjective Kâśya. This word, like Kâśika,—for which see the *Mahâbhârata*, *Udyoga-parvan*, *śl.* 5907,—means, etymologically, Káśian. But commentators on old writings explain it, and rightly, to signify "king of the Kâśis." Kâśirâja and Kâśya are used of the same person in the *Bhagavad-gîtâ*, I., 5, 17.

The *Ṛigveda* affords no warrant for connecting with the Kâśis any person whom it mentions. It speaks of Divodâsa, and it speaks of Pratardana; but only in later literature are they called father and son, and rulers of the Kâśis; and, where Kâtyâyana, in his *Ṛigvedânukramaṇikâ*, characterizes the latter as *Kâśirâja*, he may have expressed himself metachronically, under the influence of a modern tradition which he and his contemporaries accepted. As to the former, we find, indeed, in post-vaidik books, two Divodâsas; into whom a single personage seems to have been parted. One of them is son of Badhryaśwa, as in the *Ṛigveda;* but it is the other, the son of Bhîmaratha, and father of Pratardana, that is called king of the Kâśis. It may be added, that there is no ground for considering Badhryaśwa and Bhîmaratha to be two names of one and the same person. See the English *Vishṇu-purâṇa*, Vol. IV., pp. 33, and 145, 146. Badhryaśwa, not Bahwaśwa, is the reading of the *Vishṇu-purâṇa*. Correct accordingly Professor Wilson's translation of the *Ṛigveda*, Vol. III., p. 504, note 1. See, further, the *Mahâbhârata*, *Anuśâsana-parvan*, Chapter XXX.

struct anything approaching a history. The kingdom of the Kâśis, and its rulers, as is evinced by the frequency of reference to them, enjoyed, from distant ages, more or less of notoriety; and this is, substantially, all that the Hindu memorials teach us.

The Purâṇas specify but one dynasty of Kâśi kings; a goodly catalogue, beginning, in the most authoritative of those works, with the son of Kâśa.[1] To Kâśa, by a lapse of perhaps two centuries, succeeded Divodâsa, in whose reign Buddhism seems to have been still acting on the aggressive.[2] In this synchronism there is no discernible improbability; and, with some likelihood, it embodies an historic fact. A reflexion of actual events may, likewise, be afforded in the story of the burning of Vârâṇasî by the discus of Vishṇu.[3] Of the age of Ajâtaśatru, as of other very early leaders of the Kâśis, none but most vague indications have, as yet,

[1] A Kâśa is named in the *gaṇa* on Pâṇini, IV., I., 10.

According to my five wretched copies of the *Vâyu-purâṇa*, Kâśa was followed by Kâśaya (???), Ràshṭra (??), Dîrghatapas, Dharma, Dhanwantari, Ketumat, Bhîmaratha, Divodâsa.

The *Brahmâṇḍa-purâṇa* has, in one place, Kâśa and Kâśîya, as sire and son, and, a little further on, instead of them, Kâśika and Kâśeya. Kâśika, as evolving Kâśeya, must be considered as an optional elongation of Kâśi.

[2] See the English *Vishṇu-purâṇa*, Vol. IV., pp. 30–40.

We read, in the *Vâyu-purâṇa*:

दिवोदास इति ख्यातो वाराणस्यधिपोऽभवत् ।
एतस्मिन्नेव काले तु पुरीं वाराणसीं पुरा ।
शून्यां विवेशयामास क्षेमको नाम राक्षसः ॥

Then follows an account of the expulsion of Divodâsa from Vârâṇasî. So far as we know, he was the only king of the Kâśi family that had to do with that city.

[3] See the *Vishṇu-purâṇa*, Book V., Chapter XXXIV.

been discovered. Some of these personages ruled, not at Benares, but at Pratishṭhâna;[1] and, at the time of the Muhammadan conquest, Benares and the surrounding country appertained to the throne of Kanauj.[2]

[1] Its site was near Allahabad. Pûru's capital was Pratishṭhâna, in the kingdom of the Kâśis, according to the *Râmâyaṇa, Uttara-kâṇḍa*, LIX., 18, 19:

चिदिवं स गतो राजा ययातिर्नहुषात्मजः ॥
पूरुश्चकार तद्राज्यं धर्मेण महतावृतः ।
प्रतिष्ठाने पुरवरे काशिराज्ये महायशाः ॥

Before Pûru, his father, Yayâti, "lord of all the Kâśis," reigned at Pratishṭhâna. *Mahâbhârata, Udyoga-parvan, śl.* 3905 and 3918.

Purûravas received Pratishṭhâna in gift from his father Sudyumna. English *Vishṇu-purâṇa*, Vol. III., p. 237. Also see Burnouf's *Bhâgavata-purâṇa*, Vol. III., Preface, pp. XCVII.-XCIX.

Pratishṭhâna appears as a district of the kingdom of which Kanauj was the metropolis, in comparatively recent times. *Vide supra*, p. xxii., note 4.

Pratishṭhâna is the name of a kingdom, or of part of one, in the *Kathâ-sarit-sâgara*, VI., 8.

[2] *Vide supra*, p. xxii., note 4. Several Sanskrit land-grants have been published,—two among them by myself,—from which it appears that the kings of the latest dynasty of Kanauj, from Madanapâla to the unfortunate Jayachandra, were masters of Benares, in succession to their predecessors; and that they were so is fully made out by the Muhammadan historians.

In the fifth volume of the *Asiatic Researches* is a professed transcript of a short inscription from a stone, now long disappeared from sight, which was exhumed near Benares, in 1794. We read, therein, of a king of Gauḍa, Mahîpâla, father of Sthirapâla and Vasantapâla; and, at the end, the date 1083. An easy credulity may accept these statements, no longer possible of verification; but there still remains the question as to the era of the year 1083, whether Vikramâditya's, or Śalivâhana's—better, Sâtavâhana's,—or Harsha's, or whose. Not only are the blunders in this inscription, as printed, so many and so gross that we are forbidden to suppose they were in the original; but they provoke the surmise that the interspersed patches of the record which read as if correct

Flagrant as is the exaggeration of the Hindus, it is surpassed by that of the Buddhists. The Brahmadatta who figures so largely, in their sacred writings, as king of Benares[1] very likely was not a mythe;[2] but there is no ground for crediting that Gautama ever governed that city at all, notwithstanding that they represent him to have reigned there during nineteen several states of existence.[3] In a similar spirit, they assert, that, at the same capital ruled, in turn, eighty-four thousand monarchs descended from Aśoka.[4] From these specimens it is manifest that the Buddhist scriptures are little to be trusted for throwing light on the history of Benares. That Buddhism, or any Buddhist king, ever dominated there is altogether problematical.

Some relevant details, scant, but interesting as far as they go, are derivable from the itinerary of Hiouen Thsang,[5] a Buddhist pilgrim from China, who visited

may be, to a large extent, equally products of ignorant mistake and misrepresentation. A good deal of weight has been allowed to this inscription; and it has been, from time to time, honoured as a piece of genuine historic evidence. Uncritically enough, I once followed the herd, myself, in this respect: see the *Journal of the Asiatic Society of Bengal*, for 1862, p. 8, first foot-note. It now appears to me rash to see, in it, proof that Benares was subordinate to Gauḍa, or anything else whatever claiming reliance.

[1] Burnouf's *Introduction à l'Histoire du Buddhisme Indien*, Vol. I., p. 140; and Mr. R. S. Hardy's *Manual of Budhism*, p. 101.

[2] Another king unknown to the Hindu records is spoken of by the Buddhists. His name is Bhîmaśukla. See *Der Buddhismus*, translated from the Russian of Professor Wassiljew, Part I., p. 54.

[3] Mr. R. S. Hardy's *Manual of Budhism*, p. 134.

[4] So states the *Dîpavaṁśa*. See the *Journal of the Asiatic Society of Bengal*, for 1838, p. 927.

[5] *Mémoires sur les Contrées Occidentales*, Vol. I., pp. 353, *et seq.*

India in the first half of the seventh century. At that date, as he informs us, the kingdom of Vârâṇasî had a circuit of eight hundred miles,[1] while its capital measured nearly four miles by somewhat more than one. The inhabitants of the kingdom were, for the most part, Hindus. These were, mainly, worshippers of S'iva; and among them were two classes of ascetics.[2] Their temples amounted to a hundred, which gave lodgement to about ten thousand devotees.[3] The Buddhists, who

[1] "About four thousand *lis*." On the length of the *li*, consult Father Vivien de Saint-Martin, in *Mémoires*, etc., Vol. II., pp. 256–259.

[2] On M. Julien's own showing, both in the *Mémoires* and in the *Méthode*, one of these classes, that of naked mendicants, has the name, in Chinese transliterating, of *ni-kien-t'o, i.e., niggantha*, or even *nigânth*, —a Prakrit word softened from the Sanskrit *nirgrantha*, which the French translation exhibits. Nowhere in his works does M. Julien acknowledge, what he must have known full well, that he constantly puts into the mouth of Hiouen Thsang Sanskrit words, where he really used Prakrit. But there was a theory to support; and facts must be fitted to it.

[3] In the first instance, M. Julien wrote: "On compte une centaine de temples des dieux (*Dêvâlayas*) où habitent environ dix mille hérétiques, qui, la plupart, adorent le dieu *Ta-tseu-t'saï-t'ien* (*Mahêçvara dêva*)." And there should seem to be no improvement in his later rendering: "On voit une centaine de temples des Dieux. Il y a environ dix mille hérétiques qui, la plupart, révèrent le dieu *Ta-tseu-thsaï* (Mahêçvara Dêva)."

The Chinese does not, to be sure, as the translator at first expressed it, literally quarter the aforesaid heretics in the temples, or, rather, monasteries; and yet its indefiniteness easily endures this interpretation. So I am informed by Professor Summers, my obligations to whom I shall presently acknowledge in connexion with a matter of graver import. And this construction alone quadrates with the previous context. For Hiouen Thsang makes Benares a large kingdom, and one in which the Hindus much outnumbered the Buddhists; and there must, then, have been many times ten thousand of the former.

are stated to have been much in the minority, kept up thirty religious houses, tenanted by three thousand inmates, all of the Sammatîya sect. In the capital[1] were twenty Hindu temples, and a latten statue of Śiva, a hundred feet in height. We are not apprised whether there were any sacred edifices of the pilgrim's fellow-religionists in the capital itself; and the obvious inference is, that there were none, or none worth commemorating. On the monasteries, towers, and reservoirs of the immediate vicinity,[2] hallowed by Buddhist

One need do no more than collate M. Julien's two versions of Hiouen Thsang's short account of Benares, to be satisfied that the translator's notion of the sense of his original is, sometimes, of the vaguest.

[1] Its name is not specified. Fă Hian—of the beginning of the fifth century, and so an earlier traveller than Hiouen Thsang,—is translated as speaking of "la ville de *Pho lo naï*, dans le royaume de *Kia chi.*" *Foĕ Kouĕ Ki*, p. 304.

[2] Two of these remembrancers of the Buddhist faith, towers at Sârnâth, beyond the Varaṇâ or Burna, are still conspicuous landmarks. The larger of them is called, by the natives, Dhamekh,—a corruption, in all likelihood, of an old word involving *dharma* as its first factor.

On the word of M. Stanislas Julien, Hiouen Thsang locates a monument "au nord-est de la capitale, et à l'occident du fleuve de *Po-lo-ni-sse* (Vârâṇaçî)," and tells of a certain monastery at the distance of "environ dix li au nord-est du fleuve de *Po-lo-ni-sse* (Vârâṇaçî)." In a foot note, the phrase "à l'occident du fleuve de *Po-lo-ni-sse* (Vârâṇaçî)" is explained to signify "à l'occident du Gange."

As the Chinese pilgrim again and again names the Ganges, it seemed to me unlikely that he should anywhere speak of it by a periphrasis like that of "the river of London." I had observed, too, that, instead of "environ," etc., M. Klaproth had written: "Au nord [*sic*] de la ville coule la rivière *Pho lo nă* (Varaṇâ); sur son bord, à dix *li* de la ville," etc.; *Pho lo nă sse* being, as he says just before, Hiouen Thsang's name for Benares. Moreover, in M. Julien's associations, Hiouen Thsang dwells at great length, and with that lingering and minutiose reminiscence which marks a credulous and fervid piety.

That, in very early days, Benares attained to promi-

"Liste des Mots Abrégés ou Corrompus," I noticed the entry "*Po-lo-naï*, faute pour *Po-lo-ni-sse* (Vârâṇaçî);" and I was thereby unavoidably misled to the conclusion that *Po-lo-naï*, the so-called shortened or depraved form of *Po-lo-ni-sse*, must be employed in the original, the passage or passages containing it being left undesignated by the translator.

No one can give much thought to the labours of M. Julien, without detecting that they were never executed in contemplation of circumspect perusal. Warned by my past experience, and weighing the premises just recited, I at once suspected management, issuing in the obliteration, in two places, of the river Varaṇâ. I had recourse to Professor James Summers, a distinguished Sinologist; and my suspicion was changed into certitude.

Especially ought M. Julien to have abstained from mending his text here by guess, above all unconfessedly, inasmuch as, where the name *Po-lo-ni-sse* is first introduced, there is, in the Chinese, a gloss,—delusively appropriated by the translator, as we have seen,—notifying that the kingdom so named had aforetime been called, by mistake, *Po-lo-naï;* the spelling, in passing, of the *Foĕ Kouĕ Ki.* It was not, surely, to be expected, that, close to this notification, we should find—and not once only, but twice,—*Po-lo-nie* (Varaṇâ), if *Po-lo-ni-sse* (Vârâṇasî) had been intended. M. Julien, however, deemed otherwise; and he unavowedly took for granted, besides, that, in both these instances, *Po-lo-nie* was a corruption of the already corrupt *Po-lo-naï.*

Father Vivien de Saint-Martin, in his geographical commentary on M. Julien's translation, is pleased to substitute, for "fleuve de *Po-lo-ni-sse* (Vârâṇaçî)," "rivière *Po-lo-ni-ssé* (Varâṇasî);" and he proceeds to suggest,—as I have shown above, in note 2 to p. xviii.,—that the city of Benares borrowed its appellation from that of this imaginary stream, held, by him, to be identical with the Ἐρέννεσις of Arrian.

More than this, M. Julien, in one of his Indexes, writes "Vârâṇaçî, rivière, aujourd'hui Barna, l'Erinésès des Grecs;" and the violence which Father Vivien de Saint-Martin does to his text has, thus, his

nent fame is a conclusion scarcely indicated by documentary evidence. And so it was during the period of the Buddhists. So far as we know, these sectaries, unlike the Muhammadans, never assumed an attitude of

implied acquiescence. So important an alteration of opinion as that herein involved certainly called for specific acknowledgment in his "Errata Alphabétique," a list which extends to seven pages.

In fine, M. Julien has no Sanskrit authority whatever for his "Vârâṇaçî," *i.e.*, Vârâṇaśî. *Po-lo-ni-sse* may, indeed, stand for Vârâṇaśî, but — so indeterminate is the Chinese alphabet, — may just as well disguise Vârâṇasî, Varâṇasî, Varaṇasî, Bârânaśî, and scores more of quadrisyllables. M. Julien allows us an option between *Po-la-na-sse*, *Po-lo-ni-sse*, *Po-lo-ni-se*, and *P'o-lo-ni-sse*, and between "Varâṇaçî" and "Vârâṇaçî." It cannot be proved that Hiouen Thsang did not hear, and do his best to spell, as the names of the river and city, Barṇâ—the very word now used,—and Barâṇas. Indeed, the balance of probability is overwhelmingly in favour of the position, that the Indian proper names transletterred by Hiouen Thsang were Prakrit, not Sanskrit. Perhaps it is not strange that M. Julien, in drawing up his suicidal *Méthode*, and even earlier, chose to shut his eyes to this presumption. *Vide supra*, p. xxvii., note 2.

"With M. Julien's method, mathematical certainty seems to have taken the place of learned conjectures." So we read, in the *Saturday Review*, Vol. XI., p. 247 (1861), in an article lately republished as Professor Max Müller's. Finding M. Julien's method to be much more precarious than it appears at first sight, I took occasion, some years ago, with ample detail of reasons, to reclaim against this heedless hyperbole of encomium. Continued examination has multiplied my arguments of protest; and I am convinced that one will do well to use M. Julien's volumes, valuable and instructive as they are, with constant caution.

That M. Julien, for all the self-complacent air of his *Méthode*, has struck out a single idea, save of detail, that was unknown to M. Rémusat and the editors of the *Foĕ Kouĕ Ki*, I have not succeeded in discovering.

Mémoires sur les Contrées Occidentales, etc., Vol. I., p. 354; Vol. II., pp. 345, 360, 361, 479, 562: *Foĕ Kouĕ Ki*, p. 307: *Histoire de la Vie de Hiouen-Thsang*, etc., pp. 83, 132, 429, 464: *Chips from a German Workshop*, Vol. I., p. 296: *Journal of the Asiatic Society of Bengal*, for 1861, pp. 334–336.

vehement hostility as against the Hindus. Not only was the character of their religion pacific, but at no time during their presence in India[1] were they, albeit in the ascendant, beyond doubt a majority of the people. It

[1] How the Buddhists came to leave India has not yet been shown satisfactorily. The *Śankara-digvijaya* of Mâdhava—which professes to abridge an older work, but which, perhaps, has no better basis, for the most part, than oral tradition, eked out by romance,—bears witness, it is true, to a ferocious spirit of opposition to those religionists; and such a spirit, if entertained after they had become strangers to the country, may have been entertained while they were still face to face with Hindus. Nevertheless, we have no historical proof that India was ever the theatre of a Buddhist persecution. Few Sanskrit manuscripts exist that were copied more than four or five centuries ago, at which time Indian Buddhists must have been very rare, if there were any at all. Neither among the Hindus nor among the Jainas has one ever observed anything like that liberality of literary curiosity which would be at much pains to perpetuate, by transcription, the holy writ of an antagonist creed; and the fact of a persecution of the Buddhists cannot, accordingly, be deduced from the fact that their books are now but very rarely met with in the possession of natives of India.

Considering the character of their respective beliefs, the Buddhists and the Hindus were under no obligation to be truculently inimical to each other. There is even reason to believe that there were medieval Indian kings who, from motives of policy, adiaphorized between the two great classes of the faithful into which their subjects were divided. For instance, a position of practical indifference in respect of the prevailing superstitions seems to be ascertained with reference to Harsha, king of Kanauj in the seventh century. Hiouen Thsang speaks of him much as if he were a Buddhist; and Bâṇa, in the *Harsha-charita*, writes of him as if of a Hindu. Further, we find that monarch figuring as dedicatee of the *Nâgânanda*, and also of the *Ratnâvalî*, two dramas, severally Buddhist and Brahmanical.

For the *Harsha-charita* and the *Nâgânanda*,—of which I discovered copies, after these works had slumbered neglected for many generations,—see my *Vâsavadattâ*, Preface, pp. 12–18 and 50–54; and the *Journal of the Asiatic Society of Bengal*, for 1862, pp. 12, 13. See, further, on the Buddhists in Southern India, Professor Wilson's *Mackenzie Collection*, Vol. I., Introduction, pp. lxiii.–lxvi.

was but natural for their founder, in the course of his mission, to take thought of the centres of population; and the spots which he and his disciples signalized by their teachings were reverently regarded, in after ages, as consecrated ground. These spots were, however, in the neighbourhood of cities,—as Gayâ, Mathurâ, Ayodhyâ, and Benares,[1]—rather than in the cities themselves; and it was not till after Buddhism had passed its prime on Indian soil, that these towns acquired the special repute which now attaches to them. As for Benares, the attribution to it of peculiar sanctity seems to date from the period of the Purâṇas;[2] and some of these compositions may, unquestionably, claim a very respectable antiquity.

A diligent perusal of the copious inanity of the *Kásí-khaṇḍa* might lead to the discovery of its era,[3] and

[1] It is very true, that, all the way between Benares and the towers at Sârnâth, the fields are thickly strewed with bricks and other remains of former buildings. But I am not aware that Colonel Wilford has any authority for speaking of "the old city of Benares, north of the river Burna," which old city, he says, is sometimes called S'oṇitapura. *Asiatic Researches*, Vol. IX., p. 199.

[2] Professor Wilson asserts, characteristically, that Benares "has been, from all time, as it is at present, the high place of the S'aiva worship." Translation of the *Vishṇu-puráṇa*, Book V., Chapter XXXIV., last note.

In the twelfth century, as we learn from the *Haima-kośa*, Benares was already distinguished as S'ivapurì, "the city of S'iva;" and we may thence gather that the worship of S'iva especially predominated there at that time.

[3] "There is every reason to believe the greater part of the contents of the *Kásí-khaṇḍa* anterior to the first attack upon Benares by Mahmûd of Ghaznî." Thus pronounces Professor Wilson, in his translation of the *Vishṇu-puráṇa*, Vol. I., Preface, pp. LXXII., LXXIII. It would be interesting to be put in possession of even a single reason out of those to which the Professor alludes.

to other chronological determinations. In so recent a composition, and one having to do with real localities, there must, almost of necessity, be many facts interwoven with the fictions: the attempt to discriminate them would, perhaps, be remunerated. The Benares of the present day offers numerous and varied objects of interest[1] to the contemplation of the devout Hindu; and yet, a very few of them excepted, to speculate touching their age, in reliance on the data hitherto made available, would be much too perilous for prudence.

[1] Unless we are deceived by identity of names, scores of these are enumerated in the *Kâśî-khaṇḍa.*

In the last chapter of that work, cycles of pilgrimages are prescribed, as means to particular ends, precisely as at this hour. Thus, there is one round to warrant the practitioner from liability to further metempsychosis; another, to secure the attainment of Rudrahood; a third, to ensure emancipation before death. These for samples.

Saints whose aspirations are less ambitious are promised store of good things in future for repeating the *Panchatîrthikâ* daily. This consists in: (1) ablution, without disrobing, in the pool of Chakrapushkariṇî, with a propitiation-service addressed to the gods, manes, Brahmans, and beggars; (2) reverential salutation to Âditya, Draupadî, Vishṇu, Daṇḍapâṇi, and Maheśwara; (3) visual contemplation of Ḍhuṇḍhivinâyaka; (4) a dip of the fingers in the Jnânavâpî well, with adoration of Nandikeśa, Târakeśa, and Mahâkâleśwara; and, finally, (5) a second visit to Daṇḍapâṇi.

Of seven preeminently holy places Kâśî is named first; the others being Kântî, Mâyâ, Ayodhyâ, Dwâravatî, Mathurâ, and Avantikâ:

काशी कान्ती च मायाख्या त्वयोध्या द्वारवत्यपि।
मथुरावन्तिका चैताः सप्त पुर्यो ऽत्र मोक्षदाः॥

VI., 68.

Mâyâ is Hurdwar. I am not sure whether or not Kântî is the same as Kânchî. The rest are well known. These places are, all,

To the early Arab and Persian travellers Gangetic India was an unexplored tract.[1] Albirûnî, who wrote about A.D. 1000, had, however, heard of the holy fame of Benares, which he compares, not inaptly, to Mecca.[2] Mahmûd of Ghaznî is said, on doubtful warrant, to have advanced as far as Benares, and to have made a few converts there, during his ninth incursion.[3] In 1194, Shihâbuddîn, after defeating the Kanaujan monarch, Jayachandra, marched on that city, where he is reported to have demolished near a thousand Hindu temples.[4] The subsequent history of the place, for

named in the *Ayeen Akbery*, in Mr. Gladwin's translation of which, Vol. III., pp. 255, 256, Mathurâ and Avantikâ are disguised as Mehtra and Ownitka.

At least thirty or forty epithetical designations of Benares are scattered through the *Kâśî-khaṇḍa*. Half of that number, or thereabouts, from this or some other work or works, have been noted by native lexicographers. One of them, Panchanadatîrtha, "the quinquamnian resort," refers to five rivers, the Kiraṇâ, Dhûtapâpâ, Saraswatî, Gangâ, and Yamunâ :

किरणा धूतपापा च पुण्यतोया सरस्वती ।
गंगा च यमुना चैव पञ्च नद्यो ऽत्र कीर्त्तिताः ॥
अतः पञ्चनदं नाम तीर्थं त्रैलोक्यविश्रुतम् ।

LIX., 114, 115.

Four of these streams, in small quantities, are believed to emerge into the Ganges, through subterraneous channels, just in front of the Panchagangâ landing.

[1] *Relation des Voyages*, etc., by M. Langlès and Father Reinaud, Vol. I., Preliminary Discourse, pp. XLVIII., XLIX.

[2] Father Reinaud's *Mémoire Géographique, Historique et Scientifique sur l'Inde*, etc.,p. 288.

[3] English *Ayeen Akbery*, Vol. II., p. 35.

[4] Major Stewart's *History of Bengal*, p. 36. Elsewhere we read, that, "having broken the idols in above a thousand temples, he purified and consecrated the latter to the worship of the true God." Colonel Briggs's translation from Farishta, Vol. I., p. 179.

many centuries, is well-nigh a blank. Its religious character was not, in the eyes of its Islamite masters, a thing to recommend it; and commercial or political importance it had none.[1] Even Akbar, with all his toleration of Hinduism, and occasional partiality to it, did nothing to prop the sinking fortunes of Benares. Its decline was uninterrupted; and, under Aurangzeb, who changed its name to Muhammadâbâd,[2] it reached, at last, the depth of its ignominy. At the command of that harsh bigot, its principal temples were laid in ruins,[3] and mosques, constructed from their materials, were reared on their half-destroyed foundations. The Observatory, built by Mânasiṁha[4] about A.D. 1600, is, it may be, the only noteworthy Hindu edifice of the

[1] Fiscally, too, it had come, in the days of Akbar, to be of very secondary note. See the *Ayeen Akbery*, Vol. II., Appendix, p. 28.

[2] I have met with this substitute for Benares in an Urdû book written within the last hundred years. It was originally meant, of course, as a poignant insult. Deservedly, it never obtained, it is believed, any currency.

The Muhammadan names of Delhi, Agra, and Patna are of every-day use. Less familiar are Jahângîrâbâd, Mustafa'âbâd, Islâmâbâd, and Mûminâbâd, for Dacca, Rampoor, Chittagong, and Brindabun.

[3] Captain Orlich, in the tenth letter of his *Reise in Ostindien*, says that Akbar entertained the project of establishing a mosque over the Jnânavâpî well. No one at all acquainted with Akbar's character could give this silly legend the least credence. The story looks like an addition to the tale, that, when Aurangzeb threw down the old temple of Viśweśwara, its phallus cast itself, unassisted, into the Jnânavâpî.

[4] Raja of Ambherî. One of his descendants, Jayasiṁha II., who flourished rather more than a century after him, provided the Observatory with astronomical instruments. From Raja Mânasiṁha the building was called, from the first, Mânamandira, now corrupted into Mânmandil.

city, still entire, of so great antiquity. For nearly all that is striking in its architectural embellishment, Benares is beholden to the Marathas; and to the zeal and enterprise of the same energetic race the resuscitation, in the decline of Hinduism, of much of its former influence is, in large measure, indebted. There is no ground for believing that Benares, in comparison of what we now see it, with its thousand temples,[1] and their concomitants of holy harpies and willing victims, can ever have boasted a larger population, a prestige of greater potency, or more affluent prosperity.

F. H.

July, 1868.

Bishop Heber uninquiringly states that the Observatory was "founded before the Musalmân conquest." Captain Orlich says it was founded by Jayasiṁha: he does not distinguish which Jayasiṁha. But it would be endless to point out the mistakes of careless travellers.

Even Mr. James Prinsep,—*Benares Illustrated*, Second Series,—from consulting Tavernier with insufficient attention, refers the conversion of the Mânmandil into an Observatory to Jayasiṁha I.

An excellent account of the Benares Observatory, by Pandit Bâpû Deva Śâstrin, is given in the *Transactions of the Benares Institute for the Session* 1864–65, pp. 191–196.

[1] Such was Mr. James Prinsep's estimate in 1828–1829. As to the extent of the city, "the measured length along the banks of the river, by survey, is barely three miles; and the average depth does not exceed one mile." *Benares Illustrated*, p. 12. Hiouen Thsang found Benares, in the seventh century, of not far from the same dimensions. *Vide supra*, p. xxvii.

THE SACRED CITY OF THE HINDUS.

CHAPTER I.

EARLY history of Benares.—Sanctity of the city.—Mythic character of Indian history. — Ancient Buddhist records respecting Benares. S'ákya Muni, or Buddha, preached the doctrine of Buddhism first in Benares.—Antiquity of Benares.—Hiouen Thsang's account of his visit to the city in the seventh century of the Christian era.—Macaulay's description of Benares. — Connexion of Benares with the religious history of half the human race.—Its connexion with Buddhism.—Life and labours of Buddha.—Benares subsequently to the fall of Buddhism in India.—The Brahman.—Sons of the Ganges. —Devotees and pilgrims.—Benares, the religious centre of India.

THE early history of Benares is involved in much obscurity. It is, indisputably, a place of great antiquity, and may even date from the time when the Aryan race first spread itself over Northern India. Although such a supposition is incapable of direct proof, yet the sacred city must, undoubtedly, be reckoned amongst the primitive cities founded by this people. When it was first built, and by what prince or patriarch, is altogether unknown. But of its great antiquity, stretching back through the dim ages of early Indian history, far into the clouds and mists of the Vedic and pre-historical periods, there is no question. It is certain that the city is regarded, by all Hindus, as coeval with the birth of Hinduism, a notion derived both from tradition and from their own writings. Allusions to Benares are exceedingly abundant in ancient Sanskrit literature; and perhaps there is no city in all Hindustan more frequently referred to. By reason of some subtle and mysterious charm, it has linked itself with the religious sympathies of the Hindus through every century of its existence. For the sanctity of its inhabitants—of its temples and reservoirs—of its wells and streams—of the very soil that is trodden—of the very air that is breathed—and of everything in it and around it, Benares has been famed for thousands of years. The Hindu ever beholds the city in one peculiar aspect, as a place of spotless holiness and heavenly beauty, where the spiritual eye may be delighted and the heart may be purified; and his imagination has been kept fervid, from generation to generation, by the continued presentation of this glowing picture. Believing all he has read and heard concerning this ideal seat of blessedness, he has been possessed with the same longing to visit it as the Mohammedan to visit Mecca, or the Christian enthusiast to visit Jerusalem; and, having gratified his desire, has left the memory of his pious enterprise to his children, for their example, to incite them to undertake the same pilgrimage, faithfully transmitting to them the high ambition which he himself received from his fathers.

Unfortunately, Hindu writers have shown a singular neglect of chronology, and an utter distaste for noting and recording historical facts in a simple and consecutive manner. This is the more remarkable, when it is remembered that many of them have been accustomed to close thought, and have prided themselves on their intellectual acumen; that they have originated numerous systems of philosophy, and made great pretensions to logical accuracy; and that the habit of the nation generally, for thousands of years, has been to reverence the past, and to reflect upon and observe, with punctilious nicety, its religious ceremonies and social usages.

Were the Hindus proverbially reckless in their statements and opinions, and had they never produced any great work exhibiting minuteness of detail, together with clearness, consistency, and truth, there might not be so much cause for wonder. But they have astonished the world by their achievements in a department of learning usually regarded as dry and uninteresting. I refer to the subject of Grammar. Carefully collecting the facts brought to light by critical and painstaking observation, they have elaborated a system of Grammar, of gigantic dimensions, far surpassing anything that has ever been effected, in this branch of study, in any country or age of the world. Their greatest and most brilliant champion in this science is Páṇini: yet many other grammarians helped to rear the stupendous fabric which now excites the admiration of mankind. And, while they emulated the genius of the Greeks in generalizing upon the results of their observations, they far outshone them in the correctness and extent of their investigations.

One would have imagined that they who were exact in one subject would be exact in another; and that, having acquired the habit of calmly noting points of agreement and difference, and of rigidly adhering to them, it would be a moral impossibility for them to act in direct opposition to such a habit. Yet this does not hold good in regard to the Hindu race. While excellent grammarians, they are meagre historians. They possess no single record, among the ten thousand separate manuscript works of which their ancient literature is said to be composed, on the historical correctness of which one can place much reliance. Legendary stories are so intermingled with real events, and the web of the one is so intimately inwoven with the woof of the other, and the two form so homogeneous a whole, that the finest microscopic intellects of Europe, after patient and long-continued examination, have been well-nigh baffled in the attempt to discover which is fiction and which is fact. A few threads of truth have rewarded their pains, and perhaps a few others may occasionally be drawn forth; but that the gaudy-coloured fabric of Hindu history, manufactured by themselves, will ever be satisfactorily separated into its two component parts, is as hopeless as to expect that the waters of the Jumna will ever cease to mingle with the waters of the Ganges. Were only the epoch or epochs of the Mahábhárata satisfactorily settled, and were it really known what elements of that great work are pre-Buddhist and what post-Buddhist, the minds of men would be at least freed from the despair which possesses them in reference to this subject.[1]

The result is, that this city of Benares, whose antiquity is very great, is robbed of much of the glory which is justly her due. Thanks to a rival creed, however,—which sprang into existence probably in the sixth century before the Christian era,—whose annals have been kept with some decent amount of trustworthiness,

[1] See Prof. Max Müller's History of Ancient Sanskrit Literature, p. 62.

we gain certain specific information respecting this city at that early epoch.

It is a fact, admitting of no dispute, that S'ákya Muni, the last and only really historical Buddha, on attaining the mysterious condition of Buddhahood under the Bodhi tree in the neighbourhood of Gayá, travelled to Benares, and proceeded to the Íśipattana Vihára, or monastery, now known as Sárnáth. This may have been in the sixth century B.C. Here he announced the change which had come upon him, and the transcendental and superhuman, not to say divine, state in which he imagined he found himself. The five Bhikshus, or religious hermits, men of considerable note in the early history of Buddhism, who had formerly been associated with him, but had subsequently abandoned him, and who happened, at that time, to be at the Íśipattana monastery, embraced the new religion, and became disciples of Buddha. At Sárnáth S'ákya Muni first began to "turn the wheel of the Law," in other words, to preach the famous doctrines of Dharma and Nirváṇa, which were destined, in later years, to exert such an extraordinary influence over a large portion of the human family.

The Rev. R. Spence Hardy, in his erudite and valuable work, "A Manual of Budhism," quoting from Ceylon records, gives the following account of the visit of Buddha to Íśipattana:—"When Budha looked to see unto whom he should first say *bana*, he saw that the ascetics Alára and Uddaka were worthy; but when he looked again to discover in what place they were, he perceived that the former had been dead seven days, and that the latter had died the day before; and that as they were now in an *arúpa* world, they could not receive its benefit. With affection for the ascetics who were dead, he looked to discover in what place Kondanya was, and the four other recluses with whom he had practised austerities; and when he saw that they were in the Isipatana wihára, near Benares, he resolved that unto them first *bana* should be said. At the end of sixty days, in the eighth week after he became Budha, Gótama went from the Ajápála tree to Isipatana alone, a distance of 288 miles." P. 184. The brief inaugural discourse which he there delivered is stated to have been as follows:—"Then Budha opened his mouth, and preached the Dhamsak-pæwatum-sútra (Dhamma-chakka). 'There are two things,' said he, 'that must be avoided by him who seeks to become a priest; evil desire, and the bodily austerities that were practised by the (Brahman) ascetics.'" P. 187.

It is plain that Benares must have been, at this time, a city of power and importance, the weight of whose opinions on religious topics was very considerable in the country generally; and, therefore, that it was of the utmost consequence to secure its countenance and support on any great subject affecting the religious belief of the entire nation. That this was the real reason why Gautama wished to commence his career from Benares, admits of no controversy. But, if Benares was so celebrated at that era, we must look away from it to preceding ages for the date of its foundation.

The Buddhists themselves give us some glimpses of intelligence respecting the history of this city prior to the year of S'ákya's visit; and these, although liable to some suspicion, have, nevertheless, in all probability, a basis of truth. The information which they incidentally furnish rests partly upon the statements of no other than Buddha himself, corroborated, in some measure, by their own observations. This wonderful personage, considering that some of the leading dogmas which he expounded were borrowed from Hinduism, and had been advocated and set forth by various teachers previously to his time, cleverly availed himself of the prestige of these earlier instructors, by pronouncing each in succession to have been an incarnation or manifestation of Buddha; thereby coolly attaching to himself and his creed the sanction of their authority and the weight of their names.

In any case, Benares is a city of no mean antiquity. Twenty-five centuries ago, at the least, it was famous. When Babylon was struggling with Nineveh for supremacy, when Tyre was planting her colonies, when Athens was growing in strength, before Rome had become known, or Greece had contended with Persia, or Cyrus had added lustre to the Persian monarchy, or Nebuchadnezzar had captured Jerusalem, and the inhabitants of Judæa had been carried into captivity, she had already risen to greatness, if not to glory. Nay, she may have heard of the fame of Solomon, and have sent her ivory, her apes, and her peacocks to adorn his palaces; while partly with her gold he may have overlaid the Temple of the Lord. Not only is Benares remarkable for her venerable age, but also for the vitality and vigour which, so far as we know, she has constantly exhibited. While many cities and nations have fallen into decay and perished, her sun has never gone down; on the contrary, for long ages past it has shone with almost meridian splendour. Her illustrious name has descended from generation to generation, and has ever been a household word, venerated and beloved by the vast Hindu family. Notwithstanding her destruction by fire, applied by the hand of Kṛishṇa, which may or may not be true, and the manifestations, in her physical aspects, of repeated changes, shiftings of site, and resuscitations, yet, as a city, no sign of feebleness, no symptom of impending dissolution, so far as I am aware, is apparent in any of the numberless references to her in native records. As a queen, she has ever received the willing homage of her subjects scattered over all India; as a lover, she has secured their affection and regard.

Hiouen Thsang, the celebrated Chinese traveller, who, as a Buddhist pilgrim, visited India in the seventh century of the Christian era, describes Benares as a kingdom "about four thousand *li* (six hundred and sixty-seven miles) in circumference. To the west is the capital,—near the Ganges,—which is from eighteen to nineteen *li* (three miles and upwards) long, and from five to six *li* (about one mile) broad. The villages lie very near together, and contain a numerous population. Families of great wealth, whose houses are filled with rare and precious things, are to be seen. The people are gentle and polished, and esteem highly those who are devoted to a studious life. The greater portion of them believe in the heretical doctrines (of Hinduism), and few have respect for the Law (religion) of Buddha. The climate is temperate, grain is in abundance, the fruit-trees are luxuriant, and the earth is covered with tufted vegetation. There are thirty (Buddhist) monasteries, containing about three thousand monks. . . . . There are a hundred temples of the (Hindu) gods, and about ten thousand heretics (Hindus), who, for the most part, worship the god *Ta-tseu-thsaï* (Maheśwara). Some cut off their hair; others preserve a tuft upon the crown of the head, go naked, and are destitute of any kind of clothing. Some besmear their bodies with ashes, and practise zealously severe austerities, in order to obtain release from life and death (that is, from transmigration). In the capital there are twenty (Hindu) temples of the gods."[1]

And now, after the lapse of so many ages, this magnificent city still maintains most of the freshness and all the beauty of her early youth. For picturesqueness and grandeur, no sight in all the world can well surpass that of Benares as seen from the river Ganges. Macaulay's graphic description of her appearance towards the close of the last century is, for the most part, applicable to her present state. He speaks of her as "a city, which, in wealth, population, dignity, and sanctity, was among the foremost of Asia. It was commonly believed that half a million of human beings[2] was crowded into that labyrinth of lofty alleys, rich with shrines, and minarets,

[1] See Appendix B.

[2] This conjecture regarding the population of Benares is not correct. The Government census gives less than two hundred thousand; but this is too low an estimate. The number of pilgrims annually visiting the city, moreover, is very large, being one hundred and fifty or two hundred thousand, and perhaps more, while the population of the surrounding villages is exceedingly dense.

and balconies, and carved oriels, to which the sacred apes clung by hundreds. The traveller could scarcely make his way through the press of holy mendicants, and not less holy bulls. The broad and stately flights of steps which descended from these swarming haunts to the bathing-places along the Ganges, were worn every day by the footsteps of an innumerable multitude of worshippers. The schools and temples drew crowds of pious Hindus from every province where the Brahminical faith was known. Hundreds of devotees came thither every month to die; for it was believed that a peculiarly happy fate awaited the man who should pass from the sacred city into the sacred river. Nor was superstition the only motive which allured strangers to that great metropolis. Commerce had as many pilgrims as religion. All along the shores of the venerable stream lay great fleets of vessels laden with rich merchandize. From the looms of Benares went forth the most delicate silks that adorned the balls of St. James's and of Versailles; and in the bazaars, the muslins of Bengal and the sabres of Oude were mingled with the jewels of Golconda and the shawls of Cashmere."[1]

The connexion of Benares with the religious history of one half the human race, inhabiting the countries of Eastern Asia, is a subject of surpassing interest. Previously to the introduction of the Buddhist faith into India, she was already the sacred city of the land,—the centre of Hinduism, and chief seat of its authority. Judging from the strong feelings of veneration and affection with which the native community regard her

[1] Macaulay's Warren Hastings, p. 55.

in the present day, and bearing in mind that the founder of Buddhism commenced his ministry at this spot, it seems indisputable that, in those early times preceding the Buddhist reformation, the city must have exerted a powerful and wide-spread religious influence over the land. Throughout the Buddhist period in India,—a period extending from seven hundred to a thousand years,—she gave the same support to Buddhism which she had previously given to the Hindu faith. Buddhist works of that era have abundant allusions to Benares, and clearly establish the fact that the Buddhist of those days regarded the city with much the same kind of veneration as the Hindu does now. The sacred writings of Ceylon, called the Játakas, which contain an immense number of tales relating to the life of Buddha and to the early history of his religion, are replete with references to Benares; indeed, each Játaka is almost invariably connected with a Brahmadatta, king of Benares. When Buddha delivered his first discourse at Íśipattana, near Benares, not only the five Bhikshus, as already stated, but also Yaśu, son of Sujáta, and his fifty-four royal companions or princes, embraced the new religion, and became believers in Buddha. Thus these sixty persons were the first, or amongst the first, disciples of this remarkable personage; and to them he gave instructions to proceed in different directions, and announce to the world that the Supreme Buddha had appeared. Starting from the sacred city, these emissaries of Buddhism, in obedience to his injunctions, went forth, and became the forerunners and pioneers of that wonderful missionary enterprise to other cities and towns, and to other and distant lands, which terminated in the conversion to the Buddhist creed of the vast and densely-peopled countries of Eastern Asia.

When the immense influence which he has exerted upon mankind is considered, it may be safely affirmed that the career of S'ákya Muni or Buddha is unparalleled in mere human history. That he, a solitary man, prince of a royal house, becoming an ascetic, and, seating himself down under a tree, should have remained there in meditation for five years and upwards, pondering over the religion, the priestcraft, false dogmas, loose morality, uncertainty, doubt, and confusion of his times, under which the nation groaned; that he should have come to the conclusion that the existing religion was a delusion, baseless and pernicious; that he should have devised an entirely new system, of which himself was the centre, should have thought it out and put it in order, so as to be able to meet objectors and to overcome their arguments; that, at the expiration of this period, he should have risen up and journeyed to Benares, and there delivered his primary discourse respecting the new doctrine; should have thence gone forth to the gradual conquest of India, until the whole land substantially became converted to Buddhism, and sent forth missionaries to Ceylon and other parts, by whose agency that island, the empire of China, Japan, Burmah, Nepal, and Tibet, with their four or five hundred millions of people, received the extraordinary dogma, the gigantic blasphemy, that there was no separate, self-existent Supreme God, but that each individual man, by contemplation, could rise into the divinity; that all this was the ultimate result of that one man's energy, sagacity, and resoluteness of will, is, assuredly, one of the most astounding events in the annals of the world. Buddha surpasses immeasurably every other mere uninspired man in the extent and consequences of his achievements. Mahomet cannot compare for a moment with him. He forced his religion on mankind by the sword; and, after all, his adherents are much less than half as numerous as the devotees of Buddhism. Buddha was a philosopher, a reasoner, a calm disputant, employing no physical force whatever; while the morality which he enforced was the purest the world ever saw, apart from the sublime code found in the Sacred Scriptures.

Although Buddhism continues to be the paramount religion of most of the countries to which it was carried by the agency of its missionaries, yet, strange to say, with the exception of Nepal, where it maintains a struggling existence, it has long been expelled from the land whence it originally sprang. Benares, however, notwithstanding this circumstance, has not ceased to retain her position as the sacred city. From the period of the revival of Hinduism down to the present moment, her influence has continued undiminished. It is exceedingly difficult to convey a correct idea of either the nature or extent of this influence. Throughout the country, Benares is regarded with superstitious reverence by every genuine Hindu; and the name produces in his breast a kind of fascination and charm. "Holy Káśí! would that I could see the eternal city, favoured of the gods! Would that I might die on its sacred soil!" Such are his thoughts and aspirations.

There is no other city which so appeals to his sympathies, which so entwines itself round his spirit, which so stirs his soul to its inmost depths.

As Benares is the religious centre of India, it is natural that priestly influence should there be exceedingly powerful. Everywhere in India, and not merely in this city in particular, the Brahman is a character, a study. No one, not even a foreigner newly arrived in the country, can make a mistake in regard to him. Light in complexion in comparison with the rest of the people, frequently tall in stature, with the marks of a clear, penetrating intelligence depicted plainly and sometimes in a striking manner upon his countenance, erect, proud, self-conscious, he walks along with the air of a man unlike any I have ever seen, in which self-sufficiency, a sense of superiority, and the conviction of inherent purity and sanctity are combined. He needs not the *upavíta* or sacred Brahmanical cord thrown over the right shoulder, or even the streaks, in honour of his favourite deity, painted upon his forehead, to point him out. In his very gait and step you trace his claim to his superiority; and, did we but know the thoughts dwelling in his mind, we should possess the real secret of his majestic demeanour. With the idea constantly before his inner self, that he is himself a god, and deserves divine honours,—which is not a mere freak of a deluded imagination on his part, but is acknowledged by all Hindus, some of whom, as he pursues his way, will stop him, and then offer to him the adoration due only to the Almighty, which he receives complacently, as his right,—how is it possible he should comfort himself otherwise than as though the earth were hardly worthy of his tread, and the crowd about him were, in his presence, a vile, unclean, and abominable race? Though mingling with the vulgar herd, he takes care to avoid contact with them, lest he should contract some ceremonial impurity. He is most particular on this point. Should a low-caste man, by mistake, or from the pressure of the throng, approach too near to him, he cries out sharply and decisively, though not angrily; and, in case brazen vessel in his hand, filled with water from the the Ganges, which he is taking to drink or for sacrifice, be touched by such a person, he immediately throws the water away, and scours the vessel thoroughly before using it again. When he prepares his food,—for he cooks it himself,—should a man of inferior caste, by inadvertence, or from any cause, happen to touch it, the whole is considered as spoiled, and is thrown away. Indeed, so rigidly observant of the rules of their order are some of the Brahmans, that, even should the shadow of such a man, or of a Christian, fall upon their food while being cooked, it is altogether rejected. This mysterious notion of divinity, permeating the entire life of the Brahman, originates, not only in the minds of the people, but also in his own mind, a marvellous idea of his spiritual authority and power. Let any man be so infatuated as to cherish a real conviction within him that he is in some sense divine, and he will of necessity assume a bearing and demeanour different from those of ordinary mortals.

In Benares there are not fewer than from twenty to twenty-five thousand Brahmans. They have control over the temples, the sacred wells, streams, and reservoirs, and other holy places about the city. They superintend the worship of the people, and give directions respecting the numberless ceremonies which are performed. Every sacred spot has some peculiarity connected with it; and it is of great moment that no punctilio should be omitted. They receive the offerings, the alms, the public dinners, and the good things which devout Hindus are ever ready to bestow. Some of them—not a few in number—are termed "Sons of the Ganges," and are chiefly found on the banks of that stream, aiding the devotions of the numerous worshippers daily resorting thither.

Devotees and pilgrims, separately, or in crowds, are seen entering or departing from the city constantly throughout the year, especially on occasion of great festivals. They come from all parts of India. Many carry back with them the sacred water of the Ganges, in small bottles hermetically sealed, placed in baskets hanging from the extremities of poles, which they bear upon their shoulders. The poor deluded sensualist, whose life has been passed in abominable courses, or the covetous *mahájan* or native banker, who has made himself rich by a long course of grinding extortion, or the fanatical devotee, more simple than a babe, yet sometimes guilty of the foulest crimes, still comes, as of old, from the remotest corners of India, as the sands of time are slowly ebbing away, and, fearful lest the last golden grains should escape before his long journey is ended, makes desperate efforts to hold on his course, till, at length, arriving at the sacred city and touching its hallowed soil, his anxious spirit becomes suddenly calm, a strange sense of relief comes over him, and he is at once cheered and comforted with the treacherous lie, that his sins are forgiven and his soul is saved.

In Benares, therefore, Hinduism may be said to dwell at home, in the bosom of its best friends and admirers, courted by princes and wealthy natives, and aided and sustained by innumerable resources and appliances of a material character, which give symbolical significance to its existence and authority. Her thousands of temples, her myriads of idols, her swarms of pilgrims, her hosts of daily worshippers, together with the pomp and circumstance and multifarious representations of idolatry, in their vast aggregate, cause the Hindu religion to be visible to the eye, in this city, in a manner and degree unknown elsewhere. Were a stranger, visiting Benares, to wander about amongst its shrines and sacred places, and to take note merely of the manifold signs and manifestations of Hinduism which he would find there, and then to quit the city without inquiring further, without turning his attention to those silent and unobtrusive, yet potent, influences which are undermining it in every direction, and are in operation throughout all classes of native society, even in this capital and fortress of idolatry, he would imagine that the city was wholly devoted to the practice and ceremonies of heathenism, that no ray of light had penetrated its midnight darkness, and that it was an impracticable and impossible task to attempt its enlightenment and reformation.

We come, therefore, to this conclusion,—justified, I think, by the foregoing observations,—that there are few cities in the world of greater interest to the Christian and the philosopher than the sacred city of the Hindus. Calcutta, Madras, and Bombay are commercial centres of India, directing, to a large extent, the trade of the country. But they do not speak to the masses, who never ask their opinion, and are never guided by their authority on any subject connected with their social or religious usages. Benares, on the contrary, is the living oracle of the nation, and governs the Hindu with a despotic hand, in all his sacred rites and practices, about which he is vastly more concerned than about anything else. Presiding over the religious destinies of one hundred and eighty millions of people, whom she inspires with her spirit, and controls at pleasure, it is a matter not merely of curiosity, but also of great importance, to know what part she is likely to take in that extraordinary movement of mental awakening and religious reform which has already commenced in India. It is not for her to fall back, and resign her position of influence. Her place is in the front rank. While all India is making progress, intellectually and morally, she must advance likewise. But she must do more. She has always been a leader of the people, in everything sacred: such she will, I hope and believe, continue to be. And, judging from the eagerness of many of her sons in the pursuit of knowledge, from the quickened moral perceptions of the population generally, and from the sympathy which multitudes cherish for the new and liberal ideas that are spreading over the country at large, she bids fair to fulfil the predictions of her truest and sincerest friends.

CHAPTER II.

No Architectural remains dating prior to the third century before Christ yet found in India.—Ancient Hindu Edifices of the primitive period, not of a rude character.—Did the Hindus borrow from the Assyrian and Persian Sculptors? — Ancient remains found chiefly in the northern quarter of the city.—Mohammedan lust for Hindu edifices. —Shifting tendency of the modern city.—Origin of the appellation "Benares."

THE great antiquity of Indian civilization is proved, directly and indirectly, in so many ways, that it has come to be regarded as one of the ordinary truisms about which all the world is agreed. Yet it is remarkable that, although it admits not of the smallest question, no evidence in its favour should be afforded by any monument of art hitherto discovered in the country. There is no known specimen of architecture existing, of any character, the date of which carries us back beyond the third century before Christ. The pillars of Aśoka, which belong to this period, are the very earliest sculptured remains yet found. "Of these," says Mr. Fergusson, "one is at Delhi; having been re-erected by Feroze Shah in his palace, as a monument of his victory over the Hindus. Three more are standing near the river Gunduck in Tirhoot; and one has been placed on a pedestal in the fort of Allahabad. A fragment of another was discovered near Delhi, and part of a seventh was used as a roller on the Benares road by a Company's engineer officer."[1] There is reason for supposing that some of the Bhilsa topes may be assigned to this epoch, while others are, undoubtedly, of a somewhat later date. Of the cave-temples, so interesting not only to the archæologist, but likewise to all lovers of the curious, not one was excavated earlier than the first century before Christ. The great Kárleṅ cave dates from the beginning of the Christian era. The Ajunta caves belong to several epochs; and some may be as recent as the ninth or tenth century A.D. The Viśwakarman cave at Ellora is of the seventh or eighth century A.D. Among the caves in Behar there is one called from Lomaśa the Ṛishi, which, from certain peculiarities in its construction, may, it is conjectured, have been excavated prior to the Christian era, although the inscription which covers it is referred to a period so late as the fourth century after Christ.

It has been asserted, on strong authority, that no ancient temples or religious monasteries, apart from the cave structures, exist in India, on the ground that the pre-Buddhist Hindus were as yet simple and unsophisticated, and performed the rites of their religion, to a great extent, without idols or temples; or, if with them, those objects were made of perishable material. The fact of no temples or other edifices having been discovered is regarded as a powerful reason in substantiation of this assertion. Now, to say the least, it is exceedingly premature to hazard such an opinion founded on such a basis, inasmuch as the study

[1] Fergusson's Handbook of Architecture, p. 7.

of Indian antiquities with exactness is only of yesterday. Scarcely a generation has passed since Prinsep deciphered the inscription on Aśoka's pillars, and ascertained its date. Moreover, the spirit of archæological inquiry has but slightly manifested itself among the British rulers of India. Of the large number of educated Englishmen who have visited the country during the last hundred years, and have resided in it for a longer or shorter period, perhaps not one in a thousand has taken the smallest practical interest in bringing to the light of day its hidden historical treasures. It is a hopeful sign of the times, that curiosity on this subject is now being extensively excited; but it has hardly yet passed into the stage of eager desire, displaying itself by earnest and persistent effort in the pursuit of archæological investigations. The discoveries of the last few years have been so remarkable and abundant, and have contributed so many additions to our small stock of knowledge respecting ancient India, that the appetite for these researches has become more and more strongly whetted, and the belief has originated that the Indian mine is rich and deep, and is ample enough to repay the efforts of a whole army of explorers.

The ancient structures of India with which we are acquainted are not of that primitive and rude character which would lead us to imagine that they were the very first productions of Indian architectural skill. On the contrary, they indicate an advanced stage, both in the knowledge and application of permanent material, and in devising and executing elegant designs in it. No one can look upon Aśoka's monoliths and believe for an instant that the knowledge of architecture which they display was developed wholly during that monarch's reign. Nor can it be credited that the beautiful cave-temples were without their predecessors. It may be replied, however, that, from a minute and careful examination of Indian, Assyrian, and Egyptian architecture, the conclusion may almost be demonstrated, that the archetypes of the two former styles were originally wooden, while those of the last-mentioned were of stone, and that, therefore, there is a necessary limit to our investigations, beyond which it is useless to attempt to go; for that the wooden archetypes have mostly, if not entirely, perished, and the stone are of a later period. Granting that this theory is, in the main, true, we are not compelled to believe that the earliest stone erections in India were as recent as the third century before Christ; or, if there were any before that date, that they have all been destroyed. Of the ancient Assyrian palaces discovered by Layard, those most elaborately sculptured were built about B.C. 700, while others, in a less ornamented style, were erected still earlier: and even these were preceded by wooden buildings. If this be correct, why should not at least the same antiquity be conceded to Indian sculptures subsequent to the wooden period? Is it at all likely that the Aryan race existed in India for between one and two thousand years, that they conquered a large portion of the country, that they attained to greatness and glory, and made wonderful progress in civilization, equalling, if not surpassing, their contemporaries in other parts of Asia, and yet, that, during all this time, they were satisfied with only transitory symbols of greatness, and never conceived the idea of leaving behind them durable monuments of their power, which should hand down their name to many generations? They must have heard of the vast structures erected in Egypt, and of the splendid palaces, and stairs, and pillars, and other edifices, with which the Assyrian monarchs adorned their cities. They were not lacking in genius, or in the desire for knowledge; on the contrary, their minds investigated the highest subjects, and whatever was of interest to humanity in general, they regarded as of importance to themselves.

But, it may be said, the Hindus borrowed their architecture from the Assyrians; or the architecture of the two races was of a common origin. Both suppositions may be true; and, in my opinion, it is almost certain, that, in whatever way it was brought about, both countries in some respects followed the same models. Whether Assyrian or Persian sculptors were the architects of the earliest Hindu buildings, is open to question; but, if they were, it seems absurd to suppose that they should have erected edifices altogether of wood, while in their own country the public buildings were, to a large extent, of stone; especially seeing that various kinds of durable stone were easily procurable in India. If, on the other hand, the architects were natives who had learnt the principles of their art chiefly from Assyria or Persia, or from a common source, it appears equally strange that they should have perpetuated the construction of wooden buildings in India for centuries after they must have known them to have been abandoned in other countries, and to have given place to vast edifices of wood and stone combined, covered with carvings and sculptures.

We arrive, therefore, at this conclusion, that, as there is every reason to believe that solid buildings partly if not entirely of stone were erected in India several hundred years preceding the third century B.C.,—the earliest date, as already remarked, of any monuments hitherto discovered,—the probability is, that, if a diligent search were instituted, some fragmentary remains of them would be found. It is a circumstance highly favourable to the prosecution of this search, that the ancient abodes of the Aryan race in India have been, for the most part, well ascertained. All these places will, I hope, in the course of time, be thoroughly examined, and every object of interest tending to throw any light on the subject before us, or on the ancient history of India generally, noted and described.

It is natural to believe, that, *primâ facie*, Benares offers as fair a field for archæological investigation in regard to the earliest forms of Hindu architecture as any city in India. It is confessedly true, however, that no very ancient remains have yet been found there; but the reason may be, because they have not been properly sought after. Only within the last few years, so far as I am aware, have any inquiries been made, in a regular manner, after old buildings in Benares. Mr. James Prinsep, the great Indian archæologist, was a resident in the city for about ten years; but it does not appear that he made any important discoveries in it.

His "Views of Benares" are chiefly of a popular cast, and do not give evidence of any extensive observation or research of this nature. Major Kittoe, the late Government archæologist, and the architect of the Government College,—a beautiful Gothic structure in the suburbs of the city,—although interesting himself in the excavations of Sárnáth, some three miles to the north of Benares, did not, so far as is known, examine the city itself. Indeed, so inattentive was he to its claims to antiquity, that he removed many cart-loads of heavy stones, some of which were curiously carved, from Bakaríyá Kuṇḍ, on the confines of the city and not more than a mile from the college which he was erecting, without reflecting that they might possibly be relics of ancient buildings formerly situated on that site. As a fact, they were originally connected with a series of Buddhist edifices covering perhaps as much space as those structures the foundations and remains of which are found at Sárnáth. A third archæologist, Mr. Thomas, late Judge of Benares, and a distinguished numismatist, trod in the same footsteps, only taking interest in the coins discovered in the city and in the Sárnáth explorations. As instances of ruthless spoliation, I may here remark, that, in the erection of one of the bridges over the river Barna, forty-eight statues and other sculptured stones were removed from Sárnáth and thrown into the river, to serve as a breakwater to the piers; and that, in the erection of the second bridge, the iron one, from fifty to sixty cart-loads of stones from the Sárnáth buildings were employed. But this vandalism hardly equals that of Babu Jagat Sinh, who, in the last century, carted away an entire *tope*, or sacred tower, from the same vast store-house, with which he built Jagat Ganj, a ward or district in the suburbs of the city.

The chief reason why Benares has been thus neglected is, in my judgment, attributable partly to its great extent, and partly to the general ignorance as to the position of its ancient portions; and, consequently, the explorer, in commencing his task, has been in considerable doubt where to begin. Now, it is necessary to state, that much of the existing city has been erected in comparatively modern times, and, with the exception of an occasional bit of old frieze or cornice, or a broken bass-relief or statue, inserted into recent walls, deposited over drains, or lying neglected by the side of the road, there is nothing of an ancient character visible throughout a very large section of it. Yet all the northern quarter of the city, a district little frequented by European visitors, exhibits in abundance isolated specimens of architectural remains of various stages of antiquity. Independently of a few separate buildings, or parts of buildings, here and there to be seen, of an early style of Hindu architecture, sculptured stones of many kinds are distributed amongst the walls and foundations of the modern houses, and in all places wherever solid masonry is required, in such great profusion, that it is impossible not to believe that on this site stood an older city or, at least, a portion of it. Moreover, the very scattered nature of these remains shows that a considerable period has elapsed since they occupied their proper places in their own original edifices. It might be utterly impracticable to collect the entire materials of any one building; but this is not necessary, seeing that the age of a building can be commonly determined by observing merely a fragment of its ruins. In the case, however, of ancient Hindu remains, so little has been done in their investigation, especially in comparing one with another, that the question of their antiquity cannot be at once decided. From an ignorance of primitive types, mistakes of five hundred or a thousand years or upwards may be easily made. In judging, therefore, of the age of the relics found in Benares, we have, in reality, very little to guide us.

If there be anything in the argument based on the simplicity of a style, or on its ornamentation, as bearing on its greater or less antiquity, then we can predicate of the buildings which formerly stood in this part of Benares various stages of antiquity. Some of the capitals, pillars, bases, architraves, and mouldings are most severely simple in their type, while others are crowded with ornamentation; and both species are very different from the styles in modern use. The first species is, doubtless, the forerunner of the second, but at what interval, it is at present impossible to affirm.

There is no question that a large proportion of the ancient remains in Benares are of Buddhist origin, but of various epochs; and, in some cases, those on the same site are of different ages. For instance, the Buddhist monastery and temples, of which traces are found at Bakaríyá Kuṇḍ, differ in their styles of architecture. Of the two small temples, parts of which, though possibly altered and transposed, are still standing, the pillars of the one are square and without ornament, while those of the other, situated about three hundred yards off, are square below, then eight-sided, and then sixteen-sided, and are adorned with exquisitely-carved devices. Moreover, from the quarry-marks engraved upon many of the stones found here, it is manifest that a portion of the buildings was erected about the era of the Gupta dynasty, or perhaps from the first or second to the third or fourth century A.D.

There are several ancient edifices in Benares, which, if not original, are certainly to a large extent built of old materials. In these, more especially in their columns, may be traced a gradation of style. When we compare the simple bracket or cruciform capital and its plain square shaft and base, such as we find in the pillars of the cloisters around the platform of Aurungzeb's mosque behind the modern Bisheśwar temple, and also in the pillars of a Mohammedan cemetery in the neighbourhood of Tiliyá Nálá, with the elaborately ornamented columns of the mosque in the Ráj Ghát Fort, we are at once struck with the contrast, and at the extraordinary development which the style—the same fundamentally in both instances—has received. Various intermediate stages of diversity are represented in other buildings; but I cannot now further enlarge on them. The first class of pillars, however, must, I contend, be of a much earlier date than the other. Yet it does not follow that this latter class belongs necessarily to a recent epoch. The mosque in which the columns are found consists, apparently, of two Buddhist cloisters, or, possibly, of two divisions of a Buddhist temple, and has been, at times, so extensively altered and repaired that it is hard to say that any one column stands exactly as originally placed. The columns are four in each row, and are seventy in number. They are all carved, as also, with a few exceptions, are the architraves; and the carvings in one division are uniform. The carvings in the other division are bolder and more profuse, but, nevertheless, are totally free from degeneracy of style. Some of the pillars are of striking beauty, and, for grandness of conception, and correctness of execution, are scarcely surpassed anywhere in India. Now, as some of the beautifully carved pillars at Bhilsa were set up in the second or third century before Christ, we must be careful in our estimate of the date to which the Ráj Ghát pillars, which are of singular excellency and purity of style, ought to be assigned, although I do not propose to claim for them so high an antiquity.

But I do not suppose that the architectural remains scattered, for the most part in fragments, over this quarter of Benares, are all of Buddhist origin. At the same time, I must not forget the remark of Fergusson ("Handbook of Architecture," p. 100), that "the earliest authentic building that we have of the Hindu religion in Hindustan is the great temple of Bhobaneswar (in Orissa), built by Lelat Indra Kesari, A.D. 657," which, if true at the time he wrote, is hardly true now. The same eminent writer has elsewhere hazarded the observation, respecting Buddhist structures, that no built examples whatever exist in India of Buddhist temples (chaityas) and monasteries (viháras); and has, besides, apparently confounded Jaina and Buddhist monuments.

Previously to the Buddhist supremacy in India, we know that Benares was a Brahmanical city; and there is no proof that, at any period of that supremacy, Brahmanism was entirely extirpated. For my part, I am inclined to believe that some of these ancient remains may be attributed equally to Hindu and Buddhist origin. The simple style of architecture, to which I have referred, was, without doubt, the earliest introduced into Benares, perhaps into Hindustan; and, whether the work of Buddhists or of Hindus is, doubtless, of high antiquity. Yet how it found its way here is open to question. This part of the existing city, as already stated, is much older than the rest; but, after all, there is good reason to believe that only a small portion of even this quarter belonged to the most ancient city, in which case the above-mentioned fragmentary remains of a very old type, may have been chiefly brought from the primitive city, or may have been relics of buildings erected after models found there. This entire subject will be discussed in subsequent chapters, towards the close of this volume, in which some account of the archæology of Benares and its neighbourhood will be given in detail.

It is worthy of notice, as illustrating the nature of Mohammedan rule in India, that nearly all the buildings in Benares, of acknowledged antiquity, have been appropriated by the Musulmans; being used as mosques, mausoleums, dargáhs, and so forth; and also that a large portion of the separate pillars, architraves, and various other ancient remains, which, as before remarked, are so plentifully found in one part of the city, now contribute to the support or adornment of their edifices. Not content with destroying temples and mutilating idols, with all the zeal of fanatics, they fixed their greedy eyes on whatever object was suited to their own purposes, and, without scruple or any of the tenderness shown by the present rulers, seized upon it for themselves. And thus it has come to pass, that every solid and durable structure, and every ancient stone of value, being esteemed by them as their peculiar property, has, with very few exceptions, passed into their hands. We believe it was the boast of Aláuddín, that he had destroyed one thousand temples in Benares alone. How many more were razed to the ground, or transformed into mosques through the iconoclastic fervour of Aurungzeb, there is no means of knowing; but it is not too much to say, that he was unsurpassed, in this feature of religious fanaticism, by any of his predecessors. If there is one circumstance respecting the Mohammedan period which Hindus remember better than another, it is the insulting pride of the Musulmans, the outrages which they perpetrated upon their religious convictions, and the extensive spoliation of their temples and shrines. It is right that Europeans should clearly understand, that this spirit of Mohammedanism is unchangeable, and that, if, by any mischance, India should again come into the possession of men of this creed, all the churches and colleges, and all the Mission institutions, would not be worth a week's purchase.

When we endeavour to ascertain what the Mohammedans have left to the Hindus of their ancient buildings in Benares, we are startled at the result of our investigations. Although the city is bestrewn with temples in every direction, in some places very thickly, yet it would be difficult, I believe, to find twenty temples, in all Benares, of the age of Aurungzeb, or from 1658 to 1707. The same unequal proportion of old temples, as compared with new, is visible throughout the whole of Northern India. Moreover, the diminutive size of nearly all the temples that exist is another powerful testimony to the stringency of the Mohammedan rule. It seems clear, that, for the most part, the emperors forbade the Hindus to build spacious temples, and suffered them to erect only small structures, of the size of cages, for their idols, and these of no pretensions to beauty. The consequence is, that the Hindus of the present day, blindly following the example of their predecessors of two centuries ago, commonly build their religious edifices of the same dwarfish size as formerly; but, instead of plain, ugly buildings, they are often of elegant construction. Some of them, indeed, are so delicately carved externally, are so crowded with bass-reliefs and minute sculpturing, are so lavishly ornamented, that the eye of the beholder becomes satiated and wearied. In regard to size, there is a marked difference between the temples of Northern and Southern India; the latter being frequently of gigantic dimensions. Yet, in respect of symmetry and beauty, the difference is immensely in favour of the Northern fanes.

The present city of Benares, like the earlier one, exhibits a tendency to shift its site. If any person will take the trouble to ride through the city from north to south, and then all along its extensive suburbs, from the ancient fort at the junction of the Barna and the Ganges, down the road leading towards the cantonments, thence making a detour as far as Durgá-kuṇḍ until he again reaches the Ganges, he will at once be convinced that the aspects of the city differ greatly from one another. He will be especially struck by the apparent newness and freshness of the houses on the southern side, as compared with those on the northern side; and his attention will be, or ought to be, powerfully arrested by the venerable appearance of many of the buildings on the cantonment road just alluded to, and in its neighbourhood.

There is still a scattered population on the southern bank of the Barna, living in small villages or hamlets; and, to the north of the present city, between it and the Barna, mausoleums, dargáhs, mosques, and even Hindu buildings, most of which are in ruins, are found in abundance, showing that, as late as the Mohammedan period, this portion of the city, now become its suburbs, was possessed of considerable magnificence, and, indeed, was a favourite place of resort to its Mohammedan rulers. The tendency of Benares to change its boundaries—for it shifts continually in a south-westerly direction—is well illustrated by the position of the three fortresses which the Rajas of Benares have occupied at various periods of its history. The oldest fort was situated at Barna Sangam, or the confluence of the Barna and the Ganges; and a few remains of it are still standing. In its day it no doubt formed a part of the city, and was its chief defence; but now it is only a remote suburb, with a mere handful of people in its immediate neighbourhood. The second in point of time is the fort at S'iválá Ghát, some four miles further south-west in the midst of a dense population: it was the residence of Cheit Singh, in the time of Warren Hastings, but is no longer inhabited by the Rajas of Benares. The third fort is that in which the present Raja dwells, and is situated at Rámnagar, upwards of a mile to the south-east of S'iválá Ghát, on the opposite side of the river, where a considerable population has sprung up.

At present, as has long been the case, the city is known by the two names of Káśí and Benares; the latter designation being a corruption of the Sanskrit Váraṇasí, Varáṇasí and Varaṇasí.[1] On these words, as significative terms, we have only uncertain grounds for speculation. Káśí, the name most favoured by the Hindus, is considered to mean 'splendid.' Varaṇasí is explained as a compound of Varaṇá and Así, which refer, it is conjectured, to the two streams bearing these names, and severally flowing into the Ganges to the north and south of the city, of which they thus constitute to some extent a natural boundary. In some late Brahmanical writings, Benares is spoken of as lying between the Varaṇá and the Así; but, in fact, it lies at a considerable distance from the Varaṇá in one direction, and in the other, while it has passed over the small rivulet of the Así, and now embraces it within itself, it is evident that at one time it was a long way distant from that stream. The Varaṇá (or Barna, as it is popularly called,) contains a considerable body of water in the rainy season; but the Así continues a small stream all the

[1] वारणसी, वराणसी, वरणसी.

year round. There is another derivation current among the natives, perhaps worthy of mention. It is said that a certain Raja Banár formerly ruled over Benares, and gave his own name to the city.

It would appear, that, with the followers of Buddha, the popular name of the city was not Káśí, but Benares; and, on the other hand, that, while the city commonly bore the name of Benares, the circumjacent country was called Káśí. The Chinese pilgrim Fa Hian, who travelled in India at the commencement of the fifth century A.D., remarks, in the journal of his travels, that, following the course of the river Heng (Ganges) towards the "west, he came to the town of *Pho lo nai* (or Benares), in the kingdom of *Kia shi*."[1] The ancient Buddhist writings of Ceylon also make reference to the Sárnáth portion of the old city as existing "in the kingdom of Káśí." At one time, therefore, during the prevalence of the Buddhist religion in India, the territory surrounding Benares, and including the city, was called the Káśí kingdom or country; and it is not unlikely that both Káśí and Váráṇasí were terms interchangeably employed to designate the surrounding country even after the decline and downfall of the Buddhist religion in India. Dr. F. Hall concludes, I find, that so late as the eleventh century A.D., "at a period when Káśí was, presumably, the more popular name of the city of Benares, the circumjacent territory was known as Váráṇasí."[2] Indeed, the inscription which gave rise to this remark makes use of the word Váráṇasí as de-

[1] Laidlay's Pilgrimage of Fa Hian, p. 307.

[2] Bengal Asiatic Society's Journal for 1862, page 5, Note.

noting the 'circumjacent territory.' This use is found in a land-grant issued by Raja Vináyakapála, and may be as late as the middle of the eleventh century.

Further information respecting the ancient city, being, for the most part, derived from the examination of ruins found in various places, and therefore of a technical character, and not perhaps of interest to the general reader, although of much importance to the archæologist and to all concerned in the physical aspects of old Benares, is given in several chapters towards the close of the volume. I proceed now to a description, in detail, of some of the noteworthy characteristics of the city as it at present exists. I would premise, however, that such of the peculiarities of the city as are about to be referred to are by no means intended as an exhaustive catalogue of the whole. There are very many others, more or less remarkable, which any one on the spot, interested in the subject, would, very likely, find to be deserving of his attention.

CHAPTER III.

Puranic form of Modern Hinduism.—Increase of Temples in Northern India.—Number of Temples in Benares.—Temple of Bisheśwar, the idol-king of Benares.—Ancient Temple of Bisheśwar, now a Mohammedan Mosque.—The Well Gyán Bápí.—Temple of Ád-Bisheśwar.—The Well Kásí Karwaṭ.—Temple of Saníchar.—The goddess Annpúrṇá and her temple.—Temples of Gaṇeś and S'ukreśwar.

The form of religion prevailing among the Hindus in Benares, and throughout a large portion of India, is Puranic, which, in all probability, originated in the country generally at the time when the Buddhist religion began to lose its hold upon the people, or about the fifth or sixth century A.D. Vedantism more or less tinctures the philosophical creed of many; but the staple religion of the masses is the lowest and grossest form of idolatry—the worship of uncouth idols, of monsters, of the linga and other indecent figures, and of a multitude of grotesque, ill-shapen, and hideous objects. Some of them are wild parodies on the animal kingdom, representing imaginary creatures made up in a variety of ways. There is no city in India in which the reverence paid to images is more absolute and complete than in Benares. It is remarkable, too, as showing the extent to which the spirit of idolatry has permeated all classes, that pandits and thinking men, who ought to know better, join in the general practice. The only persons that do not heartily engage in it are converts to Christianity, to whom we may add many of the young men educated at the public colleges and schools, who either abandon it, or, while mechanically performing, out of deference to their parents and friends, the prescribed religious duties, have already perceived the hollowness and absurdity of Hinduism, and do not scruple occasionally to betray their sentiments, and even to scoff at their own religion. To this class, which is constantly increasing, should be added those persons,—the number of whom may be large, but which it is impossible to calculate, who have paid serious attention to the exposition of Christian truth by missionaries, and who, although not outwardly accepting Christianity, are yet to some extent convinced of the falsity of Hinduism.

Since the country has come into our hands, a great impetus has been given to the erection of temples, and to the manufacture of idols, in Northern India. In Benares, temples have multiplied at a prodigious rate; and this rate, at the present moment, is, I believe, rather increasing than diminishing. Judged merely by its external appearances, Hinduism was never so flourishing as it is now. With general prosperity and universal peace, and with a Government based on neutral principles, and largely tolerant of the national religious systems, Hinduism, under the leadership of men of the old school, —princes, pandits, banyas (tradespeople), and priests,—is making extraordinary efforts to maintain its position against the new doctrines of European civilization and religion, which they now begin to recognize as formidable opponents. The remarks of the Rev. Dr. Mullens, on the extension of Hinduism, materially and outwardly, in "Christian Work" for July, 1864, strongly bear out the preceding observations:—

"There can be little doubt," he says, "that a hundred years ago, the temples, mosques, and shrines of India, belonging to all the native religions, were by no means in a flourishing condition. Large numbers, indeed, must have been in a state of decay. The anarchy that prevailed throughout the Mogul empire after the death of Aurungzeb, the constant wars, the terrible visits of foreign armies, the civil contests, the struggles of petty landholders, all tended to produce a state of insecurity which paralysed trade, which even hindered agriculture, and involved all classes in a poverty which the empire had not suffered for many years. Never were invasions more fierce; never were famines more cruel. Though freed from the persecutions of the bigoted emperor, the temples suffered grievously from the general want; and it was, probably, only in the Mahratta provinces that Hinduism flourished; in them realizing its prosperity from the plunder of successful Mahratta armies, whose piety rewarded the shrines of their protecting divinities with a shower of endowments and offerings which remain in measure to the present day. Hinduism now is, externally, in a much more flourishing condition than it was then. All over North India especially, the native merchants and bankers who have prospered by English protection, by contracts with English armies, by the security given by English law to their extensive trade, have filled Benares and other cities with new and costly shrines; and many a Raja, and many a banker, when visiting in state the holy city, has poured into the lap of the attendant priests unheard-of sums, which must have satisfied even their covetous and grasping souls. Thus strangely has the revival of prosperity under English rule added something of external strength to the ancient idolatry, the resources of which had, in so many places, begun to fail. The new school, enlightened and doubting, ceases to build new temples, or endow the old ones. The old school, prospering in trade, growing in wealth, still trusting to the ancient superstitions, and anxious to earn merit for themselves, build new temples and present new gifts; though feeling that the days of their faith are numbered, and that other views are gradually pressing their own into oblivion."

This temple-building movement, singular as it is, is really no ground for discouragement whatever, and must not be permitted to blind our eyes to the great transforming work which is being accomplished in Benares and in Northern India generally. I regard it as a movement, to a large extent spasmodic, intended to counteract the Christian influences which, in so many ways and in so many places, are operating upon the community. Undoubtedly, it is quite true that the religious sentiments of a Hindu would prompt him to devote a considerable portion of his wealth, acquired in times of tranquillity and national prosperity, to sacred purposes. At the same time, he is quickened and stimulated in this desire, at the present day, by a strong and painful conviction that his religion is in danger, that his children are growing up unsound in the Hindu faith, and that a new creed, to which the foreign rulers and governors of his country are attached, is moving the hearts of multitudes of his own race and tongue, which he must resist with all his might, and must do so now or never. Notwithstanding, therefore, all that is being done by Brahmans, Hindu priests, and other determined idolaters, to sustain Hinduism, and to thwart Christianity, it is a fact, admitting of distinct proof, that the one is on the decline and the other is in the ascendant, the one is decaying and crumbling to pieces, while the other is daily becoming stronger and more influential.

It remains to be seen whether the new religion or the

old—Christianity or Hinduism—is the more powerful. The contest between them has already commenced. It is felt throughout all the divisions of native society. It is filling with anxiety the higher castes, and is calling forth all the subtlety of the Brahmans, all their intellect, and all their mysterious authority. We must expect the opposition to Christianity to be, in many places, organized and systematic, determined and dogged. But, if Christians in India be faithful to themselves and to their Divine Master, the triumph of their cause is certain.

Upwards of thirty years ago, Mr. James Prinsep, then stationed at Benares, took a census of the city, and also made a computation of the number of temples and mosques existing in it. From his calculation, which was made with considerable care, there were, at that time, in the city proper, exclusive of the suburbs, 1,000 Hindu temples and 333 Mohammedan mosques. But this number of temples, which has since been much increased, did not include, I imagine, the small shrines, the niches in the walls, the cavities inside and outside many of the houses, and the spaces on the gháts, in which images in immense multitudes were and are still deposited. These secondary shrines, if they be worthy of this designation, each occupied by one or more idols, are, in some parts of the city, exceedingly numerous. Figures of all forms, from a plain stone to the most fantastic shape, whole and mutilated, painted and unpainted, some without adornment, others decorated with garlands, or wet with sacred water, meet the eye in every direction. These remarks especially refer to the neighbourhood of the bathing gháts and of the principal temples. But the abundance of idols and fanes all over the city gives it a strange and repellent appearance.

By a more recent estimate than that made by Mr. Prinsep, the following results have been arrived at, the accuracy of which, however, I am unable to vouch for, though I dare say they may be taken as approximately correct :—

Districts of the City.	Temples.	Mosques.
Koṭwálí	261	19
Kál Bhairo	216	20
Ádhampurá	48	54
Jaiṭpurá	30	97
Chetganj	53	32
Bhelápurá	154	16
Dasáśamedh	692	34
	1454	272

The Hindus have a strange fancy for accumulating idols in certain spots. Not content with depositing an image in a temple, they ornament its portico and walls with deities, or arrange them in rows in the temple enclosure. You may sometimes see twenty, fifty, and even a hundred of these idols in one place, many of which will perhaps receive as much homage as the god who is exalted to the chief seat within the temple itself. If it would be difficult to count the small shrines and sacred niches abounding in the city, it would be incomparably more so to enumerate the idols actually worshipped by the people. These inferior shrines were, on one occasion, by a curious contrivance, immensely increased; and yet the increase could hardly have been generally perceived. Raja Mán Sinh, of Jeypore, wishing to present one hundred thousand temples to the city, made this stipulation, that they were all to be commenced and finished in one day. The plan hit upon was, to cut out on blocks of stone a great many tiny carvings, each one representing a temple. The separate blocks, therefore, on the work being completed, exhibited, from top to bottom, and on all sides, a mass of minute temples. These blocks are still to be seen in various parts of Benares, the largest being situated above the Dasáśamedh Ghát, near the Mán Mandil Observatory. In regard to the number of idols of every description actually worshipped by the people, it certainly exceeds the number of people themselves, though multiplied twice over: it cannot be less than half a million, and may be many more. Indeed, the love for idolatry is so deep-seated and intense in the breast of the Hindu, that it is a common thing for both men and women to amuse themselves, with a pious intent, with manufacturing little gods from mud or clay, and, after paying divine honours to them, and that, too, with the same profound reverence which they display in their devotions before the well-known deities of the temples, to throw them away.

I recall to mind a remarkable instance of this. One day on entering the courtyard of the temple of Annpúrṇá, the goddess of plenty, my attention was arrested by an aged woman seated on the ground in front of a small clay figure, which, I ascertained, she had, with her own hands, manufactured that morning, and to which she was solemnly paying homage. Close by was a brazen vessel containing water, into which every now and then she dipped a small spoon, and then gently poured a few drops upon the head of the image. She then reverently folded her hands, and muttered words of prayer, occasionally moving one hand to her face, and with finger and thumb compressing her two nostrils, in order that, holding her breath as far as possible, she might increase the merit of her worship and the efficacy of her prayer. I did not stay to the end; yet I well knew the result, as the same thing is constantly done in Benares. Having completed her devotions, she rose, took the image which she had worshipped in her hands, and threw it away, as of no further use.

Benares, like Athens in the time of St. Paul, is a city "wholly given to idolatry." The Hindu, it should always be remembered, is, in his own fashion, a religious man of very great earnestness; but his religion takes the form of idolatry. Idolatry enters into all the associations and concerns of his life. He can take no step without it. He carries his offerings publicly in the streets, on his way to the temple in the morning, and receives upon his forehead, from the officiating priest, the peculiar mark of his god, as the symbol of the worship he has paid him, which he wears all the day long. As he walks about, you may hear him muttering the names and sounding the praises of his gods. In greeting a friend, he accosts him in the name of a deity. In a letter on business, or on any other matter, the first word he invariably writes is the name of a god. Should he propose an engagement of importance, he first inquires the pleasure of the idol, and a lucky day for observing it. At his birth, his horoscope is cast; when he is ill, the gods must be propitiated; when he is bereaved, the idol must be remembered; at his death, his funeral rites are performed in the name of one or more deities.

In short, idolatry is a charm, a fascination, to the Hindu. It is, so to speak, the air he breathes. It is the food of his soul. It is the foundation of his hopes, both for this world and for another. He is subdued, enslaved, and befooled by it. He is, however, a willing slave, a willing devotee; for he loves idolatry, together with its superstitions and ceremonies, with all the ardour of religious frenzy. Moreover, it is of great importance to bear in mind, that, as a man can hardly be better than his religion, the nature of the Hindu partakes of the supposed nature of the gods whom he worships. And what is that nature? According to the traditions handed about amongst the natives, and constantly dwelt upon in their conversation, and referred to in their popular songs, which, perhaps, would be sufficient proof for our purpose, yet, more especially, according to the numberless statements and narratives found in their sacred writings, on which these traditions are based, it is, in many instances, vile and abominable to the last degree; so that the poor idolater, when brought completely under its influence, is most deplorably debased. Virtue, truth, holiness, civilization, enlightenment, human progress, all that contributes to individual happiness and to a nation's prosperity, cannot be properly appreciated by him. His soul's best affections are blighted, and his conscience is deeply perverted. Idolatry is a word denoting all that is wicked in imagination and impure in practice. These remarks are especially true of rigid and thorough Hindus, like the Gangá-putras, or "sons of the Ganges," who may be regarded as representing, in their own persons, the complete results of their strange religion. To speak plainly, and yet without extravagance, the moral nature of such Hindus has become so distorted, that, to a large extent, they have forgotten the essential distinctions of things. Their idol-worship has plunged them into immoralities of the grossest forms, has robbed them of truth, has filled their minds with deceit, has vitiated their holy aspirations, has greatly enfeebled every sentiment of virtue, has corrupted the common feelings of humanity within them, has disfigured and well-nigh destroyed the true notion of God which all men in some shape are believed to possess, has degraded them to the lowest depths, and has rendered them unfit alike for this world and for the next. Idolatry is a demon—an incarnation of all evil—but, nevertheless, as bewitching and seductive as a Siren. It ensnares the depraved heart, coils around it like a serpent, transfixes it with its deadly fangs, and finally stings it to death. Idolatry has, for many centuries, drunk the life-blood of the Hindu with insatiate thirst, has covered with its pollutions the fair and fertile soil of India, has drenched the land with its poisoned waters, and has rendered its inhabitants as godless as it was possible for them to become.

Most of the temples are of modern date; but many of them occupy, in popular belief, the sites of immemorial shrines long since displaced by their successors. It is, therefore, a common reply which one receives, on inquiring the date of any given shrine, that it is without date, and has always existed. These original sites are numerous; and each has a history of its own. For instance, the pandits say that Gaṇeś is worshipped in fifty-six places, the goddess Yoganí in sixty-four, Durgá in nine, Bhairo in eight, S'iva in eleven, Vishṇu in one, and the Sun in twelve; all which date from the mythical period, when Divodása, the famous Raja of Benares, whose name is a household word among the people, was prevailed on to permit the gods to return to their ancient and sacred home. But these places do not, by any means, represent the present number of shrines at which these deities are venerated. Gaṇeś especially, the god of wisdom, son of S'iva and Párvatí, is very extensively worshipped in Benares; and there is scarcely a temple in some niche or corner of which his monstrous figure may not be found.

The temple receiving the highest meed of honour in the whole city is that dedicated to the god Bisheśwar, or S'iva, whose image is the linga, a plain conical stone set on end. Bisheśwar is the reigning deity of Benares, and, in the opinion of the people, holds the position of king over all the other deities, as well as over all the inhabitants residing, not only within the city itself, but also within the circuit of the Panchkosí road or sacred boundary of Benares, extending for nearly fifty miles. In issuing his orders, he acts through Bhaironáth, who is the deified *koṭwál* or god-magistrate of Benares and its extensive suburbs. Every matter of importance is presumed to be brought in a regular manner by the *koṭwal* before his royal master. The agents of the *koṭwál* are stationed all along the Panch-kosí road, and are the gods or idols located there, who are supposed to act as *chaukidárs* or watchmen over the entire boundary. The office of these watchmen is to ward off all evil from the sacred city, to contend with such enemies as they may meet with endeavouring to break in upon the outer inclosure, and to send in their reports to the god-magistrate Bhaironáth.

Bisheśwar, in his capacity of idol-king of Benares, demands the homage of his subjects, and will not resign his rights to the other deities who throng his dominions. His subjects must, first of all, worship him, and must bring their offerings to his shrine, of which he, or rather his rapacious priests, are exceedingly fond. Although without mouth or throat, his thirst seems to be great; for one of the most plentiful offerings presented to him is that of Ganges water, with which, in the hot season, he is kept perpetually drenched.

It is no matter of surprise, therefore, that Bisheśwar should receive more adoration than any other idol in Benares. Not only the permanent inhabitants of the city, but also pilgrims and other travellers, may be seen pressing into the temple during the greater portion of the day. The worshippers are of all classes and conditions, and present a singular, and even picturesque, variety of appearance. Among the most prominent of these is, we need hardly say, the proud, half-naked Brahman,—with shaven head, save a long tuft depending from his crown behind, the sacred cord being thrown over one shoulder or ear, and the symbol of S'iva being displayed upon his forehead,—who performs his devotions with punctilious nicety. The faqír, too, in almost primitive nakedness,—his hair dyed and matted together, and his body bedaubed with ashes,—though scarcely noticed by other people, arrests the attention of the stranger. Few of the men have much clothing upon their persons; yet many of them, by their carriage, and by the jewels and gold with which they are adorned, show that they occupy a very respectable position in native society. The women are, for the most part, thoroughly clothed; and, some of them, occasionally, are profusely decorated with gold and silver ornaments studded with precious stones. All the worshippers carry offerings in their hands, consisting of sugar, rice, ghee (or clarified butter), grain, flowers, water, etc. One of the most beautiful of the flowers presented is the lotos, the form and colour of which bear some resemblance to those of a large tulip or water-lily.

Over the narrow doorway which constitutes the chief entrance to the temple, is a small figure of Gaṇeś, upon which some of the worshippers, as they pass in, sprinkle a few drops of water. As one enters the enclosure, several shrines are visible. The worshipper pays his homage to any god, or to all, as he may elect; but he must of necessity approach the paramount deity of the place, that is to say, the plain conical stone already spoken of. He makes his obeisance to the god either by bowing his head—his hands being folded in adoration — or by prostrating himself upon the ground; after which he presents his offering, and rings one of the bells suspended from the roof of the temple. This is to attract the attention of the god,—for it is possible he may be asleep, or otherwise occupied,—and to fix it upon himself. The adoration of an idolater is sometimes distressingly solemn. His whole soul seems to be over-awed, but with what sentiments it is impossible to affirm; and the solemnity, if any, is singularly transient, and lasts only so long as he is in the presence of the idol. It is difficult to analyse his feelings, or to affirm precisely that they are of this or of that nature: nevertheless, there can be little doubt that his mind is occasionally filled with dread and anxiety, amounting, it may be, to alarm. The idolater cherishes no love for the idols he worships, but, on the contrary, regards them as beings to be feared, and, therefore, to be propitiated by adoration and suitable offerings. Nearly all the worshippers engage in their devotions in a quiet, orderly, and decent manner, but with manifest perfunctoriness, and with little or no thought beyond the desire to perform thoroughly the task they have set themselves, even to the minutest particular.

The temple of Bisheśwar is situated in the midst of a quadrangle, covered in with a roof, above which the tower of the temple is seen. At each corner is a dome, and, at the south-east corner, a temple sacred to S'iva. When observed in the distance, from the elevation of the roof, the building presents three distinct divisions. The first is the spire of a temple of Mahádeva, whose base is in the quadrangle below; the second is a large gilded dome; and the third is the gilded tower of the temple of Bisheśwar itself. These three objects are all in a row, in the centre of the quadrangle, filling up most of the space from one side to the other. The carving upon them is not particularly striking; but the dome and tower glittering in the sun look like vast masses of burnished gold. They are, however, only covered with gold leaf, which is spread over plates of copper overlaying the stones beneath. The expense of gilding them was borne by the late Maharaja Runjeet Sinh, of Lahore. The tower, dome, and spire terminate, severally, in a sharp point. Attached to the first is a high pole bearing a small flag and tipped with a trident. The temple of Bisheśwar, including the tower, is fifty-one feet in height. The space between the temples of Bisheśwar and Mahádeva, beneath the dome, is used as a belfry; and as many as nine bells are suspended in it. One is of elegant workmanship, and was presented to the temple by the Raja of Nepal.

Outside the enclosure, to the north, is a large collection of deities, raised upon a platform, called by the natives 'the court of Mahádeva.' They are, for the most part, male and female emblems. Several small idols likewise are built into the wall flanking this court. These are evidently not of modern manufacture. Their age, however, does not seem to be known. The probability is, that they were taken from the ruins of the old temple of Bisheśwar, which stood to the north-west of the present structure, and was demolished by the Emperor Aurungzeb in the seventeenth century. Extensive remains of this ancient temple are still visible. They form a large portion of the western wall of the Mohammedan mosque, which was built upon its site by this bigoted oppressor of the Hindus. Judging from the proportions of these ruins, it is manifest that the former temple of Bisheśwar must have been both loftier and more capacious than the existing structure; and the courtyard is four or five times more spacious than the entire area occupied by the modern temple. The architecture of the ruins seems to be of a mixed character, and composed both of Jaina and Hindu orders. Indeed, it is not impossible that a few slight traces of Buddhist architecture might be detected, also. What makes this latter supposition plausible is, that, on three sides of the perpendicular face of the terrace on which the mosque stands, Buddhist pillars, of a simple and very early type, forming recesses or rooms, but which were, originally, in all probability, cloisters, are distinctly visible.

The mosque, though not small, is by no means an imposing object. It is plain and uninteresting, and displays scarcely any carving or ornament. Within and without, its walls are besmeared with a dirty whitewash, mixed with a little colouring matter. Its most interesting feature is a row of Buddhist or Hindu columns in the front elevation. The presence of this mosque, located, from motives of insult, in a place held so sacred by the Hindus, and around which their closest sympathies are gathered, is a constant source of heart-burnings and feuds both to Hindus and Mohammedans. The former, while unwillingly allowing the latter to retain the mosque, claim the courtyard between it and the wall as their own. Consequently, they will not permit the Mohammedans to enter the mosque by more than one public entrance, which, instead of being in front of that building, is situated on one side of it. The Mohammedans have many times wished to build a gateway in the midst of the spacious platform in front of the mosque; but, although they once erected one, they were not suffered to make use of it, on account of the excitement that the circumstance occasioned among the Hindu population, which was only allayed by the timely interference of the Magistrate of Benares. The gateway still stands; but the space between the pillars has been filled up. A peepul tree, adored as a god, overhangs both the gateway and the road; but the Hindus will not allow the Mohammedans to pluck a single leaf from it. The Government, as a kind of trustee of the mosque, still pays, periodically, or did so not long since, the interest of money belonging to it, deposited in the Treasury, notwithstanding the Act lately passed forbidding such a practice.

Between the mosque and the temple of Bisheśwar is the famous well known as Gyán Bápí or Gyán Kúp, "well of knowledge," in which, as the natives believe, the god S'iva resides. Tradition says, that, once on a time, no rain fell in Benares for the space of twelve years, and that, in consequence, great distress was experienced by the inhabitants. In order to provide water for the people, and so to relieve them from the terrible calamity which had befallen them, a *Ṛishi*,—one of the mythical beings, not exactly divine, and certainly not mortal, who, to the number of many thousands, are reverenced by the Hindus,—grasping the trident of S'iva, dug up the earth at this spot, and forthwith there issued from beneath a copious supply of water. S'iva, on becoming acquainted with the circumstance, promised to take up his abode in the well, and to reside there for ever. It is stated, moreover, that, on occasion of the destruction of the old temple of Bisheśwar, a priest took the idol of the temple and threw it down for safety. The natives visit this well in multitudes, and cast in water or flowers, and other offerings, as a sacrifice to the deity below. The compound mixture thus produced is necessarily in a constant state of putrefaction, and emits a most disgusting stench. The well is surrounded by a handsome low-roofed colonnade, the stone pillars of which are in four rows, and are upwards of forty in number. The building is small, but has been designed and executed with considerable taste. It is of very recent date, having been erected in the year 1828, by "Sri Maut Baija Bai," widow of "Sri Maut Dowlat Rao Sindhia Bahadoor," of Gwalior.

Immediately to the east of this colonnade is the figure of a large bull, about seven feet high, cut in stone, dedicated to the god Mahádeva; and a few steps further east is a temple built in honour of the same deity. The bull is a gift of the Raja of Nepal; and the temple, of the Rani of Hyderabad. On the south side of the colonnade is an iron palisade, in the enclosure of which are two small shrines, one of white marble, the other of stone, and between them a scaffolding of carved stone, from which a bell is suspended.

Standing in this courtyard, the chief objects in which have been thus briefly described, and looking beyond in a north-westerly direction, the eye falls on a temple about sixty feet in height, situated one hundred and fifty yards distant from the mosque. This is Ád-Bisheśwar, that is, the temple of "the Primeval Lord of All." The natives in the neighbourhood all regard this shrine as of an epoch anterior to that of the old Bisheśwar, the ruins of which, as already stated, form a constituent portion of Aurungzeb's mosque. Hence the name attached to it. This temple is surmounted by a large dome, the decaying condition of which is visible in the gaps on its outer surface, caused by the falling away of broad thick flakes of the cement of which it is composed. The temple below, however, which is faced with slabs of stone as far as the base of the dome, has lately been extensively repaired by a tobacconist in the neighbourhood, named Gaṇpat, who has embellished its interior with paintings traced on the walls, making them look fresh and modern. There is really nothing in this temple of an ancient character; but, on the eastern side of the enclosure, the ground becomes considerably elevated, and upon it stands a mosque built of very old materials, the pillars of which date as far back as the Gupta period, and possibly earlier. May not these old stones and pillars be remains of the original Bisheśwar? Formerly a communication was open between the enclosure of Ád-Bisheśwar and the courtyard of Aurungzeb's mosque already described; but is now closed.

Káśí Karwaṭ, a sacred well of some repute, is situated a short distance to the east of Ád-Bisheśwar. Besides the vertical opening, there is a passage leading down to the water, which formerly was traversed daily by religious Hindus desirous of approaching the holiest part of the well. A few years ago a fanatic offered himself in sacrifice to S′iva, the god of the well, when the authorities caused the passage to be closed; but, on the priests representing that their revenues would greatly suffer, were it to be kept permanently shut, permission was given for it to be opened once a week, namely, every Monday.

This neighbourhood is exceedingly rich in temples of most elaborate workmanship. Some of them, from the summit to the base, are one mass of curious and intricate carving. Not that the designs represented on them, although in some cases elegant, display any very remarkable genius; yet the execution of them is a marvellous feat of chiselling. On the south side of Bisheśwar stands one such temple. The gateways leading into the court-yard and into the fane itself are, both, profusely carved; and, in addition, the latter is crowded with figures intermingled with a multitude of short gilded spires.

Proceeding a little beyond these temples, we come to a small shrine dedicated to Saníchar, or the planet Saturn. The deity within, representing the planet, exhibits a silver head, beneath which depends an apron, or what has the appearance of such. The truth is, the idol is bodiless, and the apron conceals the want. A garland of flowers hangs from either ear, falling below the chin; while above the figure a canopy is spread, designed, I imagine, to illustrate the majesty of the god. It is said of this deity, that, for seven years and a half, he troubles the life of men in general, but that he exempts his own worshippers from the trials and disasters which, for this period, he brings on the rest of mankind.

A few steps further on is Annpúrṇá, a goddess of great repute in Benares, inasmuch as, under the express orders of Bisheśwar, she is supposed to feed all its inhabitants, and to take care that none suffer from hunger. The people have a tradition, that, when Benares was first inhabited, Annpúrṇá found that the task of feeding so many persons was too heavy for her. Filled with anxiety, she knew not what step to take. The goddess of the Ganges, or Gangá, generously came to her relief, and told her, that, if she would bestow a handful of pulse on every applicant, she herself would contribute a *lotá* (a brass vessel) full of water. Annpúrṇá was comforted with the suggestion, in which she acquiesced; and the arrangement thus made produced the most satisfactory results. In honour of Annpúrṇá, "the supplier of food," a custom prevails among all classes, by which hundreds and even thousands of the poor are daily supplied with food. It is this. Those persons that can afford it put aside a quantity of pulse, and moisten it over night, and, in the morning, give it away, in handfuls, to the poor. Only one handful is given to each person; but, as he and all the members of his family can, each, procure a handful, after collecting a supply from a number of donors, they are able, by the middle of the day, to obtain, in the aggregate, a goodly quantity, which they first dry, and then either cook for food, or sell in the bazaar. I have been told that the great consumption, in this way, of this particular kind of grain is one reason why its price is so high in Benares.

On the ground in front of the entrance to the temple of Annpúrṇá, beggars are seated, during most of the day, some of whom have cups in their hands, into which the worshippers, as they go in and out of the temple, throw small quantities of grain or rice. Passing through the doorway into the quadrangle, a similar system of alms-giving and almstaking displays itself. The priests of the temple, too, receive offerings for the poor, in addition to the presents appropriated to themselves. In one corner of the enclosure is a stone box, which is the common treasury for the reception of the gifts intended for this object. In it may be seen a singular medley of rice, grain, water, flowers, milk, etc., which, though perhaps not unwelcome to a Hindu stomach, would revolt a European. Not that the whole of this medley is eaten; but the rice and grain and other edible substances are separated from the rest, and distributed among the applicants.

The temple of Annpúrṇá was erected, 150 years ago, by the Raja of Poona. It possesses a tower, and also a dome, which is carved and ornamented after the Hindu fashion. The dome is sustained by pillars; and between them a bell is suspended, which is kept almost constantly sounding; for, as soon as one worshipper leaves it, another, having performed his devotions, takes his turn in beating it. The bells, in this and other Hindu temples, are not rung, but are beaten with the clapper or tongue depending from within. The carved portions of this temple were once partially or entirely painted; and the painting in the interstices is still visible. The goddess within the temple is regarded, by the natives, as a charming creature. She exhibits the taste of her sex in her fondness for ornaments; for, besides her necklace of jewels and her silver eyes, she occasionally wears a mask of gold or burnished copper, and thus endeavours to enhance her beauty and fascinate her beholders. The temple occupies a large portion of the quadrangle, and stands in its centre. In one corner of this quadrangle is a small shrine dedicated to the Sun. The idol representing the Sun is seated in a chariot drawn by seven horses, and is surrounded by a glory indicative of the rays of light which he emits from his person in all directions. In a second corner is another shrine, in which is an image of Gaurí 'Sankar, and the stone box or receptacle before alluded to. In a third is a large figure of Hanumán, the monkey-god, in bass-relief: and, in a fourth, a figure of Gaṇeś, with the head of an elephant and the body of a man.

Not far from the temple of Annpúrṇá is the temple of Sákhí Bináyaka, or the "witness-bearing Bináyaka." Pilgrims, on completing the journey of the Pánch-kosí road, must pay a visit to this shrine, in order that the fact of their pilgrimage may be verified. Should they neglect to do this, all their pilgrimage would be without merit or profit. The temple is in a square, and was erected by a Mahratta, about one hundred years ago. On the road between these two temples is a red glaring figure of the god Gaṇeś, with silver hands, trunk, feet, ears, and poll, squatting down on the floor, which is raised a little above the pathway. The oddity of this painted monster would excite one's laughter, were the mind not distressed at the thought that it receives divine honours.

Near the temple of Bisheśwar, and to the south of Saníchar, is a small shrine, dedicated to 'Sukreśwar, which is visited by persons desirous of becoming parents of handsome sons. It is said that this god will bestow a fine son on his worshippers, even though fate should not have conferred one on them; and, so long as he lives in Benares, he will pass his time happily, and, at death, will depart to the realms of 'Siva.

CHAPTER IV.

Temple of Bhaironáth, the god-magistrate of Benares.—Dandpán, or the Deified Staff. — Temple of the Planets. — Kál-Kúp, or Well of Fate. —Image of Mahákál, or Great Fate. —The Manikarniká Well and Ghát. — Legends respecting the Well. — Temple of Tárakeśwar. — Sindhia Ghat and the Raja of Nagpore's Ghat. — Temple of Briddhkál.—Shrines of Márkandeśwar and Daksheśwar.—Legend of Raja Daksh.—Temples of Alpmriteśwar and Ratneśwar.

THE temple of Bhaironáth is situated upwards of a mile to the north of the temple of Bisheśwar. The god of this shrine, as already described, is, in public estimation, the deified *kotwal*, or police-magistrate, of Benares and its suburbs, as far as the Pánch-kosí road, within the circuit of which, under the orders of his royal master Bisheśwar, he exercises divine authority over both gods and men. He is bound to keep the city free from evil spirits and evil persons, and, should he find any such within its sacred precincts, to expel them forthwith. As it is through his care and energy that its inhabitants, and all others who may conceive the vain design of ending their days at this hallowed spot, eventually, it is supposed, obtain salvation, it is of the utmost importance that he should perform the functions of his high office wisely and well. It is a natural result, therefore, of his possessing such vast authority, that, for the execution of his orders, he should have deemed it right to arm himself with a truncheon. And this is no figment of the imagination, but a veritable cudgel, of enormous thickness; not, indeed, of wood, but, what is more terrible, of stone. It is called Daṇḍpán, from *daṇḍa*, a stick, and, in common belief, is nothing less than divine. Whether from a desire to enjoy as much tranquillity as possible, or from the universal Hindu custom to shift anxiety and trouble from one shoulder to another, I cannot say, but Bhairo has considerately issued his commands to it, to beat any person who may be found working mischief, and, having done so, has resigned himself to a life of ease. So that, in fact, this intelligent stick is, *de facto*, the divine magistrate of the city. It may seem strange, however, that the temple in which Daṇḍpán is deposited is not that of Bhaironáth, but is another, situated a short distance off. The stone representing this singular deity is about four feet in height, and is specially worshipped, every Tuesday and Sunday, by a great many people. It is set up on end, the upper extremity receiving, occasionally, the adjunct of a silver mask or face; but, when our wondering eyes beheld it, there was only the bare stone visible, with a garland depending from the upper extremity. In front of the stick, three bells were hanging; and, on one side, a priest sat, with a rod in his hand, made of peacock's feathers, with which, in the name of Daṇḍpán, he gently tapped the worshippers, and thereby vicariously inflicted punishment upon them for the offences of which they were guilty. In this temple are other remarkable objects, which will be presently referred to. The worship of Daṇḍpán, and the function attributed to this extraordinary divinity, constitute a climax of absurdity. But the Hindu is as solemn in the presence of the divine stick,—administering, as he imagines, divine justice,—as though it were the chief judge of the Sudder Adawlut, and is totally unconscious of the ludicrous position he occupies.

The worship of Daṇḍpán illustrates, very instructively, the changes that have come over popular Hinduism even within a few centuries. Daṇḍapáṇi,—to give the uncorrupted Sanskrit word,—is, properly, the name of an attendant of S'iva, and signifies 'staff in hand.' The true character of this personage has been forgotten; and his emblem has been elevated to the rank of a substantive deity.

But to return to Bhaironáth. The wall on either side of the door, leading into the enclosure, is decorated with paintings. On the right is a large figure of Bhaironáth or Bhairo (for he possesses both titles,) himself, depicted in a deep blue colour, approaching to black; and behind him is the figure of a dog, intended for him to ride on. The dog, too, is holy; and, in the neighbourhood of the temple, sweetmeat-sellers make small images of a dog in sugar, which the worshippers purchase and present to Bhaironáth, as an offering. On the left side of the doorway is a larger figure of a dog; and above it are ten small paintings, representing the ten *avatars* of Vishṇu. The door itself is carved and embellished not inelegantly. On passing through into the quadrangle, I was struck with the confined position of the temple, which fills up a large portion of the entire area; so that from the quadrangle itself it is impossible to gain more than a very limited view of its upper part.

The base of the tower is, on three sides, built of plain stone, terminating in a castellated parapet, from within which the beautifully-carved spire rises to a considerable height. The shaft is surrounded by an immense number of small domes, ascending, in successive series, up to the apex, which consists of a gilded dome.

The entrance to the temple is on the north side. In front of the shrine occupied by the idol is the porch, or, more properly, the belfry, in which four bells are suspended. This porch rests upon pillars, and is painted and decorated according to Hindu taste, and after the most approved models. A priest is seated to the right and left of the porch, with a rod of peacock's feathers by his side, with which he performs mesmeric passes over children, women, and other people, and thereby, it is believed, wards off from them imps and evil spirits who may seek to do them harm. He also keeps in a prominent position a cup made from a cocoa-nut shell, into which he expects a proper amount of coppers to be thrown, to pay for his mysterious operations. The threshold of the shrine is guarded by two idols, called, severally, Dwárpáleśwar, which stand in niches, one on either side of the doorway. The trident, too, with prongs painted red,—the symbol of Bhaironáth's authority,—stands upright by the wall. The interior of the shrine consists of a small room; and on one side of it is a diminutive shrine, made entirely of copper, which is the habitation of the god Bhaironáth. The idol is of stone; but his face is of silver. He possesses four hands, and stands in a grotesque posture. His head is encinctured with garlands, which hang down in front; and a small oil lamp is kept burning near by. A priest sits close by and applies *kundi*, a kind of dun-coloured powder, to the foreheads of the worshippers. The shrine is surmounted by a dome, which, like the shrine, is of copper; and a bell is suspended in front. As both the god and his priests have a liking for ardent spirits, this is one of the offerings presented to him. Dogs are permitted to enter the interior of his temple, which is owing, doubtless, to the circumstance of his having selected a dog for riding on; but they are not permitted to enter other temples.

This building was erected, upwards of forty years ago, by Bájí Ráo, of Poonah, on the site of the old temple, a small edifice which was thrown down to make room for the new one. Outside the quadrangle, on the south side, is a shrine remarkable for the evident antiquity of some of the idols in it. One of these is a figure of Bhaironáth himself, now much defaced by the wear and tear of time. It is not improbable that this is the original Bhaironáth, which was discarded on account of its mutilated appearance, and in order to make room for the modernized deity. There are other images in this temple; among them, Mahádeva, Gaṇeś, and Súrajnáráyaṇ.

On the west side of the quadrangle, a few paces up a narrow court, is a shrine dedicated to S'ítalá, or the goddess of small-pox. In it are seven figures in bass-relief, representing seven sisters; for this dreaded goddess is, in reality a seven-fold deity. She has four temples devoted to her worship in Benares.

A short distance east of Bhaironáth, and between it and Daṇḍpán, is a temple sacred to Naugrah, or, the Sun, Moon, Mars, Mercury, Jupiter, Venus, Saturn, Ráhu, and

Ketu. The first seven give, in Hindí, their names to the seven days of the week, beginning with Sunday. The Naugrah, in popular estimation, is a very formidable collection of deities. It is customary for the Hindus to commence every important religious ceremony, as, for instance, that of marriage, with the worship of them; for, unless they be propitiated, they may vitiate the entire ceremony. The idols are placed, in the temple, in three rows, three being in each row. The temple remains closed all the day long, but is opened every morning, when a priest comes and peforms *púјá*, that is, worships the idols and presents the necessary offerings. This is the only temple dedicated to Naugrah in Benares. Naugrah is a corruption of the Sanskrit *Nava-graha*, 'the nine planets.'

Proceeding down this narrow street, and passing under an archway to the left, you come to the temple of Daṇḍ-pán, already partially described. Here is, also, a famous well called Kál-kúp, or the Well of Fate. Over the trellis-work of the outer wall of the building is a square hole, which is so situated, in relation to the sun, that, at twelve o'clock, its rays, passing through the hole, impinge upon the water in the well below. At this hour of the day the well is visited by persons wishing to search into the secrets of the Future: and woe be to the man who is unable to trace the shadow of himself in the fatal water; for his doom, it is believed, is certainly and irrevocably fixed, and within six months from that instant he will inevitably die. The general ignorance respecting the explanation of this daily phenomenon does not speak much for the scientific knowledge of the Hindus, or even for their common sense. Under the same roof is an image of Mahákál, or Great Fate. This god virtually bestows salvation on his worshippers; for, on their departure from the world, he spreads over them the ægis of his protection, and prohibits Kál or Evil Destiny from conveying them to the regions of hell. Here, likewise, are the figures of the five brothers, or Pánch Páṇḍav, whose names are celebrated in the Mahábhárata.

No lover of the marvellous should pass through Benares without paying a visit to Maṇikarṇiká, the famous well of Hindu mythology. It is the first place sought after by the thousands of pilgrims flocking yearly to the holy city, who are drawn towards it by a mysterious and irresistible fascination. Its fetid water is regarded as a healing balm, which will, infallibly, wash away all the sins of the soul, and make it pure and holy. There is no sin so heinous or abominable, but, in popular estimation, it is here instantly effaced. Even for the crime of murder it can, it is said, procure forgiveness. No wonder, therefore, that conscience-stricken sinners should rush to this well from all quarters, and, deluding themselves by its reputed sanctity, should, by the easy process of washing in its foulness, seek to atone, in one minute, for the crimes and sins of a life-time. Yet it is appalling to think that the human soul, thus conscious of its guilt, and perhaps, in many instances, in agony respecting it, and anxious for pardon, and for reconciliation with God, should be so cruelly mocked and deceived. Of all places of pilgrimage throughout Hindostan, this well is held, by many, to be the most, or amongst the most, efficacious for bestowing salvation.

Yet the story connected with its origin is wild enough. The author of the *Káśí-khaṇḍa*, not in jest, as some might suppose, but gravely and soberly, furnishes the following account of the matter :—

"The god Vishṇu," he says, "dug this well with his discus, and, in lieu of water, filled it with the perspiration from his own body, and gave it the name of Chakra-pushkariṇí. He then proceeded to its north side, and began to practise asceticism. In the meantime, the god Mahádeva arrived, and, looking into the well, beheld in it the beauty of a hundred millions of suns, with which he was so enraptured, that he at once broke out into loud praises of Vishṇu, and, in his joy, declared that whatever gift he might ask of him he would grant. Gratified at the offer, Vishṇu replied that his request was that Mahádeva should always reside with him. Mahádeva, hearing this, felt greatly flattered by it, and his body shook with delight. From the violence of the motion, an ear-ring called Maṇikarṇaka fell from his ear into the well. From this circumstance, Mahádeva gave the well the name of Maṇikarṇiká. Among the epithets applied to it are those of Muktikshetra, 'seat of liberation,' and Púrṇaśubhakaraṇ', 'complete source of felicity.' Mahadeva further decreed that it should be the chief and the most efficacious among places of pilgrimages."

Such is the tale as found in the *Káśí-khaṇḍa*; but there is another version current among the people. It is reported that Mahádeva and his wife Párvatí were one day seated by the well, when, accidentally, a jewel fell from the ear of Párvatí into the water, on account of which circumstance Mahádeva named the well Maṇikarṇiká. Mr. Prinsep, in his "Views of Benares," makes the following remarks on this subject:—"After Kashi had been created by the united will of Iswur and Párbati, the two incorporated energies of the formless and quality-less Bruhm, the active pair determined to give their paradise the benefit of an inhabitant; and Poorooshotama (the supreme male, Vishnoo,) became manifest. Shiva gave him instructions how to behave himself, and left him to his own meditations; whereupon, as a first exploit, with his chakra or discus he dug the tank denominated, from its origin, the Chakr-pushkarni. He then engaged in the usual course of austerity, at the sight of which Shiva shook his head in astonishment, and one of his earrings fell; whence the name of the ghat Manikarnika (jewel of the ear). Vishnoo upon this spot also obtained, as a boon from Mahadeo, the privilege which Kashi enjoys, of giving *mookti* or emancipation to all objects, especially those who bestow gifts, erect *lingas*, and do not commit suicide within the holy precincts."

A series of stone steps on each of the four sides of the well leads down to the water. The seven lowermost steps are said to be without a joining, and to belong to the original well as built by divine hands; and, although the singular fact of several joinings being visible is, to the uninitiated, a slight difficulty in the way of such an assertion, yet the Hindus, brushing aside such a trivial circumstance, readily accept the explanation given by the Brahmans, that the joinings are only superficial, and do not penetrate through the stones. Upon the stairs, in a niche on the north side, is a figure of Vishṇu; and, at the mouth of the well, on the west side, is a row of sixteen diminutive altars, on which pilgrims present offerings to their ancestors. The water of the well is very shallow, being not more than two or three feet in depth. It is insufferably foul, and the effluvium from it impregnates the air for some distance around. The worshipper, descending into the water, laves his head and body with the vile liquid, and, at the same time, utters certain phrases appointed for the ceremony.

Directly in front of Maṇikarṇiká, and between it and the Ganges, is the temple of Tárakeśwar, or "the Lord Táraka." When a Hindu dies, and this god is propitiated, he breathes into his ear, they say, a charm or *mantra* of such efficacy that it delivers him from the misery of the future, and secures for him happiness and joy. The idol is in a kind of cistern, which is kept filled with water offered in sacrifice; and, consequently, the deity is invisible. In the rainy season, the swollen river flows beyond this temple, which, for several months, stands immersed in the stream. Its foundations are thereby undermined, and the blocks of stone of which it is composed incline to separate from one another. The upper part of the tower has been entirely removed, in order to lessen the weight resting upon the base of the building.

Upon the Maṇikarṇiká ghát or stairs, on higher ground than that occupied by the Tárakeśwar temple, is a large round slab, called Charaṇa-páduká, projecting slightly from the pavement; and in the middle of it stands a stone pedestal, the top of which is inlaid with marble. In the centre of the marble are two small flat

Photographed by D. Treshan , Esq.

TEMPLE AT MAṆIKARṆIKÁ GHÁT.

objects, representing the two feet of Vishṇu. The tradition is, that this deity selected this precise spot for the performance of ascetic rites and the worship of Mahádeva. It is, consequently, held in great veneration by the natives, and receives divine honours. In the month of Kártik, multitudes of people flock to Vishṇu's feet, imagining that all who worship them are guaranteed a sure introduction into heaven. Mr. Prinsep observes, that "the charan-páduka (impression of Vishṇu's feet) is said to mark the spot on which he alighted. It is distinguished by the figure of two feet cut in white marble in the centre of a round slab, probably intended to represent the *chakr* or discus; but, as the *charan* is generally thought to be peculiar to Buddha and Jain places of worship, the emblem is, probably, of modern and spurious introduction where it is here set up. There is another *páduka* near the mouth of the Barna Nála."

The Maṇikarniká ghát, while the most sacred of all the gháts in Benares, is also the intermediate point of them all; so that, were the city divided into two portions at this place, they would be nearly equal in extent. Ascending the second flight of stairs, we come to a temple of ancient reputation, but probably of modern construction, occupied by Siddha-vináyak, or Gaṇeś. Imagine a figure painted red, having three eyes, a silver-plated scalp ornamented with a garland of flowers, and an elephant's trunk, this last member being hidden behind a cloth which conceals a large portion of the idol, and, in front, is so tucked in as to resemble the cloth which a barber wraps about a man before shaving him. At the feet of the god is the figure of a rat,—the animal on which he is supposed to ride,—and also a miniature fountain. On either side of the inner shrine is a statue of a woman, one being called Siddhi, and the other, Buddhi. In this neighbourhood there is, likewise, an imposing temple, erected a few years ago by the Raja of Ahmety.

Near to Maṇikarṇiká ghát are Sindhia ghát and the Raja of Nagpore's ghát, the former of which is remarkable not only for the massiveness of its masonry, but also for the circumstance that the entire structure has sunk several feet into the earth since its erection, and is still gradually and slowly sinking. The ghát consists of three rows of low towers or turrets. The uppermost row is of two turrets, one at each extremity, which are the largest of the whole and are exceedingly massive. The second lower down has six turrets; and the third, five. These turrets are called *maṛhís* by the natives, and are used, by them, for sitting upon in the cool of the day, or for retiring to after bathing in the Ganges. They are of stone, and are connected together by walls and stairs of the same material. Before the ghát could be completed, the masonry began to sink; and, on one occasion, so violent was the motion, that a loud report like the discharge of cannon was heard. A temple to the left of the south turret is rent from the summit to the base; and the entire building is so dilapidated, that it looks as if it had been shaken by an earthquake. The ghát itself, and also the stairs leading up to the top of the huge breastwork uniting the two largest turrets, exhibit an immense rent, which is carried down to the very base of the ghát. The breastwork, likewise, to-

Photographed by D. Tresham, Esq.

RAJA OF NAGPORE'S GHÁT.

gether with the turrets, is out of the perpendicular, and has a remarkable appearance. In some places the stones are more than two feet apart. The people residing in the neighbourhood say, that the ghát has sunk some ten or twelve feet in all, and that, inasmuch as stair after stair continually, though slowly, vanishes, they know that the subsidence is still going on. The ghát was built by Baija Bai, the same lady who erected the colonnade round the Gyán Bápí well; but it is not yet completed, and there is no hope that it ever will be.

The temple of Bṛiddhkál, situated on the northern side of the city, is interesting, both for its antiquity and extent, as well as for the singular legends connected with its primitive history. It formerly possessed twelve separate courts or quadrangles; but now only seven are in existence, and several of these are fast falling into ruin. Indeed, the aspect of the entire building is that of decay. The site of the other five courts, and of the gardens once attached to the temple, is occupied by dwelling-houses. When this shrine was in its glory, it must have been a place of some magnificence. The pile of buildings now standing has a hoary appearance, the effect of which is greatly increased by its ruinous condition. The tradition respecting the origin of the temple is, that, in the Satjug, an old Raja in ill-health visited Benares, and there diligently performed ascetic rites, and religious ceremonies. The god Mahádeva was so gratified with the piety of the old man, that he not only healed his sickness, but also caused him to become young again. In honour of this deity, therefore, the Raja erected the present temple, and gave it the name of Bṛiddhkál, a corruption of two Sanskrit words, '*bṛiddha*,' or more properly, '*vṛiddha*,' and '*kála*,' the former meaning *old*, and the latter, *fate*. Mahádeva endowed it with two remarkable properties; the one, that of healing disease, and the other, that of prolonging life. The temple is one of the oldest in the city, and stands on the boundary of Benares Proper,—indisputably the most ancient portion of the existing city, where it unites itself with Káśí, a less ancient portion.

On ascending the steps, and traversing the passage running from the doorway to the inner part of the edifice, we are met by a red figure of Mahábír, the monkey-god, standing within a shrine at the corner of a court into which the passage leads. Close by, to the right, is a small temple dedicated to the goddess Kálí, a small black deity cut out of stone, dressed in a red garment, with a garland of flowers hanging from the neck. In front of her is a hollow space, in the form of a square, for the residence of Mahádeva; and outside of it is a bull, for the god to ride on.

To the right of Kálí, leaning against the wall, are figures of Gaṇeś and Párvatí; and to the left of the latter are images representing Bhairo, the Sun, Hanumán, and Lakshmínáráyaṇ or Vishṇu, and his wife Lakshmí. Immediately opposite to the temple of Kálí are two wells. The first is shallow, and contains putrid water, whose disgusting fetor fills the entire court. Into this well sick persons, and those wishing for long life, plunge their bodies. The former also take various medicines, and resort to other useful means for regaining

their health; and, should they recover, the foul well gets the credit of their restoration. Should the disease, however, be of an obstinate character, such as leprosy or elephantiasis, they must constantly bathe in the well for a period of twelve years. Instead of showing us a man who had been cured, they brought a leper who had strongly-defined marks of leprosy on his legs. He was trying the efficacy of the bath, and said he was better than when he had first arrived. The water of the well is reported to be impregnated with sulphur, in which case it would, doubtless, be very serviceable in some diseases, especially those affecting the skin. In conjunction with washing in this well, it is necessary also to drink of the water of the second well, which, unlike the other, contains sweet water, and has a raised parapet round its mouth. Near the wall of the court is a collection of stone deities, all representing the linga. They are nine in number, of which several are, apparently, very old. Two stone figures of *satís* have also been placed here, in commemoration of the self-immolation of widows on this spot in former times.

To the right of the court is a small square, with a temple in the middle, dedicated to Mahádeva. A serpent is entwined about the chief idol, which is called Nágeśwar, or the Serpent-god. The central deity is surrounded by others of smaller stature. Passing beyond this square, we come to another, in which two peepul trees and one neem tree are growing. This quadrangle has no temple in it, but is used as a residence for devotees. Close by is another quadrangle, the residence of the deity Bṛiddhkál. The shrine within contains two compartments, one of which Bṛiddhkál occupies. He sits in a cistern, while, over his head, hangs a small brass vessel, filled with water, which drops through a hole upon him, without intermission. Though only a plain stone or linga, he is regarded as a very sacred object. In a niche in the verandah is an antique image of the elephant-headed god Gaṇeś. There is another shrine in the area of this quadrangle, flat-roofed, and containing an image of Hanumán.

Returning to the court, in which the wells are situated, and passing through a corridor to the north, we come to a small enclosure, the walls of which are in a dilapidated condition. Here are two shrines, of considerable interest on account of the singular legends associated with them. That on the right is called Márkaṇḍeśwar. Márkaṇḍa was a Ṛishi, whom Mahádeva, it is said, for his piety, endowed with immortality; and who, in acknowledgment of the honour, dedicated this temple to Mahádeva. That on the left is called Daksheśwar, the legend respecting whom fills several pages of the *Káśi-khaṇḍa*. The tale, as revealing some strange events connected with the domestic life of the ruling god of Benares, is worth recounting. Raja Daksh, one of the heroes of the story, is still famous in Benares, and was, no doubt, a real personage.

The wife of S'iva, it seems, although a goddess, dies like common mortals; but, unlike them, shortly after her death, she is born again into the world, and, assuming another name on arriving at maturity, is always married to the same husband, namely, Mahádeva or S'iva. On one occasion, the story goes, Mahádeva assembled, for some purpose, all the gods of heaven and earth. His wife Satí was also there, and likewise her father, Raja Daksh. It appears that Mahádeva neglected to pay proper respect to his father-in-law in the presence of the deities; and, consequently, on departing, the Raja relieved his feelings by showering upon him the following abuse:—"You have neither caste nor habitation, and yet have taken to yourself a wife. You are naked, and wear long hair, and lie down on a tiger's skin. You never had father or mother. Your body is covered with ashes; and, at the end of the world, you will destroy everybody. I have committed a great mistake, in giving you my daughter to wife." After this mental relief, the Raja went home, and prepared a great religious festival, to which he invited all the gods and Rajas, with the exception of Mahádeva and his wife. These latter did not know what was occurring; but Nárad Muni came to them and told them all about it. On hearing of the circumstance, Satí requested permission to go to her father's house, and see, for herself, what was the real state of the case. But Mahádeva urged that she had not been invited to the feast, and, therefore, declined to permit her to go. At last he yielded to her importunity, and she went. On arriving, only her mother paid her the slightest deference; all the rest of the family treating her with marked indifference. When the feast was served, she received her portion; but her husband's share, which ought, in his absence, to have been given to her, was withheld. At this neglect, Satí became exceedingly angry, and beat her head upon the ground, in passionate frenzy.

Moreover, the heavens themselves sent down a shower of blood, in token of their sympathy with her. Several of the gods of the party, disapproving of Raja Daksh's proceeding, rose and left. On their departure, Satí, becoming still more excited, sought out the hole in which the sacrifice was being consumed, and, throwing herself into it, was burnt to ashes. When Nárad Muni brought news of this sad catastrophe to Mahádeva, his wrath rose to fierceness; and, creating an army of demons, he placed it under the command of Bírbhadra, a demon of giant strength, and sent it against the Raja, with orders to kill him, and to frustrate his sacrificial ceremony. On the way, Bírbhadra plucked up forests and mountains, and carried them along in his hands. Having reached the Raja's palace, the demons flew upon the people, slaughtered to right and left, and devoured the viands provided for the sacred feast. The invincible Bírbhadra sought out the Raja, and, finding him, seized him with his hands, and, after crying out "Why did you blaspheme the god Mahádeva?" cut off his head.

This bloody work being finished, Brahmá, the first of the three deities placed at the head of the Hindu pantheon, proceeded, in great consternation, to Mahádeva, with whom he reasoned and expostulated respecting the awful calamity that had just occurred, and prevailed on him to accompany him to the scene of the recent carnage. On reaching the place, Mahádeva's heart was smitten with compassion for the slain; and he gave orders that all the gods, Rishis, and Rajas should be again gathered together, as well the living as the dead. The heads, arms, legs, and other members that had been lopped off the killed and wounded during the conflict, were also collected, and were severally joined afresh to the bodies to which they belonged. Thus Mahádeva healed all the wounded, and restored to life all the slain. But, in the search for the amputated members, Raja Daksh's head could nowhere be found. The god, however, commanded that a goat should be brought to him, the head of which, being cut off, was stuck upon the trunk of the Raja's body, which became forthwith reanimated with its former life. After this, the sacrifice which had been so violently interrupted was completed. Mahádeva then left, with all his demons, for his residence on the Kailás mountain. The rest of the deities also departed, with the exception of Brahmá, who remained behind, in order to talk with Raja Daksh, to whom he represented, in its true colours, the heinous sin he had committed in reviling Mahádeva, and in utterly defeating the sacred festival, the sacrifice at which could not possibly be performed without the presence of that deity. He concluded by recommending the Raja to visit Benares, and there to dedicate an idol to Mahádeva, and thus try to propitiate him. In accordance with this advice, the Raja forsook his throne and his dominions, and proceeded to Benares, where he dedicated an idol to Mahádeva, and applied himself to the performance of ascetic and other religious rites. There he remained for many years. In the meantime, Satí, the wife of Mahádeva, who had perished in the sacrificial fire, was born again among mortals, under the name of Párvatí, her father this time being Raja Mount Himálaya; and, on arriving at womanhood, she was again married to her former husband, Mahádeva. The happy couple travelled to Benares, for the purpose of spending their honeymoon; and, while there, what was their surprise to see old goat-headed Raja Daksh, who was still absorbed in his religious exercises! He, too, was doubtless equally astonished to see Mahádeva, whom, of course, he recognized, although his mental eyes were closed in regard to Párvatí, whom he did not perceive to be his own daughter Satí. The Raja pleaded with Mahádeva for the forgiveness of his sin. The god heard his petition, and granted it; and the old man, filled with joy, dedicated a shrine to Mahádeva, called Daksheśwar, which is said to be that situated in the interior of the temple of Bṛiddhkál. This tale is as entertaining as many of the legends connected with the Black Forest; the only difference, though an essential one, being, that they are designed for amusement and fun, whereas this, strangely enough, is intended for the promotion of religion.

Leaving this temple, and proceeding along the street by its southern wall, we come to a shrine standing at its south-western angle, and forming part of the Bṛiddhkál edifice. Its name is Alpmṛiteśwar, from the god to whom it is dedicated, who, it is reported, is endowed with the miraculous power of prolonging the lives of persons apparently in act to die. The fame of this shrine is considerable; and it is the resort of a large number of worshippers, who seek for themselves and their friends an escape from sickness and death. In the

streets leading to the Bṛiddhkál temple, a *melá* or fair is held every Sunday; and, once a year, in the month of Sáwan, one on a large scale is held, which lasts for several days. These *melás* are partly of a religious, and partly of a secular, character; but their primary intention is the worship of some celebrated deity.

In a street leading to Bṛiddhkál, a small temple obstructs the thoroughfare, called Ratneśwar, from *ratna*, a jewel. The shrine is referred to in Hindu writings. A curious circumstance is connected with its modern history. Upwards of thirty years ago, an English magistrate of Benares, while making improvements in the city, determined that this temple should be levelled with the ground. The natives say, that, one night, the god Mahádeva appeared to the *sáhib*, or gentleman, in a dream, and, representing to him the great sin he was intending to commit, ordered him to forbear from the execution of such an evil design; and that, on awaking, the *sáhib*, in obedience to the divine admonition, laid aside his levelling project. It is reported, also, and commonly believed, that, while digging at the foundations of the temple, on this occasion, a jewel was discovered beneath it; but the natives themselves express considerable doubt about its genuineness.

CHAPTER V.

Legend respecting Divodás. — Temple of Divodáseśwar. — The Well Dharm-kúp.—Rádhá-Krishṇa.—The Nág Kúáṅ or Serpent's Well.—Old Images.—Temples of Bágeśwarí, Jwarahareśwar, and Siddheśwar.

Although the city of Benares is now regarded as sacred to S'iva, and as a place over which he exercises divine authority, yet it is commonly believed, by the inhabitants, that there was a time when such a divinity was not worshipped here, but divine honours were bestowed on a Raja called Divodás. The tradition, too, is sanctioned by the *Kásí-khaṇḍa.* It is said, that this personage, whom Brahmá raised to the dignity of Raja of Benares, and vested with jurisdiction over both gods and men, took it into his head to banish all the gods from the city. This ruthless act seems to have produced immense consternation throughout the Hindu pantheon; but the Raja possessed such supernatural power, that the deities were thwarted in all their efforts to reenter the city. Headed by S'iva, they formed a conspiracy to unseat him, and, in order to effect their purpose, attempted to inveigle Divodás into some act of sin; knowing, that, the moment the sin was perpetrated, his divine power and authority would come to an end, and they would regain their lost dignities and prerogatives. But this miserable and disgraceful design, though instigated and approved by S'iva himself, came to nothing; for Divodás was a man of unspotted purity and of the strictest integrity. At last, Gaṇeś hit upon a scheme, which was singularly cunning and successful. In the character of a great Guru or teacher, he appeared, one day, at the door of the Raja's palace, and solicited an audience with him. This the Raja granted, and, in course of conversation, was so much pleased with the intelligence, learning, and sanctity of his new acquaintance, that he wished to sit at his feet, as his disciple. With this request Gaṇeś refused to comply; but, taking advantage of the Raja's good opinion of him, he induced him to consent to follow out whatever instructions should be communicated to him in a dream. These instructions simply were, that he should quit Benares. Feeling bound to fulfil his promise, he abandoned the government, abdicated the throne, and retired from the place, and was, thereupon, conveyed, by S'iva himself, to the Kailás mountain. On his departure, the gods reentered the city, and S'iva became their supreme ruler and the head of the city. These are reported to be the old deities of Benares; and to them pilgrimages are made. The myriad deities which have been introduced, at various times, into the city, since this imaginary emigration of the gods, must, therefore, be looked upon in the light of interlopers.

In endeavouring to extract a few grains of truth out of this strange mythological story, we are led to suppose that there was a time when Benares was not imbued with Hinduism as it is now. This Raja Divodás, who, no doubt, was a real personage, may be conceived to have resisted the encroachments of Hinduism, on its first approach to Benares, but was, eventually, obliged to succumb to it, and to surrender his crown to the Brahmanical invaders; or, it may be, that, in a remote age in the history of Hinduism, the Raja may have become possessed of the city, perhaps by right of conquest, and, being attached to another creed, may have forthwith expelled the Brahmans, together with the symbols of their religion, from the place, but, after violent opposition on their part, was, at length, outwitted and supplanted by them. The second supposition contains some show of historical truth; inasmuch as it is a well-established fact, that Brahmanism was compelled to retreat before Buddhism, not only in Benares, but throughout a large portion of India; and that Buddhism, after being the paramount religion for many centuries, was compelled, in its turn, to retreat before Brahmanism. As there is no record of any other creed having become supreme in Benares besides these two, which, we know, successively were so, it is not unlikely that Divodás, who was, evidently, a sworn enemy of the Brahmans and their gods, was a Buddhist. This ejection from the city by a subtle and knavish scheme, may, perhaps, be only another mode of expressing the downfal of the religion which he had strenuously supported, and the return and triumph of the Brahmans.[1]

The temple of Divodáseśwar, in which Divodás is worshipped, stands in a court a short distance from Mír Ghát. The idol consists of a black emblem of S'iva. It is not alone, but is associated with other gods, one of whom is called Bisbáhuka, or the Twenty-handed

[1] See Appendix C.

Divinity, and is the occupant of a niche in the wall. In front of the entrance to the temple is a high *diwaṭ* or lamp-stand, on the sides of which a number of small oil-lamps are placed, on certain occasions, in honour of Divodás. In the centre of this court is Dharm-kúp, one of the famous sacred wells of Benares. Its mouth is begirt partly by a wall and partly by five small shrines standing side by side; and the entrance to the enclosure thus made is by a door opening through the wall on the eastern side. This enclosure is of narrow dimensions, yet contains several objects of interest. Close by the door is an enormous stone emblem of Mahádeva, four feet in height, fixed firmly in the ground. Each of the five shrines has a chamber or stall, in which several idols are deposited, one of which contains a representation of S'iva as Panchmukhi,—that is, the 'five-faced' god. In another, I counted as many as sixteen images; and my attention was arrested by a number of time-worn stone figures imbedded in the boundary wall. No one could furnish any reliable information respecting these interesting objects; but it was suggested that they were figures of the goddess S'ítalá or Small-pox. The well has a palisade round its mouth, and is very deep; and it is worthy of remark, that the reservoir below, holding the water, is not circular, as is usual, but quadrangular.

Dharm-kúp, the name of this well, from *dharm*, religion, and *kúp*, well, is, I am disposed to think, not of Hindu, but of Buddhist, origin. *Dharma* or *Dhammo*—the former being Sanskrit, the latter Pali—constitutes one of the three grand divisions of the Buddhist faith; and, in the Pali writings, Buddha himself is often spoken of as Dhammo. In the time of Aśoka, the common term employed to denote this religion was Dhammo, which is found inscribed on Buddhist monuments reared by him and standing to the present day. In the passage leading to the court, is a temple dedicated to Dharmeśwar, or Lord Dharma,—that is, the deity who personifies *dharm*. If Dharm be regarded as the Buddhist creed, then this appellation would refer to the supposed divine head of such creed, or Buddha. This entire Mahalla or ward of the city is called Dharm-kúp, thereby showing, that, in all likelihood, the well is as ancient as the Mahalla itself. The antiquity of the well, therefore, is placed beyond all doubt; and its connexion with Buddhism, at some period of its history, is invested with some probability. We do not forget that the term *dharma*, meaning virtue, merit, justice, duty, piety, and many other things, is in constant use among Hindus; but still, perhaps, it has hardly that strong and distinctive signification of a system of religion, of a national faith, which it had with the Buddhists in India in former times.

Returning to the street, a few steps bring us to a temple inhabited by the goddess Viśálákshí,—literally, ‘ the large-eyed," an epithet of Párvatí, S'iva's wife,—whose crowned head only is visible, the rest of her person being covered with a yellow cloth. A short distance from this spot is Mír Ghát, leading down to the river. The ghát is narrow, but strongly made; and its stairs are placed at convenient intervals for persons ascending and descending them, so as to induce as little fatigue as possible by the exercise. In passing down the ghát, you are attracted by a row of shrines on the left, embellished in strong glaring colours; and, at one angle of the ghát, a temple is seen on the right-hand side, filling up the corner in that direction, on arriving at which you come in sight of the river. It is dedicated to Rádhá-Kṛishṇa, that is, to Kṛishṇá and his wife, who are standing side by side. They are both completely dressed; Kṛishṇa has tinsel drapery about him, and presents a somewhat rakish appearance. He is playing on a flute; yet is, nevertheless, holding in each hand a marigold and a rose—not artificial, but natural flowers. The temple contains a number of small paintings, a red idol of Gaṇeś, and a tiny shrine in white marble, which cost the sum of one hundred rupees, or ten pounds.

The Nág Kúáṅ or Serpent's Well is situated in a ward of the city called after the name of the well, or Nág Ḳúáṅ Mahalla, which adjoins the Ausán Ganj Mahalla. This well bears marks of considerable antiquity; and, from the circumstance of an extensive district of Benares being designated by its name, there is no doubt that it must be regarded as one of the oldest historical places the present city possesses. The construction of this well was, probably, nearly, if not quite, coeval with the building of the Mahalla or ward itself, which, we may imagine, was described as that part of the city containing the well—the well being the most important and noticeable object there: and so, gradually, the inhabitants associated the Mahalla with the well, and called them by the same name. The ward is in the north-western part of the city, at some distance from the Ganges. The quarter lying to the east of this ward, that is, between it and the Ganges, is, as I have already remarked, in all likelihood, the oldest portion of the present city; and, therefore, the Nág Kúán ward would have been, originally, in its suburbs. It is even possible that one of the first places built in these suburbs, and frequented by the people, was this well, and that its existence was one of the reasons, perhaps the chief, for the settling of a population in its neighbourhood. No person in Benares can tell when the well was made; but there is a reference to its existence in the *Káśi-khaṇda*.

Steep stone stairs, in the form of a square, lead down to the well; and a broad wall of good masonry, six or seven feet thick, surrounds them at their summit, rising to the height of four or five feet above the ground. Each of the four series of stairs has an entrance of its own. Their junction below forms a small square, in the centre of which is the well. Descending twelve stone steps, you reach the water, which is stagnant and foul. Beneath the water is a sheet of iron, which constitutes the door leading to a still lower well, which, perhaps, may be the old well in its original state. The stairs, I suspect, are not of great date. On the inside of those to the east is an inscription, to the effect, that, in 1825 Samvat, or nearly one hundred years ago, a Raja extensively repaired the well. It is possible he may have built the stairs then. Many of the slabs of stone of which they are composed display carvings on their external surface, some of which bear unmistakeable marks of considerable antiquity. These slabs were, doubtless, taken from dilapidated buildings in the neighbourhood. A thorough examination of them, especially of the more ancient among them, would, I am satisfied, not be unproductive of interesting results. The wall was also repaired by Mr. Prinsep about thirty years ago.

At this well the Nág or Serpent is worshipped. In a niche in the wall of one of the stairs is a figure representing three serpents; and, on the floor, is an emblem of Mahádeva in stone, with a snake crawling up it. The well is visited, for religious purposes, only once in the year, namely, on the 24th and 25th days of the month Sáwan, when immense numbers of persons come to it, on pilgrimage, from all parts of the city. The women come on the first day, and the men, on the second. They offer sacrifices both to the well and to Nágeśwar, or the Serpent-god.

Near the wall of the stairs, on the south side, stands a large peepul tree; and at the foot of it are several old mutilated images, one of which has extensive carvings upon it. There is, also, a small low temple close by, containing figures of Hanumán and other deities. Outside the door of the temple are two strange antique idols, in bass-relief. One has, apparently, four legs, and is graced with a nimbus. The other is in an erect posture, with a *chatr* or umbrella over its head. I have grave doubts respecting the Hindu origin of these idols and of some of the mutilated images referred to above.

In the adjoining Mahalla of Jaiṭpurá, a short distance from the Serpent's Well, is the temple of Bágeśwari. Her face consists of a compound of eight kinds of metal, which is of a pale hue, and highly burnished. She wears on her head a large crown, surmounted with balls, like the coronets of the nobility. Her person is covered with a cloth; and from her neck depend several garlands of flowers. The goddess is seated on a lion in a recumbent posture. These figures are in a chapel in the inner chamber of the temple, which appears to have been once painted of a silvery white. The verandah leading to this chamber contains paintings, in fresh glaring colours, representing mythical subjects of great interest to the credulous Hindu. In the small quadrangle is a stone statue of a lion, the *váhan* or riding animal of the goddess, which was presented to the temple by Lál Bahádar Sinh, Raja of Amethi. This Raja has dedicated four similar statues of the lion to the service of the principal deities of four other temples in Benares: one is in the temple at Durgá Kuṇḍ; a second is in the Chausaṭhí-deví temple, in the Bengali Tola; a third is in the Siddhimátá-deví temple, in the Bulhánálá; and a fourth is in the possession of the Gujarati Pandit Gor Jí, awaiting its ultimate destination. In the niches in the wall of the quadrangle are various divinities. In one are three figures, representing Rám, Lakshmaṇ, and Jánakí, cut in black stone or marble. In another is an old figure of Agwán, the porter of Bágeśwarí; and by his side is a second figure, still older, about whom no one could give any information. A third niche holds the goddess Bindhyáchalá, seated on the back of a lion. In a chamber in one corner of the enclosure I observed a large red idol, which

I soon discovered to be the ill-formed Gaṇeś. On one side of this chamber is a row of images, and, on the floor, a singularly-carved figure, called Naugrah, which embodies in itself all the planets. On the exterior face of the temple-wall is a niche, four or five feet in height, which is filled up by the god Hanumán. He is painted bright red, and stand with hands folded; while on one shoulder sits the god Rám, and, on the other, his brother Lakshmaṇ.

In sight of this temple are two others, namely, the temples of Jwarahareśwar and Siddheśwar, which, together with Bágeśwarí, are regarded as old places of pilgrimage. *Jwara* signifies fever; *hara*, destroying or conquering: so that Jwarahareśwar is famous for his supposed power of dissipating fever. The worshipper, on approaching the idol, vows, that, should he recover, he will present to it *dúdhbhangá*, that is, *dúdh* or milk; *bháng*, leaves of hemp; and sweetmeats, mixed up together. Siddheśwar professes to grant ability to consummate any undertaking in which a man may wish to engage. Near these temples are several tombs to devotees, and also a number of mutilated figures, which, it is said, have been dug up in this neighbourhood. Several of these are placed together on a small mound of earth. They are not all worshipped, which is rather strange, considering how prompt the Hindus are to worship carved images of every kind. But the reason of their not being worshipped is, I imagine, because they are so unlike the idols that are now found in Hindu temples. They are more delicately sculptured, and are more chaste in their design, than the productions of modern Hindu art: indeed, their superiority in this respect is exceedingly noticeable. To what epoch they ought to be ascribed, it is not easy to say. I question if they are Hindu sculptures at all, and should be disposed to assign a Buddhist origin to most, if not all, of them. I was much struck with one stone, which seemed to represent, at least, two undeniable emblems of Buddha. The apex of the stone was ornamented with a circle, with radii diverging from the centre, in other words, with the Buddhist wheel. Various stones built into the wall, in this quarter of the city, are, likewise, elaborately carved. These, it is possible, are connected with the same era as the figures just referred to.

CHAPTER VI.

BENARES, Kás'í, and Kedár, the three Grand Divisions of the city.—No Old Hindu Temples in Benares.—Puranic Character of the Kás'í division of the City.—No trustworthy information concerning Ancient Buildings to be obtained either from Hindus or from their sacred writings.—Preference of the Old Fanes by Pilgrims.—Trilochan Temple.—Legends respecting Trilochan.—The Idolater's idea of the benefit resulting from Worshipping in this Temple.—Kot-Linges'war. — Nának Sháh, the Sikh Guru. — Painting in the Trilochan Temple, depicting the Punishments of Hell.—Trilochan Ghát.—Gáe Ghát.—Temples of Nirbuddhes'war and Ád-Mahádeva.—Gor Jí, the Gujarati Brahman.

WHILE the terms Benares and Káśí are alike applied to the entire city, yet some of the natives divide it into three great portions, namely, Benares, Káśí, and Kedár, to which they assign three distinct epochs. The most ancient is Benares, the northern division of the present city. To the south of this is Káśí, of less antiquity; and, to the south of Káśí, Kedár, which is, comparatively, of modern date. From what source this notion has been derived, it is impossible to say; nevertheless, it is, I believe, for the most part, correct. We shall see, in a future chapter, that the ancient Buddhist remains at Bakaríyá Kuṇḍ are situated on the northern side of the city, or in Benares Proper. In addition, there are, in this quarter, other spots, with which I am acquainted, where Buddhist ruins are to be found.

It is a remarkable circumstance, that, in the modern city,

no Hindu temples—including the temple of Bṛiddh-kál, which has, undoubtedly, an antiquity of several hundred years,—whatever exist, to which the epithets 'old' and 'ancient' can properly be applied; thereby corroborating what has been previously asserted, that the modern city has, to a large extent, shifted from its original site. The priests tell you, that, where temples now stand, others once stood, and that the deities now worshipped have been worshipped at these precise spots through all past time; but this, of course, is said with the object of extolling their gods. No dependence can be placed on tradition, in ascertaining the dates of temples, so long as your informant can only state that a certain temple, on a certain site, had a predecessor on that site, and that predecessor had a previous one, and so on, in an endless series.

There are, in the division of Benares Proper, a few Hindu temples, which, perhaps on good grounds, lay claim to an antiquity of several hundred years; but the number of such temples is very small. The central portion, or Káśí, which now constitutes the heart of the city, cannot, so far as my knowledge extends, make even such a boast. Yet it is the favourite resort of Hindus, and is literally choked with its abundant population and the pilgrims who, from all parts of India, are perpetually flocking thither. Its temples and idols, its symbols of idolatry, and its priests, are all on so vast a scale as to defy calculation; while, as if in honour of this portion of it, the entire city is spoken of, throughout India, as Káśí. But, although the Káśí division now receives the lion's share of respect and attention, and the

Benares division, except on special occasions and at special festivals, obtains only a very inferior share, there was a time when the two stood in a reverse relation to one another, and Benares Proper was the common resort of Hindu votaries, while the Káśí division was its mere suburb, and scarcely honoured at all, and the Kedár division was a jungle, where, possibly, stood a secluded temple or two, and a few austere naked ascetics resided in savage simplicity.

Although I regard the central portion of the city, or that which distinctively bears the name of Káśí, as, speaking generally, less ancient than the division to the north of it, I would not have it supposed that I doubt the considerable antiquity of a certain portion of it. I refer especially to the foundations of many of the buildings in the streets immediately adjacent to the Ganges; and I conceive it to be not at all improbable, that, even in those early ages when the city extended for miles on the banks of the great river to the north and north-east of the Barna stream, its southern extremity not only included of the modern city what I have termed Benares Proper, but also a thin band of what is now the Káśí division of the city, stretching along the Ganges in a south-westerly direction, as far, possibly, as the Daśáśamedh Ghát.

While, as already remarked in a previous chapter, the present form of Hinduism in the city is Puranic, yet I would apply that term, in an emphatic and special manner, to the Káśí division, because of the strong and very intimate association which it has with the latest development and manifestation of Hinduism in the

Puráṇas, and with the present features of idolatry amongst the Hindu race. The temples which stud the streets, the idols worshipped in them, the religious observances practised by the people, in short, the materialistic and sensuous characteristics of the Hindu faith, as exhibited there, are, to a very great extent, Puranic in their origin.

Respecting ancient Hindu buildings in the city, no definite and trustworthy information whatever can be gathered either from the lips of Hindus or from the writings which have come down to them from past ages. That remains of such buildings actually exist somewhere, admits of no question; but we are left utterly in the dark concerning them, and have to depend entirely upon personal observation, in searching them out. One would have supposed, that works written upon Benares and in its praise, such as the *Kásí-rahasya*, which numbers thirty chapters; the *Kásí-máhátmya*, which contains five; and *Kásí-khaṇḍa*, taken from the *Skaṇḍa-puraṇa*, which consists of one hundred chapters, would have shed some light on this interesting subject: but the authors and compilers of these books have contented themselves with bare generalities, and have not troubled themselves about the epoch of any one temple, or ghát, or well, or other structure to which they may have referred. It is not known, with certainty, when the above works were written; but this, however, is well ascertained, that not one of them was written till several hundred years after the date of the Buddhist edifices the remains of which have been discovered in the city.

The Hindus do not resort to all temples equally, but only to those which are well known, and which, they have reason to suppose, were frequented by their forefathers. New temples are constantly springing up in various parts of the city, some of which far surpass the old shrines in magnificence; but these are regarded as family temples, and are, for the most part, visited only by the relatives of the persons who have erected them, and by members of the caste to which they belong. The thirty-six castes,—into which Hindus are sometimes divided,—practically shun such temples, although I am not aware that they cherish any dislike to them; while all regard the other class of temples as peculiarly their own, and flock to them indiscriminately. Pilgrims also have the same feeling, and will have nothing to do with the new shrines.

One of the temples in Benares Proper, which may be regarded as not of recent date, is the well-known temple of Trilochan or the Three-eyed,—from *tri*, three, and *lochana*, an eye,—so called from the following circumstance. It is said, that, on one occasion, when S'iva was wrapt in meditation, he was visited daily by Vishṇu, who always brought with him a thousand separate flowers, which he sacrificed to S'iva when in the act of worshipping him. One day Vishṇu had brought his thousand flowers, as usual; and, having placed them ready for sacrifice, his attention was drawn off from them for a short period. Embracing the opportunity, S'iva quietly purloined one of the flowers. Ignorant of the circumstance, Vishṇu presently set about his devotions, offering his flowers one at a time, and counting the number offered. What was his surprise, when, on arriving at the nine hundred and ninety-ninth, he found that one was missing! He was totally unable to account for the loss; but, as he had no other at hand, and it was necessary to complete the sacrifice which he had begun, he removed an eye from its socket, and offered it instead. On applying the eye to the forehead of the idol, it adhered to the spot on which he placed it. S'iva immediately began to see with it, and from that time forwards possessed three organs of vision.

There is, however, another tale connected with this temple and the third eye of S'iva. Tradition affirms, that the emblem of this god, which is worshipped in his temple, having passed through the seven *pátálas* or subterraneous regions, had made its home in this place. Gaurí, wife of S'iva, was, at this time, seeking, but could not find him. S'iva, with his third eye, the eye of reflection,—distinguished from his other two eyes, which are merely eyes of observation,—perceived her. It is commonly believed, that, on the site of this temple, the three rivers, the Ganges, the Jumná, and the Saraswatí, meet. Moreover, three notable deities are spoken of as residing here, corruptly called Saraswateśwar, Jamaneśwar, and Nirbuddheśwar. The first two idols actually do exist here, and are pointed out in the enclosure of the temple; and the last has a separate temple to herself, at a short distance from the Trilochan fane. It is not at all unlikely, that, formerly, this idol was also worshipped in this place; for all three are referred to in the *Káśí-khaṇḍa*, in connexion with it.

The fruits of performing religious ceremonies in the Trilochan temple are regarded, by the idolater, as of a varied character. As, in his estimation, it is high up in the scale of sanctity, it is not surprising that he imagines great blessings are to be obtained from the worship of its idols. That mystery in Hindu idea, called spiritual emancipation, which, in this land, means the destruction of personal identity, or the annihilation of self and absorption into Brahma, preceded, it may be, by a transmigration through the bodies of other creatures, on the death of the present body, is, in his belief, as effectually secured here as elsewhere. Moreover, there is a special benefit attached, by the people generally, to the performance of religious rites in this temple; namely, that, whoever does so, should he fall ill in any other part of the country, and die, is certain not to sink into hell, but to enjoy everlasting happiness. In the month of Baisákh, should any one remain in this temple, uninterruptedly engaged in religious exercises during the whole of one day and night, without sleeping, he is promised eternal liberation as his reward.

The temple stands in the midst of a quadrangle, and is of recent date, having been built a few years ago by Náṭhú Bálá, of Poonah; but the priests state that the quadrangle itself is upwards of three hundred years old. There is little question, however, that the original Trilochan temple was earlier even than this. Some of the numerous idols deposited within the circuit of the quadrangle exhibit signs of an age equal to, if not greater than, that ascribed to the earlier fane. On entering the high-walled enclosure, the large number of images which meet the eye on both sides and in front is somewhat amusing. Most of them, though not all, are of diminutive size, and are placed in separate shrines, in groups of five, ten, twenty, and upwards. On the left, by the wall, are two temples, one of which is surmounted by a low spire or steeple, and the other by a small dome; and the tiny deities to whom they are dedicated are partly deposited upon the floors of the temples, and partly inserted into the walls. Figures of bulls, likewise, intended for these gods to ride on, are placed near. On the right-hand side is a series of shrines occupied by assemblages of idols. There is, also, an image looking like a huge club, which is not honoured with a residence, but stands apart from all the shrines. It is made of stone, and is three feet high above its base, and ten inches or a foot in thickness. Its name is Koṭ-Lingeśwar, from the circumstance that its surface is supposed to have a *koṭi* or ten millions of the emblems of S'iva carved upon it. The actual number cut out on the superficies of the stone is not more than a few hundred; but the Hindus are not particular in their definition of numbers. In the south-west corner, a peepul tree grows, near the foot of which, in a chapel or niche attached to its trunk, is a figure of the monkey-god Hanumán; and, close by, two images of Gaṇeś and S'ítalá (or the goddess of Small-pox) have been let into the wall. On the south side, a small shrine contains the black ugly figure of the goddess Bárṇarasí, presented, I was told, by Raja Banár, a reputed old Raja of Benares. There are other deities, but smaller in size, in the same shrine, such as Gaṇeś and the Sun; but these appear to hold a subordinate position in the place.

In front of the porch of the Trilochan temple, which stands in the middle of the enclosure, is a double temple. Each division is open on its three sides, and, from the number and assortment of its idols, is a veritable pantheon. It would be curious to know the reason for making such collections of deities. I believe it is simply whim or caprice, similar to that which prompts children to accumulate a large number, and a great variety, of playthings. It is, also, evidently, a childish motive which has dictated the methodical, not to say picturesque, arrangement of idols on the floors of temples, and around the walls of their enclosures. In regard to some collections of idols, however, there is no doubt that they have been gradually made by the worshippers in the temples in which they are found, who, in their zeal, have presented idols, as well as money and other gifts, to their favourite shrines.

The porch of the Trilochan temple is painted red, and is sustained by eight pillars, four in front, and four attached to the wall behind. Its roof is embellished with pictures; and on the floor, directly opposite to the entrance of the temple, is a bull, in white marble, in a recumbent posture. Two bells are suspended in the porch, which are struck by the worshippers, after performing their devotions. The wall of the temple, adjoining the porch, exhibits several curious objects. There is a figure of Gaṇeś, in white marble, in a niche in the wall on the left; and near it a painting, representing Nának Sháh, the Guru or spiritual guide of the Sikh race. As the Sikh religion is regarded, by the Hindus, in the light of a heresy, it is strange that they permit such a picture to decorate the walls of one of their principal shrines. In a niche on the right are two black figures of Náráyaṇa or Vishṇu, and his wife Lakshmí.

Here is, likewise, a remarkable painting, representing the divine vengeance executed on sinners in hell. In the foreground is the River of Death, through which persons are seen endeavouring to make their way to the other side. Some are left alone to buffet with the waves in their own strength; while others, who, when living in this world, supported Brahmans, are helped across by the sacred cow, who swims before, and drags them along by her tail, which they grasp fast hold of with their hands. This explanation was given by the priests; for, really, no cow was visible as the attendant on any one. As soon as they are landed on the opposite shore, the new arrivals are represented as immediately led away: and the remainder of the picture consists in a delineation of the punishment of the wicked. The priests stated that the poor wretches are first judged, and then punished according to their deeds. In one place, a conscience-stricken sinner, who has recently emerged from the stream, is seen strongly resisting the hand of the executioner, who is dragging him away by the leg. In another is an enormous vessel, full of boiling ghee or clarified butter, into which the wicked are plunged.

Here and there, executioners are standing, armed with prodigious clubs, with which they cruelly belabour their helpless and despairing victims. One conspicuous object in the picture is a pillar of red-hot iron, on the top of which lies a writhing and agonizing mass of humanity. This punishment is reserved exclusively for those who have been guilty of adultery and uncleanness.

The interior of the temple is very simple, and is exceedingly dirty and foul. A brazen cistern, with knobs at each corner, is let into the floor; and, in the middle of it, stands the emblem of S'iva, who is here called Lingeśwar; and near it is S'iva's wife, Párvatí. A small oil lamp is kept constantly burning not far from the idol, whose daily supply of water and flowers,—the offerings of his worshippers,—would be enough, did he possess the flesh and blood of a human creature, to suffocate and drown him.

Quitting this spot, and proceeding to Trilochan Ghát, we pass a beautiful little temple, situated at the corner of two streets, lately built by Kunú Sáhu. Its porch is supported on pillars, the elegant carving of which displays much taste and skill. Immediately opposite this is a large temple, in a quadrangle, also new. Above the ghát is a small shrine, containing a number of old images; and, a short distance down the stairs, are two more, in the walls of which idols of great age are inserted. I may here remark, that the neighbourhood of the Trilochan temple abounds with shrines.

The Trilochan Ghát is called, also, the Pilpilla Tírth, or place of pilgrimage. After bathing in the Ganges, at this ghát, the pilgrim, in order to perform this peculiar pilgrimage, proceeds to the Panchgangá Ghát, and bathes again in the river; and then, finally tracing his steps to the Maṇikarṇiká Well, washes in its loathsome waters. These ablutions being terminated, the poor deluded man is taught to believe that his sins have all been forgiven. There are two low turrets at the Pilpilla Ghát, between which the pilgrim must bathe, as the water beyond has no special sanctity.

This ghát is the last of the stairs, leading down from the city to the river, made entirely of strong masonry. The gháts to the north are constructed, in part, of a less durable substance, that is, from below towards the river; although, in the upper portions of these even, the stairs are solid, like the others. A short distance higher up the stream is Gáe Ghát, jutting out a little beyond the bank.

Two other temples in this neighbourhood are, possibly, of the same era as the Trilochan fane. The first is the temple of Nirbuddheśwar, situated only a few steps to the south-east of this structure. It is an exceedingly plain edifice, without ornament or embellishment, and is, evidently, not much visited, except by pilgrims, and on festival days. The other is the temple of A'd-Mahádeva, at the entrance of which is a tiny shrine, faced with an iron grating. A priest from Trilochan was leading the way into the enclosure, when I felt myself irresistibly detained by the curiosities in this shrine. I observed several small pillars covered with silver tinsel, and, also, a figure of Hanumán gaudily painted in red, yellow, white, and black colours; while, on the floor, other idols were lying. In this cage-like place sat an old man, squatting down beside these miserable divinities, his body occupying a large portion of the shrine. Presently he folded his hands together, apparently in deep devotion, and did homage to one or more of the images before him. He then rang a little bell, and quietly left the place. This man was the proprietor of the shrine, and had erected and dedicated it, and probably had purchased in the bazar the very idols which I saw him worship.

The temple of Ád-Mahádeva, like the temple of Nirbuddheśwar, is unadorned and plain. In the porch is a very old chair, in which, in former days, a *Vyás*, or public reader of the sacred books, used to sit and read in the presence of a congregation gathered to hear him. This ancient custom has lost ground even in Benares, which professes to be the very citadel and defence of Hinduism. In front of the porch, to the east, is a peepul tree, with a platform attached to its base, upon which is a small shrine, containing a collection of idols; while opposite to it is a stone figure of the goddess Párvatyeśwarí in bass-relief. This divinity was formerly one of considerable repute, but, from some unknown circumstance, was destroyed, together with her shrine; so that no remains of the one or of the other can be discovered. The goddess, however, I am sorry to say, has been resuscitated by a Gujarati Brahman, residing in Benares, named Gor Jí, who manufactured the present idol, and placed it in this position, as representative of Párvatyeśwarí; and it is now honoured, by the Hindus, with pilgrimages and offerings, like its predecessor. Gor Jí is a remarkable man, and has done more to revive Hinduism, in this city, of late years, than, perhaps, any other person. Having diligently read the *Káśí-khaṇḍa*, he has searched about for the temples and idols referred to in that book; and, whereever he has found old temples in decay, or abandoned, or has discovered sacred sites now neglected and generally unknown, he has endeavoured to restore them to honour and popularity. One favourite method which he adopts is to inscribe an extract from the *Káśí-khaṇḍa*, respecting a particular forsaken temple or site, on stone, and to set it up there, for the enlightenment of passers-by. In some cases, he merely writes the extract on a wall or other suitable place. This man feels, like many other rigid Hindus of the old school, that the ancient religion is falling into decay; that some of its old temples, formerly frequented by crowds, are now rarely trodden; and that many a hallowed spot, or niche, or grove, or fane, has been abandoned and forgotten.

Behind the peepul tree is a temple dedicated to Gaṇeś, the God of Wisdom, an elephant-headed, large-bellied, and very red deity, who has associated with himself a variety of deities, one of whom is a stone on which two snakes are carved in bass-relief; but the stone is broken, and the two parts are placed, side by side, against the wall.

CHAPTER VII.

Panchgangá Ghát.—Legend respecting it.—Lakshmaṇbála Temple.—The Minarets.—Temple of Kámeśwar.—The Machaudarí Tírth or Place of Pilgrimage.

The Panchgangá Ghát is one of the five chief places of pilgrimage on the banks of the Ganges. The Hindus believe that five rivers meet at this spot. Their names are Dhútapápá, Jarṇanada, Kiraṇanadí, Saraswatí, and (Gangá) Ganges. Respecting these streams, Mr. Prinsep makes the following observations:—"A virgin," he says, "named D'horátpápá, whom Brahmá pronounces to be more pure than three and a half crores of the holy *tíraths* (places of pilgrimage), having cause of complaint against her admirer Dharma, politely pronounces a malediction upon him, and turns him into the Dharmanada (river of virtue). He, in revenge, converts her into a rock; but her father, Vedásoor, in compassion, metamorphoses her again into the Chandrakánta (moon stone), which, melting in the moon, forms a stream, called D'horátpápá (channel of sin), an appropriate bride for the river of virtue. The third stream, called Kirnaddá (brook of rays), was produced from the perspiration of the Sun, while performing penance in honour of Mangulgouree (a form of Devi), on an adjoining ghát. These three, with the Ganges and Saraswatí, complete the number of Panchanada, to the satisfaction even of the deities themselves, who condescend to bathe on the spot during their residence in Kashi."[1]

Only one of these streams, namely, the Ganges, is visible; but the remaining four are supposed, by the credulous, to be somewhere under ground. The ghát is broad and deep, and exceedingly strong. Its stairs and turrets are all of stone, and, from their great number, afford accommodation to a multitude of worshippers and bathers. The turrets are low and hollow, and are employed as temples or shrines. Each one contains several deities, which are, mostly, emblems of S'iva. An ordinary observer would be in ignorance of the fact that these are filled with idols, and would scarcely imagine that he was walking upon the top of a long succession of shrines, and over the heads of hundreds of gods. He would have to descend several steps, before discovering the sacrilege which he was ignorantly committing; but, having done so, he would at once perceive that the turrets are open towards the river, and are, therefore, very convenient for devotional purposes. The platform above the ghát, along which runs a narrow, though excellent, road, is below the steep bank of the river. From the platform a number of stairs thread their way up the bank, uniting the ghát with this quarter of the city. The same remark is, for the most part, applicable to the other gháts. They are all connected together by a road, which is, in some places, paved, and in the hot

[1] Prinsep's Views of Benares—Second Series.

weather, is, in parts, covered over with an awning, under which the people walk. From this road innumerable stairs, chiefly of stone, pass up the banks, and communicate with the alleys and streets leading into the city.

One of the flights of stairs rising up from the Panchgangá Ghát enters a large building, known as Lakshmaṇbála, which it ascends, and then issues into a lane at the summit of the bank, leading into the streets of the city. The building, although presenting an extensive frontage towards the river, is, in reality, hardly more than a mere casemate to the bank. It is used as a temple, and is dedicated to Lakshmaṇbála. The principal room is in an upper story, the roof of which is supported on carved wooden pillars of a deep black colour. The walls are embellished with paintings, many of which are representations of green trees, while others are pictures set in frames. Devotees are seated in the room, counting their beads, and muttering to themselves the names of their gods. Music is also performed, the plaintive strains of which fall upon the ear pleasingly. Near the players, at one end of the room, are three idols, in a row. That in the centre is dressed in blue, and has a blue turban on his head, and a garland thrown over his shoulders, hanging down in front. On his left is a gilded disk, let into the wall, displaying nose, eyes, cheeks, and mouth, and a nimbus, and is intended as a representation of the Sun. On his right is a disk, representing the Moon, made of a pale metal, probably silver, and exhibiting the various parts of the face, as in the case of the Sun, but without gilding or glory. A few feet in front of these idols, a small lamp is kept burning. The worshippers pass in and out of this room, and perform their devotions as though it were an ordinary temple. It is the only temple in Benares, however, so far as my observation has extended, in which persons, seating themselves on the floor, engage formally in religious exercises. The temples in Benares, and in Northern India generally, with their courts, porches, and subordinate shrines, though they, in some instances, cover a considerable area, are, for the greater part, of very narrow dimensions, and contain only one small room, in which, besides the presiding deity, several inferior divinities are frequently placed, leaving not room enough for a dozen persons to present their offerings at one and the same time, and to observe the prescribed ceremonies in an orderly manner.

Ascending another series of stairs from the Panchgangá Ghát, you approach the lofty mosque of Aurungzeb, known, by the natives, as "Mádhudás ká Dewhrá." The edifice itself is above the bank of the river; but its foundations sink deep into the ground; and their enormous stone breastworks extend far down the bank. Indeed, it is said that the foundations of the mosque are as deep as the building is high. Although more than a century and a half has elapsed since this structure was reared, yet it appears as solid and strong as on the day of its completion. The massive pile is on the very edge of a steep bank or cliff; yet not a stone of it has been loosened. There is a high wall, next to the street running by the western side of the mosque,

Photographed by D. Tresham, Esq.

THE MINARETS—FROM THE GANGES.

which is continued round to the north-east corner. A door in the northern wall opens the way into the enclosure, in full front of the mosque; the latter being situated on its southern side. From the eastern side commences the long flight of stone stairs descending to the river. The enclosure is not sufficiently spacious to give the observer an ample view of the minarets; but, nevertheless, it is extensive enough to enable him to gain a satisfactory idea of their symmetry and elegance. The mosque itself exhibits nothing striking, and, indeed, can hardly be called beautiful. It is plain and common-place; and, were it not for the minarets rising above, it would not be accounted a noticeable object in Benares. The minarets themselves have a delicate gracefulness about them which it is impossible to portray in words; and my photographic representation fails to convey the exactness and exquisiteness of the reality. I do not remember their exact height; but it is not less than one hundred and fifty feet, reckoning from the floor of the mosque. When it is remembered that the bank of the river on which this edifice stands is nearly the same number of feet above the bed of the stream, it will at once be perceived that the minarets occupy a very prominent position in a panoramic view of the city. Although many of the buildings of Benares, especially those in the neighbourhood of the ghát́s, are of a great height, yet they are all overtopped by the minarets, the clear forms of which, pointing upwards to the sky, may be discerned at the distance of many miles from the city. They were, originally, some fifty feet higher than they now are, and were cut down to their present height, in consequence of exhibiting signs of weakness and insecurity. There is a staircase in each tower, from the summit of which you gain a complete view of Benares and its suburbs, and of a portion of the surrounding country; but the ascent and descent are attended with considerable fatigue.

It is astonishing that this mosque, although so much visited by Europeans, and regarded, by them, as one of the chief sights of Benares, should be almost abandoned by the Mohammedans. On Fridays, a small number of the faithful assemble within its walls for religious purposes, but on no other day; and, during the remaining six days of the week, it is handed over to the care of two men. These consist of a Mullá and his servant, who alone have charge of the building. It seems that the office held by the Mullá was formerly held by his ancestors, who received it, possibly, from Aurungzeb himself.

A small village was, at one time, in possession of the mosque, from the proceeds of which its expenses were partially paid: but it has lapsed to the Government; and, consequently, the expenses of repairing and cleaning the mosque, so far as I was able to learn, are defrayed by the contributions of visitors. Its existence in this part of city, which is almost entirely inhabited by Hindus, affords the strongest proof of the rancour and violence with which the emperor Aurungzeb opposed the idolatrous practices of the people, and endeavoured to propagate his own religion. Tradition says, that, on the site of the mosque, a temple once stood, which was removed in order to make room for it; and there is every reason to believe that the tradition is true. The Government takes care of the minarets, and keeps them in order.

The temple of Kámeśwar, in the northern division of Benares, is one of the few temples, in the city, not of comparatively modern date; and yet, like them, it by no means belongs to a very distant epoch. It is remarkable, also, for the vast accumulation of shrines and images within its boundaries. At the entrance, towards the street, is a temple, with a group of deities inside, who are supposed to guard the passage. Passing along, we come to the first court, in which is a kettle-drum, which is beaten at intervals during the day, in honour of the presiding divinity. Proceeding into the second court, an extraordinary sight presents itself. The entire area of the quadrangle is literally filled with temples, so that it seems impossible to insert another. The quadrangle is not large, when compared with some others in Benares. All the temples are painted red, and have short steeples. The principal one is dedicated to Kámanánáth, or Kámeśwar, the Lord of Desire, who, according to Hindu belief, assists his worshippers in the realization of whatever they aspire to achieve. Another temple is inhabited by the god Rám, Sítá (his wife), the goddess Lakshmí, and the Sun. The temples altogether amount to ten or a dozen, each containing several idols.

On the north side of the enclosure is a peepul tree; and on a platform, surrounding its base, is a group of idols. One of these is Narsinh, an incarnation of

Vishṇu, and a monster of horrible appearance. His birth is said to have been out of a pillar or post, which split down the middle, in order to admit him into the world. The two parts of the pillar are represented in the stone figure, one being on each side of the idol, which, in the form of a man with two horns on his head, is seated in the fork of the divided pillar, gloating over the victim who lies prostrate across his lap. This is a *daitya* or demon, whom he is disembowelling and pulling to pieces with his nails, and greedily drinking his blood. Besides other images, there is the usual emblem of S'iva, with a snake creeping up it; and on the horizontal stone, which is always connected with it, are carved ten other emblems, exact counterparts of the entire idol, with the exception of the snake. On the sides of the quadrangle, long narrow rooms open on the centre of the square; and these may be regarded as so many separate shrines, inasmuch as they are occupied by groups of deities. Two of these are filled with the peculiar emblems of S'iva; and one of them holds as many as twenty-five. A third has a figure of Narsiṅh, similar to that just described, and, also, the goddess Machaudarí, an immodest figure, seated on a peacock. There is, likewise, in the same room, an image of the Ṛishi Durvásas, whose asceticism is said to have been so vigorous, that he was raised, by its instrumentality, to an equality with the gods, and sat with Vishṇu as his peer.

The temple of Kámanánáth is connected with a depressed plain close by, which was formerly an extensive *jhíl* or pond, and was then called the Machaudarí Tírth, or place of pilgrimage, which, like other tanks in Benares, was frequented by many pilgrims, who worshipped in the temple and bathed in the pond. The *jhíl* was drained, some years ago, by Mr. James Prinsep, the famous archæologist, when stationed at Benares. Its removal must, on sanitary grounds, be regarded as a beneficial measure; and no injury has been sustained by the people, as the river Ganges flows only a few steps off. The Machaudarí Tírth is now abolished; and, consequently, the number of pilgrims frequenting the temple of Kámanánáth has greatly diminished.

CHAPTER VIII.

TEMPLE of Jágeśwar, a Resort of the Native Aristocracy of Benares.—Káśí-Deví, Goddess of the City of Benares.—Karnghaṇṭa Táláo or Tank.—Temple of the demon Bhút-Bhairo.—Temple of Bará Gaṇeś.—Jagannáth.—Satís.

IN the Iśwar-Gangí street, situated in the Ausánganj Mahalla or ward of the City, is the aristocratic temple of Jágeśwar,—more correctly, Yájeśwara, 'Lord of Sacrifice,' that is, Śiva,—to which all the nobility and gentry of Benares, from the Maharaja downwards, occasionally resort. Ascending a flight of steps, you enter the outer court of the temple, where are several shrines standing in a row, each of which contains an assemblage of small idols. This court forms a platform; and, as it is spacious, clean, and orderly, it serves as an agreeable lounge, in the cool of the day, for persons frequenting the spot. But the object of interest here is the temple of Jágeśwar, which is in a court of its own, walled in all round. The temple occupies a large portion of the enclosure; but there is, nevertheless, a narrow space between it and the walls, so that worshippers are able to carry out their favourite custom of traversing the circumference of the temple a multitude of times. The portico rests on pillars; and its floor is paved with small square slabs of polished marble. In the centre of the portico, facing the door of the temple, crouches a large bull, called Nandi, the animal on which the god rides. But what would one fancy the size and form of the idol which the *élite* of Benares, its men of opulence, of illustrious birth, of intelligence, and education, reverently worship, and before whom they beat their heads upon the threshold, and even prostrate themselves upon the floor, and to whom they pay that supreme homage and adoration due only to the Lord God Almighty? It might be supposed that it was an object of surpassing splendour, with diamond-sparkling eyes, and a body of gold, adorned with garlands, necklaces, and bracelets, of costly value and of dazzling beauty. But its pretensions are of a very different order; for it is simply an enormous block of stone, round and black, six feet in height, and twelve in circumference. The tradition is, that, on one occasion, the gods assembled to perform a great sacrifice, and that out of the burning oblation issued S'iva, in the shape of this stone. Above the temple is a capacious spout, looking not unlike a chimney, placed immediately over the shapeless idol below. In the hot weather this spout is kept filled with water, which dribbles perpetually upon the god, through one or more holes in the bottom, and keeps him cool. At the entrance to the temple from the portico are two small shrines, one on each side of the door.

Adjoining the Ausánganj Mahalla is the Mahalla of Káśípurá, where, at the junction of several narrow streets, stands a banyan tree, near which is a temple divided into two chambers. In one of these chambers, in a niche let into the wall, sits Káśí-deví, or the goddess of Benares. Pilgrims, making the tour of the city for the purpose of performing their devotions at its most celebrated shrines, do not fail to visit this tutelary deity. The spot is also interesting to the natives, as being, in their estimation, the centre of Benares, though it is exceedingly doubtful whether it is so in reality. A few steps bring us to the Karṇghaṇṭa Táláo, a tank named from the goblin Ghaṇṭákarṇa, 'Bell-eared.' This tank is in a quadrangle, between which and the neighbouring street a garden is situated. On descending a flight of steps, you enter the quadrangle. At the foot of the steps is a platform extending all round the enclosure; and from it is a succession of stone stairs leading down to the water of the tank. On the south side of the platform overlooking the tank are three temples, one of which, namely, that in the middle, is of considerable interest. It is dedicated to Vedavyás, the compiler of the Vedas, and is called Vyáseśwar. The deified compiler is seated in a niche in the wall, and is decorated with a garland, and also with armlets and anklets. There is another temple, erected in honour of this famous man, in the palace of the Maharaja of Benares at Rámnagar; but there he is associated with Śiva, and is worshipped through the emblem of the latter divinity, whereas, in the temple at Karṇghaṇṭa Táláo, he is represented by an image of his own. In the month of Sáwan, multitudes of people, especially women, visit this tank, bathe in its unclean water, and worship the peepul, kadam, and banyan trees.

A short distance to the north of Káśí-deví is the temple of Bhút-Bhairo or, more properly, Vishama-Bhairava; the former being the vulgar designation which the idol bears. *Bhút* means a demon; and Bhairo is the deified magistrate of Benares; so that the idea is, that the god Bhairo delivers his worshippers from demons and other infernal beings. The idol is dignified with a moustache, the ends of which are curved after the most approved fashion; but it is, nevertheless, an ugly object. The head and part of the neck are alone visible, the remainder of the person being hidden by an apron which reaches above the head. The court in which this temple stands contains several other shrines, all which bear the marks of age upon them. Several of those curious blocks of stone found in various parts of Benares,—to which allusion has been made in a previous chapter,—of pyramidal shape, and presenting, on their surface, rude carvings of small temples, are lying about the enclosure. I counted as many as seven; and it is likely there are others. They are in various positions; several being erect, whilst some are standing out of the perpendicular, or are lying prostrate on the ground. There is no other place in Benares, I believe, which contains such an assemblage of these remarkable stones. On one side of the courtyard is a large emblem of S'iva, about which the following singular story is told. It is said, that, about six or seven years ago, a tree fell down at this place, and, on the spot where the trunk had stood, the emblem was found in the position in which it is now seen. The figure looks old; and it is not unlikely, that, in the youth of the tree, it was inserted in the earth immediately at its base, and that, as the tree grew, it gradually enveloped the stone, which, being large and strongly fixed in the ground, was not expelled, but, on the contrary, became more firmly set by the lateral pressure of the tree. This explanation is strengthened by the supposition that the tree was the sacred peepul, the trunk of which is so strangely corrugated, as often to appear to consist of a multitude of small trees united together. Preparations were made for erecting a temple around this sacred stone; but the person who had undertaken the task died before much progress had been made in the work. Fragments of carved stones are lying about, which were, doubtless, originally destined for the new temple: but there is now little chance of its ever being raised; as no Hindu likes to prosecute an enterprise begun by another man, inasmuch as, when completed, he believes that all the merit resulting from it will go to such person and not to himself.

In the Ausánganj Mahalla is the well-known fane of Bará Gaṇeś, or the Great Gaṇeś. An alley branches off from the main road, and conducts to this temple. At an angle of the alley is a low shrine, dedicated to Jagannáth, containing three figures, of horrible ugliness. On the right is Jagannáth; on the left is his brother Balbhadra; and, in the middle, is their sister Subhadrá. The two former have arms, but no hands or feet; while the latter is destitute of arms, as well as of feet. These large-mouthed, goggle-eyed, round-faced deities are equal in frightfulness to some of the idols made and worshipped by the savages of the Fiji Islands in the South Seas. In another place, in a corner of this alley, are two Satís, that is to say, two figures of women, in bass-relief, placed upon a square pedestal, in commemoration of the cremation of widows on the funeral pile of their husbands at this spot. In addition to the Satís, there are two other objects of interest placed upon the pedestal. One is a bass-relief sculpture of a small figure, much worn by time. The other presents, in a small compass, most elaborate chiselling; the design illustrated being of a complicated character. There is a central figure, in an erect posture, but headless; and, in the back-ground, a nimbus surrounds the space formerly occupied by the head. On either side are several other figures, but of smaller stature, and also a column, with a capital, on the summit of which is a diminutive statue of a man. Between the columns, but raised above them, in a line with the central object beneath, is, likewise, another small statue of a man. Altogether, this delicate piece of statuary exhibits ten human figures, besides various other objects, all which are defined with considerable nicety. It is not easy to comprehend the general design which the sculptor had before his mind, or to furnish a satisfactory account of this work of art. It is, certainly, far superior to modern productions of Hindu art; and I suspect it is not, properly, of Hindu origin at all.

The towers of two temples are seen rising high above the Satís; and in the adjoining enclosure stands the temple of Bará Gaṇeś. The quadrangle is open to the sky; but it has a covered verandah, supported on pillars, running round the four walls, on their inner side, opposite to the temple, in the centre. In the midst of the temple is a large idol of Gaṇeś, the elephant-headed god, with silver hands and feet. The head is decorated with a gilded nimbus. Inside the temple, four bells are suspended; and immediately over the doorway, and in front of the idol, three small mirrors are placed, the object of which, possibly, is to produced a threefold image or reflexion of the idol; for even a reflexion of a god is accounted a sacred object, and worthy of veneration. On either side of the threshold, leading into the temple, is another idol of Gaṇeś; but both are well worn, and, evidently, many centuries old. The present temple was erected only some twenty-four years ago; but the priests say that these two figures have always existed here. The extensive verandah of the quadrangle contains several other figures of Gaṇeś, of, apparently, as great antiquity as those just described.

CHAPTER IX.

THE Piśách-Mochan Tank. — Legend of the goblin Piśách. — The Festival of Loṭá-Bhanṭá, or the Egg-plant.—The Gháts and Temple of Piśách-Mochan.—Súraj-Kuṇḍ or Tank of the Sun.—The Hom or Burnt Sacrifice.—The god Ashṭáng-Bhairo.—Temple of Dhruveśwar or the Pole Star.

IN the outskirts of the city, on its western side, is a large square tank or reservoir, called Piśách-Mochan, built in a regular manner, with gháts or stone stairs leading down to the water. On the bank, towards the road, are several temples, containing a great many images of various deities. Piśách-Mochan is a noted place of pilgrimage among the Hindus. All pilgrims coming to Benares must visit it; and all the residents in the city must bathe in its waters at least once a year. These waters are considered to have a peculiar efficacy in ensuring deliverance from the power of demons and all kinds of evil spirits, in preventing horrible dreams, or destroying their bad effect, and in removing sickness. The word Piśách means ghoul or bad spirit, and Mochan, release or deliverance. The history of this sacred place is said to be as follows. On one occasion, a very powerful demon had the temerity to approach the holy enclosure in which Benares is situated. He was, however, stopped, at the Panchkosí road, by the deities stationed there. But, although they contended bravely with him, yet, being stronger than they, he overcame them, and, crossing the road, entered the enclosure. He then pursued his course, until he reached the spot where the Piśách-Mochan tank is now situated, and would have effected an entrance into the holy city itself, had not Bhaironath, the *koṭwal* or deified Chief Magistrate of the place, met him there. An encounter immediately commenced between these two worthies, which ended in the magistrate cutting off the head of the common enemy. Having performed this act of valour, Bhaironath conveyed the head to his royal master, Bisheśwar, and stated all the circumstances of the conflict. But the demon, though overcome and bodiless, had lost neither his life nor his tongue; and, therefore, he implored Bisheśwar not to banish him from the city, but to allow him to reside on the spot where he was decapitated. He also had the boldness to request, in addition, that all pilgrims proceeding to the city of Gayá should be directed first to visit him. To this the king gave his consent, but stated that he should allow no other evil spirit to visit Benares, and that he, the demon, was to take care that none ever did so.

Such is the quaint story which the Hindus believe respecting this place. The great ugly head of the demon, carved in stone, is seen on the top of the ghát by the side of one of the temples. All pilgrims, too, proceeding to Gayá, pay honour to this Piśách; and in case any, travelling from distant parts of the country, should, from ignorance or other causes, reach Gayá without having first come to Piśách-Mochan, in Benares, they are immediately questioned on the matter. To obviate the necessity of their travelling to Benares, and then returning to Gayá, another Piśách-Mochan has been erected in the latter place, as representative of that in Benares, where they may perform *pújá* or religious rites, and thus, after the payment of the prescribed fees to the priests (a *sine qua non*), acquire the full stock of merit which would have accrued to them had they really visited the Piśách in Benares.

In addition to several small *melás* or festivals, a very large one is held every year at Piśách-Mochan. This *melá* is called Loṭá-Bhanṭá, from the singular custom which prevails, on that occasion, of grinding the vegetable called *bhanṭá*, or egg-plant, and mixing it with flour, forming it into cakes, which are eaten at the *melá*. The tank is a square, with gháts or stairs on the four sides. A portion of the ghát, to the east, was erected, about eighty years ago, by Gopál Dás Sáhu; and the remaining portion, and also a temple on the bank, by a Hindu lady, named Mirch Bai, about the same time. The ghát and wall, to the west, date from the same period; the former, together with the tower rising above it, having been erected by a Hindu, Balwant Rao Bákirá, and the latter, by a Mohammedan, Mirza Khurram Sháh, of Delhi. The ghát to the north was built more than a hundred years ago, by Raja Muralídhar; and that to the south, which bears upon it the marks of age, partly by Raja S'iva Sambar, some three hundred years ago, and partly by Binaik Rao, a few years since.

On the eastern bank of the tank, occupying a prominent position, are two temples, one of which is a modern structure, and was built by Nakku Misr, a servant of the Government; and the other is that erected by Mirch Bai, already spoken of. The latter only presents features of interest. The foundations of this temple are raised some distance above the level of the neighbouring street. Its roof is flat; and, in the centre of it, a peepul and a banyan tree have fixed their roots, while their trunks rise up high into the air. On all the four sides of the temple are small shrines or niches, containing a great collection of idols. Here is Śiva; next to him, the hideous head of the demon Piśách-Mochan; and, beyond it, the four-handed god Vishṇu, holding in one hand a conch, in another a lotos, in a third a club, and in a fourth a discus, while a garland of lotoses hangs from his neck. Next to him is his wife Lakshmí, who has an image of the Sun on her left; beyond which is the figure of a Brahman, in stone. Then comes a shrine in which is a large red idol representing the Monkey-god Hanumán. All these are on one side of the temple; and immediately round the corner to the east is a curious figure of the god Gaṇeś, who, instead of one elephant's trunk, which he commonly possesses, has, in this case, five. All the remaining sides are similarly decorated with deities, with the exception of the west side facing the tank, which has fewer in number than the rest. Away from the temple itself, but resting upon the raised pedestal on which the temple stands, is one of those curious stones representing a multitude of tiny shrines, found in various places in Benares.

Súraj-kuṇḍ is a large tank situated on the south-west side of the city, and originally consisted of twelve wells dedicated to the Sun. Two of the wells are still traceable beneath the surface of the water. A temple is above the tank; and on the same side are stairs leading down to the water. A few paces distant is a temple to the Sun, called, by the natives, Súraj-Nárá-yaṇ, which was erected by the Raja of Kotah-bundi, who is the owner of the land in this neighbourhood. On the floor of the temple is a large round flat stone, of ancient appearance, which is worshipped as the solar deity. The day for the special worship of the Sun is Itwár or Sunday. A small building stands detached from the temple, and, in a hole in its floor, the ceremony of the *hom* is performed, which consists in certain offerings consumed by fire. Wood is first placed over the hole, upon which the offerings are scattered, and are then burnt to ashes. While the sacrifice is going on, it is customary for a Pandit to read portions of the Súrya-puráṇa, or the Puráṇa inscribed to the Sun. This shrine is also called Sámbádit, from *Aditya*, the Sun, and *Sámba*, son of Jámbavatí, a wife of Kṛishṇa. Tradition states, that one day this youth committed a very serious offence, for which his father pronounced a curse upon him, so that he became a leper. Whereupon his mother pleaded with Kṛishṇa for him; and, at length, the god said, that, if he proceeded to Benares and practised asceticism, if he built a tank and bathed in its waters, and if he made an image of the Sun and worshipped it, he should be healed of his disease. All this he is reported to have done; and, the tradition adds, he was healed. Hence, it is affirmed, the round stone above referred to is called Sámbádit.

A mutilated figure of the god Ashṭáng-Bhairo stands near Súraj-kuṇḍ, in a small temple open in front. There are eight idols bearing the name of Bhairo in Benares, to each and all of which pilgrims resort. This image was mutilated by that fierce iconoclast, the Emperor Aurungzeb.

The temple of Dhruveśwar, or the Pole Star, is also in this quarter of the city. It is said that Dhruv, a Ṛishi or Saint, afterwards the Pole Star, once visited Benares, and that S'iva, honouring his sanctity and devotion, united his name with his own, so that they might be worshipped in the same temple, as a united and individual deity. But this legend is an outgrowth from popular etymology; for the word *íśwar*, in Dhruveśwara, 'Lord Dhruva,' has been ignorantly confounded with a familiar synonym of S'iva, *i.e.*, *Íś-war*, or 'Lord' by eminence. The old temple of Dhruveśwar fell down some time since; and, in its place, a new one has been erected, which stands on an elevation at the corner of an extensive enclosure, in the midst of which is a large temple dedicated to S'iva; built by some Gosains or devotees, upwards of seventy years ago.

CHAPTER X.

The Mán-Mandil Ghát.—Temple of Dálbhyeśwar.—Temple of the Moon or Someśwar.—The Mán-Mandil Observatory erected by Raja Jay Sinh—Description of its Instruments.—The Nepalese Temple.

The Mán-Mandil Ghát is principally remarkable for the old Observatory, situated upon the banks of the Ganges at this spot, and which will, presently, be more particularly referred to. This lofty building gives a noble appearance to the ghát, and commands a fine view of the river. Near the entrance to it is a collection of ancient idols which have been worn away by time and perpetual sacrificial ablutions. Several of these are figures of monkeys, representing the god Hanumán. A flag waves from the top of a high staff at this spot, in honour of the Raja of Jaypore,—the proprietor of this entire Mahalla or ward of the city,—whose ancestor Raja Jay Sinh erected the Observatory. In a lane leading to the ghát is the temple of Dálbhyeśwar, which deity is supposed to exercise great power over the clouds, in procuring rain. The image is in a cistern, low down in the centre of the temple. If the idol is properly worshipped and kept drenched with water, pious Hindus believe that he will look with favour on the prayer for rain. As the heat is now daily increasing in intensity, and the rains, both for the cooling of the atmosphere and for the fertilizing of the soil, are beginning to be desired, the god was lately treated to a delightful bath, which he is imagined to have received with prodigious satisfaction. Not only the cistern, but also the entire temple, up to the threshold, was filled with water. This event, which was noised abroad among the natives, has considerably heightened, in their estimation, the probability of rain.[1] Dálbhyeśwar is also known as the Poor Man's Friend; for, should a man in straitened circumstances visit this shrine, and duly perform the prescribed ceremonies, his poverty, they say, will disappear, and his wants be relieved. One would have thought that the squalid and indigent people inhabiting the sacred city and resorting thither would have flocked eagerly to this temple, had they had the smallest particle of faith in the god there. Associated with Dálbhyeśwar are Chaturbhuj or Vishṇu, S'ítalá (the goddess of Small-pox), and other deities.

Close by is Someśwar Mandil or the Temple of the Moon, from *Soma*, the moon. Here, it is imagined, diseases of every character may be healed; and, while the god is regarded in the light of an all-powerful physician, his temple is spoken of as a hospital. It need hardly be remarked, that, since these are the sentiments of the people, their practice strangely belies

[1] This was written as the summer was advancing, before the rains commenced.

such sentiments; for, instead of thronging to this shrine, they visit, in great numbers, the European hospitals and their own native doctors. The wonder is, that, although, after worshipping this god, they are not healed, but remain as they were, their faith in him continues unabated. Such is the force of habit uninfluenced by considerations of reason. A short distance from this temple, in an alley running into one of the streets, is the shrine of Baráhan Deví, who is worshipped in the morning, and is held to be a very potent goddess. On approaching the temple, I was requested to take off my shoes, in order not to defile the hallowed spot, an honour I declined to render to the goddess. The peculiar virtue ascribed to this deity is, to heal all such of her worshippers as are afflicted with a swelling in the hands or feet.

The Observatory is a substantial building, rising high above the ghát. The approach to it is not from the ghát, but from a street leading to it, at a considerably higher elevation than the foundations of the edifice. Passing up the steps, you enter a court, one side of which faces the river. From this you ascend a staircase, which brings you to that part of the building devoted to astronomical purposes.

The Observatory was erected by Raja Jay Sinh, who "succeeded to the inheritance of the ancient Rajas of Ambheri, in the year of Vicramaditya 1750, corresponding to 1693 of the Christian era. His mind had been early stored with the knowledge contained in the Hindu writings; but he appears to have especially attached himself to the mathematical sciences; and his reputation for skill in them stood so high, that he was chosen, by the Emperor Mahommed Shah, to reform the calendar, which, from the inaccuracy of the existing tables, had ceased to correspond with the actual appearance of the heavens. Jayasinha (Jey Singh) undertook the task, and constructed a new set of tables, which, in honour of the reigning prince, he named Zeej Mahommedshahy. By these, almanacks are constructed at Delhi, and all astronomical computations made at the present time."[1] For the accomplishment of this undertaking, and the promotion of astronomical investigations, Jay Sinh erected five observatories; namely, at Delhi, Benares, Mathura, Oujein, and Jeypore, remains of which exist to the present day. But he himself has described the object he had in view in their erection, in his preface to the Zeej Mahommedshahy. In the Asiatic Researches, Vol. v., this preface is given entire. A few quotations from this curious production may not be uninteresting.

Since, he says, "the well-wisher of the works of creation, and the admiring spectator of the theatre of infinite wisdom and providence, Suvai Jey Singh, from the first dawning of reason in his mind, and during its progress towards maturity, was entirely devoted to the study of mathematical science, and the bent of his mind was constantly directed to the solution of its most difficult problems, by the aid of the Supreme Artificer, he obtained a thorough knowledge of its principles and rules. He found that the calculation of the places of the stars, as obtained from

[1] Asiatic Researches, Vol. v., pp. 177, 178.

the tables in common use, such as the new tables of Seid Goorganee and Khaeanee, and the Insheelat-Mula-Chand-Akber-shahee, and the Hindu books, and the European tables, in very many cases, give them widely different from those determined by observation; especially the appearance of the new moons, the computation of which does not agree with observation. Seeing that very important affairs, both regarding religion and the administration of empire, depend upon these, and that, in the time of the rising and setting of the planets, and the seasons of the eclipses of the sun and moon, many considerable disagreements of a similar nature are found, he represented it to his Majesty,—of dignity and power, the sun of the firmament of felicity and dominion, the splendour of the forehead of imperial magnificence, the unrivalled pearl of the sea of sovereignty, the incomparably brightest star of the heaven of empire, whose standard is the Sun, whose retinue the Moon, whose lance is Mars, and his pen like Mercury, whose threshold is the Sky, whose signet is Jupiter, whose sentinel Saturn, the Emperor descended from a long race of kings, an Alexander in dignity, the shadow of God, the victorious king, Mahommed Shah,—may he ever be triumphant in battle!"

"Thereupon the Emperor graciously ordered him to labour for the ascertaining of the point in question, that the disagreement between the calculated times of those phenomena, and the times in which they are observed to happen, may be rectified." "Finding that brass instruments did not come up to the ideas which he had formed of accuracy, because of the smallness of their size, the want of division into minutes, the shaking and wearing of their axes, the displacement of the centres of the circles, and the shifting of the planes of the instruments, he concluded that the reason why the determinations of the ancients, such as Hipparchus and Ptolemy, proved inaccurate, must have been of this kind. Therefore, he constructed, in Dar ul Kheláfet Shah Jehanabad, which is the seat of empire and prosperity, instruments of his own invention, such as Jeypergás, and Rám Junter, and Semrát Junter,—the semi-diameter of which is of eighteen cubits, and one minute on it is a barleycorn and a half,—of stone and lime, of perfect stability, with attention to the rules of geometry, and adjustment to the meridian, and to the latitude of the place, and with care in the measuring and fixing of them, so that the inaccuracies from the shaking of the circles, and the wearing of their axes, and displacement of their centres, and the inequality of the minutes, might be corrected. Thus an accurate method of constructing an Observatory was established; and the difference which had existed between the computed and observed places of the fixed stars and planets, by means of observing their mean motions and aberrations with such instruments, was removed. And, in order to confirm the truth of these observations, he constructed instruments of the same kind (as those constructed in the observatory at Delhi) in Suvai Jeypore, and Mattra, and Benares, and Oujein. When he compared these observatories, after allowing for the difference of longitude between the places where they stood, the observations and calculations agreed." "He found the calculation to agree perfectly with the observation. And, although, even to this day the business of the Observatory is carried on, a table under the name of His Majesty, the shadow of God, comprehending the most accurate rules and most perfect methods of computation, was constructed; that so, when the places of the stars, and the appearance of the new moons, and the eclipses of the sun and moon, and the conjunctions of the heavenly bodies, are computed by it, they may arrive as near as possible to the truth, which, in fact, is every day seen and confirmed in the Observatory."

Such is the account of the erection of the Benares Observatory and the invention of its instruments, written by the native astronomer himself, whose genius planned and carried out this important enterprise. Some of the instruments are of gigantic size, and are built of strong masonry capable of lasting for ages, and yet of such delicate adjustment as, for the most part, to continue serviceable according to the original purpose of their designer. But little use, I fear, is now made of them, beyond the calculation of eclipses, festival days, horoscopes, and other matters of practical interest to the people. Many Europeans passing through Benares visit this famous Observatory; and, doubtless, the Brahman in charge of it reaps a considerable harvest thereby. One would naturally suppose, that, if not the celebrity of the place, at least the emoluments which they derive from European and other sight-seers, would be an inducement to the Brahmans to keep the building and its instruments in repair, and so prevent them from falling into decay; but they seem to be utterly careless on these points, and are allowing the hot sun and the drenching rains of summer to play upon exquisitely enamelled surfaces, the parts of which are divided and subdivided into regular distances with the nicest accuracy, without attempting to restore the breaches in the mortar, and to keep the instruments from injury.

On entering the Observatory, the first instrument you come to is the Bhittiyantra, or Mural Quadrant, which consists of a wall, eleven feet high, and nine feet one and a quarter inches broad, in the plane of the meridian. By this instrument the sun's altitude and zenith distance, at noon, may be ascertained; and, also, the sun's greatest declination, and the latitude of the place. Not far distant are two large circles, one built of stone, the other of lime; and also a large square, built of stone. These may, perhaps, have been used for the purpose of ascertaining the shadow of the gnomon cast by the sun, and the degrees of azimuth; but all the marks upon them are obliterated.

There is an enormous instrument, called Yantra-samráṭ (or prince of instruments), whose wall is thirty-six feet in length, and four and a half feet in breadth, and is set in the plane of the meridian. One extremity is six feet four and a quarter inches high, and the other, twenty-two feet three and a half inches, sloping gradually upwards, so as to point directly to the north pole. By the aid of this instrument, the distance

Photographed by D. Tresham, Esq.

THE NEPALESE TEMPLE.

from the meridian, and the declination of any planet or star, and the sun, and also the right ascension of a star, may be known. There is, also, here a double Mural Quadrant, and, to the east, an Equinoctial Circle made of stone. There is, likewise, another Yantra-samráṭ, of small dimensions.

Hard by is the Chakrayantra, between two walls, an instrument used for finding the declination of a planet or star; but it is now out of order. In this immediate neighbourhood is a gigantic instrument, called Digaṅśayantra, constructed to find the degrees of azimuth of a planet or star. It consists of a pillar four feet two inches high, and three feet seven and a half inches thick, surrounded by a wall of exactly its own height, at a distance of seven feet three and a quarter inches, which is again surrounded by another wall, double its height, and distant from it three feet two and a half inches. The upper surfaces of both walls are divided into three hundred and sixty degrees, and are marked with the points of the compass. On the south side of this instrument there is another Equinoctial Circle; but the marks and divisions upon it are totally effaced.

I am indebted to the interesting paper of Pandit Bápú Deva Śástrí, — Professor of Mathematics and Astronomy in the Government College, Benares, — which he contributed to the Benares Institute, for this information respecting the instruments found in the Mán-Mandil Observatory.

The Nepalese Temple, rising from the banks of the Ganges, at no very great distance from the Mán-Mandil

Ghát, is a strikingly picturesque object, and does not fail to arrest the attention of every visitor to this quarter of the city. In its external appearance, it is altogether unlike the shrines erected by the Hindus for the practice of their religion.

CHAPTER XI.

DAŚÁŚAMEDH Ghát and Temple.—Legend of Daśáśamedh.—Siddheswarí Temple.—Chandra-Kúp, or Well of the Moon.—Temple of the goddess S'ankaṭá Deví.—S'ankaṭá Ghát.—Rám Ghát.

To the south of the Mán-Mandil Ghát is the Daśáśamedh Ghát, a spot exceedingly venerated by the natives of the city, as well as by pilgrims and devotees, and much frequented for its supposed sanctity. It is one of the five celebrated places of pilgrimage in Benares. The other four are Así Sangam, Maṇikarṇiká, Panchgangá, and Barná Sangam. These five places, in addition to their proper attractions, are associated together, and furnish the devotee with a complete course of pilgrimage, in the same manner as a journey to Jagannáth, or Gayá, or Benares, or Hardwár, is regarded as such. Proceeding from Así Ghát or Sangam, at the extreme south of the city, the pilgrim, having already performed proper religious ceremonies at this ghát, arrives at Daśáśamedh, and worships the gods in the temple there, and, passing thence to Maṇikarṇiká, bathes in the well. Having done this, he advances to Panchgangá, and on to Barná Sangam, the northern extremity of the city, at both which places he bestows the customary offerings, and pays reverence to the deities peculiar to them. He has thus traversed the city from south to north, having kept upon the bank of the river throughout the whole distance, and passed over every ghát. This pilgrimage is called the Panch-tírth, to perform which is considered a very meritorious act.

The legend connected with the Daśáśamedh temple and ghát, as the foundation of the sanctity of both, and on account of which the Hindus regard them as the very gateway to heaven, must not be omitted here. It is another of the legends connected with the famous Divodás. It is said that S'iva and Gaurí (his wife) were sitting together, one day, on the Mandaráchal mountain, when the former exhibited great distress of mind at not having received any intelligence from Benares for some time. The city was then in the hands of Raja Divodás, who, as already narrated, on accepting its sovereignty, had expelled from it all the gods, and S'iva, the head of them all, amongst the number. Although S'iva had sent several persons, successively, to inquire into the state of the city, yet none of them had returned; inasmuch as, on reaching it, every one had been so captivated with its tranquillity and blessedness, as to have been powerless to quit so happy a region. In his anxiety, S'iva thought to himself, that, should I send Brahmá (the first god of the Hindu triad), who is a dear friend of mine, he will, without fail, bring me word again about its condition. He then fixed his thoughts on Brahmá, who, in obedience to the secret summons, was immediately at his side. On arriving, S'iva unburthened his mind to him, and wished him to proceed to Benares, and, when there, to devise some plan for the expulsion of Raja Divodás from the government of the city. Brahmá was quite ready to do what he could towards assisting his friend, and so took his departure for Benares, mounted on a goose. On reaching the holy city, he was enraptured with its appearance. He went all about it, and visited its temples, bazars, and gháts, with ever-increasing delight, and, at last, selected a spot for his own residence, and transformed himself into the form of an aged Brahman. After a time he sought an interview with the Raja, and was received by him with much respect. The Raja begged he would ask of him whatever he wished to have. Brahmá replied to this kind solicitation, that he would take nothing from him, but that he had come to Benares for the performance of ascetic rites. While conversing together, it struck Brahmá, that, if he could cause the Raja to commit a sin, no matter how small, he would be obliged to lay down his authority over the sacred place, and to quit the kingdom. He, therefore, requested the Raja to give him all the essential materials for a special sacrifice, hoping that some little mistake would be made in the number or quality of them. These materials consisted of water taken from twenty-seven wells, leaves plucked from twenty-seven trees, and a multitude of other ingredients, twenty-seven times told, and derived from twenty-seven different sources. The Raja, in reply, said, "Good, take materials, not for one sacrifice merely, but for ten." Presently, Brahmá left the Raja, and went and sat down upon the banks of the Ganges, where materials for ten such sacrifices were brought to him. Not one ingredient was missing; all were perfectly complete. Brahmá then offered the ten sacrifices; and at each of them, a horse was consumed. The spot on which the ten sacrifices were offered Brahmá called Daśáśwamedha Ghát, or ghát of the ten horse-sacrifices,—from *daśa*, ten; *aśwa*, a horse; and *medha*, sacrifice,—which became, thenceforward, in Hindu estimation, a place of eminent sanctity, and endued with the power of conferring a multitude of blessings on all who sacrificed and bathed there.

Brahmá constituted Daśáśamedh the prince of places of pilgrimage, equal to Prayág (Allahabad). Should a Hindu, therefore, wishing to proceed to Prayág, at the time of the *melá* or religious festival there, not be able to undertake the journey, he may, at this ghát, obtain all the merit which he would have acquired, had he actually completed the pilgrimage to Prayág, and bathed at the sacred junction of the Ganges and the Jumna. Brahmá also dedicated two images in honour of Śiva, one of which he called Daśáśwamedheśwar, and the other, Brahmeśwar. The former is a plain black stone, of enormous dimensions, being not less than five or six feet in girth, and three or four in height, in front of which is a bull, also of large proportions. The other image is much smaller. Whoever worships Daśáśwamedheśwar will, it is supposed, escape all future transmigration; and his soul, instead of passing into a man, a mouse, or a frog, will go straight to paradise,—that is, the heaven of Śiva. In like manner, he who worships Brahmeśwar will, it is said, at death, fly at once into Brahmaloka, or the sphere of Brahmá. In the temple which contains these idols, there is a great assemblage of other images, consisting, for the most part, of *lingas*, representing S'iva, which are chiefly arranged by the wall, and form, what the natives term, a *kachahrí* or court of gods. In the latter half of the month of Jeṭh, a great many persons bathe at this ghát, and, also, in a small tank, near by, called Rudrasar, which shares in the sanctity of the neighbourhood. For fifteen days the bathing and practice of religious ceremonies continue, the virtue of each day increasing in an arithmetical series; so that the virtue acquired on the fifteenth day is fifteen times as great as that acquired on the first; and the aggregate virtue amassed during the entire fifteen days, consequently, amounts to the virtue of one hundred and twenty days.

After terminating the ten sacrifices, it occurred to Brahmá, that he had not effected his object with Raja Divodás, in inducing him to commit sin. How could he, therefore, return to S'iva? And, enamoured with all he saw around him, and flattered by Divodás, who built for him a house of great beauty, he settled the difficulty by determining to remain where he was, until S'iva came to him.

In the Siddheśwarí Mahalla are two temples, held by devout Hindus in great repute. One is the Siddheśwarí temple itself, to which is attached the ancient well known as Chandra-kúp; the other is the temple of S'ankaṭá Deví. The former consists of two small quadrangles, in the first of which, in the centre of the open space, is Chandra-kúp, or the well dedicated to the moon,—from *chandra*, the moon, and *kúpa*, a well. In the month of Chait, on the day of the full moon, this spot is visited by pilgrims, who cast their offerings into the well, in honour of the lunar deity. They also resort thither whenever a new moon occurs on a Monday; as that day is sacred to this luminary. In the sacred quadrangle a figure of the goddess Durgá is seen in a niche at the base of the wall, on the right-hand side as you enter. With one hand she grasps a lotos, and, with another a sword; the third hand rests upon a lion, and the fourth, upon a buffalo. A verandah extends along two sides of this enclosure, supported on pillars, the walls of which are decorated with paintings in vivid colours, several of which represent incarnations of the god Gaṇeś. Behind the verandah is the shrine of Siddheśwarí, the goddess who contributes perfection. Oppressed with the ills and trials of life, the Hindu approaches the goddess, and presents to her newly-gathered flowers, and water from the Ganges, hoping to obtain the promised blessing. He retires, believing in the virtue of his sacrifice, yet sick at heart, with his sorrows unrelieved and his sins unforgiven.

Śankaṭá Deví is another goddess who is thought to bestow similar favours on her votaries. Her shrine is situated on one side of a spacious quadrangle, in the middle of which, raised upon a platform, is an assemblage of temples and idols; and, on the western side of the platform, a bell hangs, suspended from the stone scaffolding. A portion of the quadrangle is

Photographed by D. Tresham, Esq.

RÁM GHÁT.

appropriated to a *maṭh* or Hindu monastery. Among the persons attached to the monastery are certain devout Hindus who have come to the sacred city to die; but by far the larger number of residents are young men receiving instruction in the Hindu S'ástras. The Sankaṭá Ghát, leading down to the river, is a short distance from this place. On the stairs stands a large figure of Mahábír, the monkey-god; and lower down is a domed temple, containing an emblem of S'iva, over which a goblet is suspended, from which water drops incessantly upon the idol, through a hole in the bottom.

To the north of Sankaṭá Ghát is Rám Ghát, on the steps of which is a temple, or, more properly, a room, filled with the most grotesque collection of deities to be found in Benares. The images are dressed in bright-coloured garments interwoven with tinsel, and are of various shapes and forms. Some present a hideous appearance, having large eyes and mouths, and being destitute of hands and feet. The whole collection looks like a doll-shop of a very vulgar description. It is difficult to understand how persons in their senses can pay divine homage to such frightful objects; yet, on conversing with the priests, they boldly defended the adoration of them, and perceived, or pretended to perceive, neither the absurdity nor the degradation of such a proceeding.

Most of the gháts leading from the streets of the city down into the river have been built by Rajas or other powerful natives, and are, generally, provided with one or more temples, especially *S'ivályas*, or temples dedicated to S'iva.

CHAPTER XII.

The Bengali population of Benares.—The popular Temple of Kedáreśwar.—Legend of Kedár.—Mánsarwar Tank and surrounding Temples.—Bálkṛishṇa and Chaturbhuj Idols.—Máneśwar Temple.—The Great Image of Tilubhaṇḍeśwar.—Ancient mutilated Statue.—Temple of Duláreśwar.—Peepul tree at Chaukí Ghát—Swinging gods.

The Bengalis inhabiting Benares form a considerable community. They reside, for the most part, by themselves, in a quarter of the city called the Bengali Tolá, and are noted chiefly for the superior education which many of them have received, in comparison with the Hindustani portion of the population. Not a few among them are more or less acquainted with the English language, and pride themselves on this circumstance, and on the various kinds of knowledge which, through its instrumentality, they have acquired. In their social habits, however, many of this class are not much, I fear, in advance of their neighbours; although, I rejoice to be able to say, there is reason to believe that some have made considerable progress in such matters, of late years. Being more enlightened than Hindus generally, it is strange that, in many respects, their inner domestic life is scarcely better than theirs. Some of them are beginning to educate their wives and daughters, and are anxious for their intellectual improvement. Yet the uneducated portion of the Bengali community adhere to the customs of

Hindu society just as rigidly as other inhabitants of the city, cling with equal pertinacity to caste, and exhibit the same blind and senseless attachment to idol-worship. A great difference is observable amongst Bengalis, however; and numbers of them are utterly unsound in the faith of Hinduism; for their understandings, having been strongly affected by their English studies, have become sufficiently cleared to perceive the foolishness of idolatry. These occupy the position of great social and religious reformers, and are engaged in a very important work, which is none other than the entire regeneration of native society. I look upon this class of Bengalis, together with the educated Parsees, as in the van of national improvement and progress.

The Bengali Tolá, with its neighbourhood, is bestrewn with shrines and deities, which seem to be as numerous here, or nearly so, as in that quarter of the city occupied by the temple of Bisheśwar. But the temple most frequented by the Bengalis, and which holds the position of a cathedral or chief ecclesiastical edifice in this district of the city, is the temple of Kedáreś-war, or, as it is called, with equal propriety, Kedár-náth. This is a large building, rising from the banks of the Ganges, from which a fine stone ghát descends to the bed of the river. It stands in the middle of a spacious court, at the four corners of which are four temples crowned with domes. The verandah running round the inner side of the enclosure contains several small shrines and a numerous collection of idols. Most of these latter are of a diminutive size, but not all; for two figures in brass, covered over with cloth, so far as

I could judge, appeared to be of imposing dimensions. They stand in a cage-like looking place; but why they are so concealed from the public gaze by the wrappings about them, it is hard to say. Perhaps it is in order to protect them from the dust and filth of the enclosure, or because they have not been, as yet, properly consecrated and transformed into deities worthy of worship, by means of certain ceremonies prescribed by the sacred books and performed by the Brahmans, which, as is fondly asserted, are capable of producing such an astounding and impossible result. The principal temple in the centre of the quadrangle, like the temples at each of its corners, is surmounted by a dome. Its outer walls, as high as the ceiling of the court, and, indeed, all the walls of the court and passages, and the pillars of the inner verandah, are painted red and white, the former colour predominating. The entrance to the temple itself is on its eastern side, from which a broad path leads down to the Ganges. Two black stone statues in bass-relief, six feet in height, stand on either side of the doorway, and are supposed to guard the approach to the inner chamber. The figures are exceedingly well executed, and have a striking and life-like appearance. Each has four hands, and, in form and posture, is the exact counterpart of the other. In one hand they hold a trident, in the second a club, in the third a flower, while the fourth is empty, and is raised for the purpose of attracting attention, one finger being extended as though expressive of prohibition or warning. The meaning of this peculiar position of the finger is, I understand, as if these doorkeepers stopped the worshipper, wishing to cross the threshold into the sacred chamber where the idol dwells, and addressed him as follows:—"Wait a little, and, when you get permission from the god, then you may enter." This may explain the circumstance, that the door of the temple is, for a certain time in the day, kept closed, and the worshippers have to remain outside until it is thrown open again, when they are allowed to enter.

Between the statues is a door leading into the interior of the shrine, and to its outer framework sixty-seven small lamps are attached, which are lighted up with oil every evening. Within the temple is the god Kedáreśwar, who is represented simply by a stone, the emblem of Śiva; for Kedáreśwar is, strictly speaking, only another name for this divinity. Kedár is, properly, no name of a person, but of a place in the Himalayas. Śiva, it is believed, resided there; and hence is called Kedáreśwar or Kedárnáth, 'Lord of Kedár.' Yet, in Benares, there is a tradition, that Kedár was a devout Brahman, who, in company with the Muni Vasishṭha, visited a mountain forming part of the Himalaya range, where he died. At his death, it is said, Śiva endowed him with the attributes of deity, and allowed him to be worshipped in conjunction with himself, and through the same symbol. Appearing to Vasishṭha in a dream, he said he would comply with any request he might make; whereupon Vasishṭha requested that he would take up his residence in Benares. Such is the origin of the temple here, as given in the *Káśí-khaṇḍa.* There is a temple dedicated to Kedáreśwar near the famous temple of Harináth, on Mount Himáchal, to which so many pilgrims yearly resort, besides that in Benares.

Other idols are also associated with the presiding divinity here, such as Lakshmínáráyaṇ, Bhaironáth, Gaṇeś, and Annpúrṇá. Upon the wall of the passage leading to the ghát is a long inscription, in Bengali and Hindi characters, setting forth the glory and excellency of Kedáreśwar. Just within the passage, and near to the threshold, I observed a man, of respectable appearance, lying prostrate on the ground across the path. He had thrown himself there, as an act of homage to the idol. The outer enclosure of the temple is frequented by large numbers of poor persons, who sit by the side of the passages, in a row, spreading out their laps, or pieces of cloth, or extending their hands for food and money. In this respect, the Kedáreśwar shrine reminds one very much of the temple of Annpúrṇá, where crowds of beggars are to be seen. The ghát descends from the eastern wall of the temple. Upon its staircase are several small shrines; and, at its base, is a well, in the shape of a parallelogram, containing water. This well is called Gaurí-kuṇḍ; and its water is famous for the imaginary virtue of removing three kinds of fever.

To the west of Kedárnáth temple, at the distance of about one-third of a mile, is Mánsarwar, which consists of a deep tank and a large collection of shrines all around it. These shrines are not fewer than fifty in number, each containing one idol, at least; and several, a great many. One of the most considerable is dedicated to the brothers Rám and Lakshmaṇ. In a niche in the enclosure of this temple is an idol of

Dattátreya. This Yogí, with the Moon and Durvásas for brothers, was son of Atri. He is a rare object of homage in the present day. Mánsarwar was built by Raja Mán Sinh. At this one spot there are, I conjecture, upwards of one thousand idols.

Near the eastern entrance of Mánsarwar, at the corner of a street, are two antique figures, one of which stands on a pedestal, while the other is inserted in the wall of a house. The former is Bálkṛishṇa, who is kneeling down, while his head and chest are thrown back so as to assume a very remarkable appearance; the head being in a horizontal instead of a perpendicular position. The other is Chaturbhuj. A few steps further off is Máneśwar, a temple erected by the same Raja Mán Sinh spoken of above. The Raja was influenced, most probably, by his own name, in selecting the divinity he has here honoured with a shrine.

In this neighbourhood, but in a south-westerly direction from Mánsarwar, is the monstrous idol Tilubhaṇḍeśwar, which is, by measurement, fifteen feet round and four and a half feet high. It is simply a large stone, and resembles the idol Jágeśwar, in the Ausánganj Mahalla of the city, to which, as already observed, the gentry and nobility of Benares pay their devotions. Tilubhaṇḍeśwar is so called because, it is said, the god daily increases in size to the extent of one *til*, a seed of sesamum, from which oil is extracted and sold in the shops. The god inhabits a temple, the basement of which, together with a small piece of ground in connexion with it, is raised to a considerable height above the streets in the neighbourhood, the ascent being effected by steps. The temple, consequently, is a prominent object in this quarter of the city. A sculptured bull lies crouching in the verandah opposite the idol. On either side of the entrance to the temple are small shrines, containing a number of idols, one of which bears the strange name of Sámkátik. This idol is rare in the Benares temples. Passing round to the east side of the temple, several niches in the wall are seen. These contain numerous idols. In one is a representation of the sole of Vishṇu's foot, in marble, besides three snake-gods, three emblems of Mahádeva, and an old figure of Gaṇeś. Another has a large black idol of S'iva, with head, hands, and feet. This idol is very seldom found in Benares; as S'iva is almost always worshipped through a phallic symbol, which is the commonest and most popular object of adoration in every quarter of the city. The idol is good-looking, and is seated in a meditative posture, its hair falling in ringlets upon its shoulders. A plantain-tree, carved in stone, stands on either side of him; and, in a corner, is a figure of Sámkátik who is reading to S'iva. The verandah of the temple was once beautifully embellished; but the small and delicate paintings which crowd the roof and capitals of the pillars are exceedingly faded.

On a second platform, lower than that on which the Tilubhaṇḍeśwar temple stands, is a peepul tree, resting upon which is a large mutilated statue. Its head is two feet in height, and a foot in breadth; and its body is of proportionate size. The height of the head is partly owing to the mode in which the hair is arranged upon it; for it is plaited and bound round the crown, so as to have the appearance of a high head-dress. The face is round, and not at all of the Hindu expression. The Brahmanical cord passes over one shoulder, and descends to the waist; but, notwithstanding this circumstance, I am strongly inclined to think that the figure is rather of the Buddhist than of the Hindu era. The presence of the cord is no difficulty in the way of this supposition; inasmuch as several of the pre-historical Buddhas were Brahmans. The hair is arranged in a manner altogether different from that which the modern Hindus practise. It is said that Aurungzeb mutilated this statue. The thighs are imbedded in the ground; but the legs, I was told, from the knees downwards, are not in existence. The statue is symmetrically proportioned, and its parts are finely chiselled. Hindu sculptors of the present day are utterly incapable of producing such a piece of workmanship; and, therefore, one is curious to know how it came here, and from what place it was brought. The priest in attendance gave it the name of Bírbhadra, a famous messenger of Śiva. A multitude of idols, not fewer than thirty, are placed around him and the trunk of the tree against which he leans. There is a neem tree a few paces off, at the foot of which reclines the eight-handed goddess Ashṭbhují; and close to her is a collection of nine deities. In the enclosure of this temple are several images of considerable antiquity. A bull, especially, in the lower enclosure, bears marks of immense age, and formerly, it is said, stood in front of the idol Tilubhaṇḍeśwar.

On the way from Kedárnáth temple to Daśáśamedh temple various objects of interest are to be seen. At one place several strange idols have been fixed into the walls, from which they jut out in bass-reliefs, and catch an occasional sprinkling of holy water, or flower blossoms, from the passers-by. Among them are the Naugrah, or planets, represented as deities. The temple of Duláreśwar, also, although modern, is worthy of notice. It was erected by a Bengali, named Sátu Bábú, more than fifty years ago, and is dedicated to S'iva. It contains a large symbol of this divinity, in jet-black stone or marble, from which a slab, of the same kind of stone, projects at right angles. The lofty temple stands in the centre of the enclosure; and on either side is a row of seven temples, all built uniformly, with towers above, and conical symbols of S'iva below. The god in each of the fifteen temples in this enclosure is decorated with a white streak, made with sandal-wood, which is renewed and obliterated daily.

At Chaukí Ghát, on the banks of the river, is a peepul tree, part of the trunk of which is encompassed with masonry, to the height of several feet; and out of its centre the tree seems to spring. The pedestal thus formed is literally crowded with idols. Several are figures of snakes; and one represents the heads of five snakes in a row, the necks being erect, and the heads curved, as though in the attitude of springing. All are in stone; and the entire collection does not number fewer than fifty. In front of this peepul tree is the temple of Rukmeś-war; and several other temples are close at hand. In A'hyabar Galí, a narrow street, is a banyan tree, which has a pedestal round its base, somewhat similar to that of the peepul tree just described; but, in this case, a small shrine is attached to the pedestal. Near it is an old figure of Gaṇeś. In Kewal Galí a swing is hung up in what, at first sight, appears to be a shop. Beyond the swing, by the opposite wall, sits the ten-armed goddess Durgá, with a crown on her head, decorated with gay clothing, and set off by a nimbus painted on the wall behind; her priest having intended her to look, not like a mere queen of earth, but like the queen of heaven. By the swing sits the priest, who, when so disposed, places in it some of the idols of the shrine, but not Durgá herself, and gratifies them with a swing.

The idols and fanes in the Bengali Tolá, and, indeed, in this neighbourhood generally, are exceedingly numerous. All the latter, with, perhaps, one exception, and most of the former, are of comparatively recent date. In regard to the temples, it is possible that part of the Tilubhaṇḍeśwar temple may be old. The priest told me, that, at the back of one of the small shrines at the entrance to the temple, was an inscription, which stated that the temple was erected by a Raja upwards of four hundred and sixty years ago. He rubbed off part of the whitewash, in order that I might see a portion of it. The horizontal lines of the inscription, however, were intercepted by the idol in the shrine; and, therefore, it was impossible to interpret what was written. It would be interesting to have the entire inscription copied; for, if the temple is really of the date traditionally assigned to it, this quarter of the city must have been frequented, if not partially inhabited, at the same epoch. The few idols of an ancient appearance found in this part of Benares, prove, in themselves, nothing; as they may have been brought from other parts of the city, or, indeed, from elsewhere. Some of them are stuck into the walls, and the sides of houses, built ten or twenty years ago; while others are placed by the trunks of trees, planted within the memory of living men, or upon, or in, the walls of the pedestals of masonry formed round their base. Neither the Kedár nor the Káśí quarter of Benares contains, so far as my investigations have gone, any *bona fide* remains of ancient temples, such as the Trilochan or Benares quarter presents, unless it may be the walls of the former temple of Bisheśwar, now part of a mosque, built by Aurungzeb, and the temple of Bṛiddhkál, on the boundary between the Káśí and the Benares quarters. Still, it must be confessed, that time-worn idols do exist in the Kedár quarter, as well as in the two remaining quarters of Benares. These, no doubt, furnish a strong proof of the antiquity of the city itself, though not of this individual portion of it; and their existence, to a small extent, in it throws no light upon its real epoch. On the contrary, however, temples and other buildings which are stationary and immoveable, so long as they stand, do determine the era of their own neighbourhood, and furnish some reasons for supposing that other edifices may possibly be found near them, of equal antiquity with themselves.

CHAPTER XIII.

Durgá Kuṇḍ Temple. — Bloody Sacrifices; their meaning. — Sacred Monkeys.—Legend of Durg and Durgá.—A Devotee.—Durgá Kuṇḍ or Tank.—Kurukshetr Táláo or Tank.—The Lolárik Kúáṅ or Well.—Ancient Sculptures.

One of the popular and most frequented temples in Benares is that of Durgá, wife of Mahádeva or S'iva, situated at the southern extremity of the city. Bloody sacrifices are offered to the goddess in great abundance, by persons wishing to obtain her aid in cases of sickness, under the impression that she will accept the life of an animal in exchange for the life of a human being. Not that they have any notion whatever of atonement effected thereby, or of the sacrifices having any connexion with sin and its forgiveness; but their simple idea is, that the goddess delights in blood, that she takes pleasure in the sickness and death of mankind, and that she can only be appeased, if appeased at all, by an irrational creature being dedicated to her, in the place of a rational one, whom she had doomed to sickness or death. Sacrifices are also presented to her for all kinds of objects. For instance, men out of employment will offer a kid to Durgá, in order that, through her, they may speedily obtain work. Formerly, a small shrine was situated on this spot, in the midst of what, it is asserted, was then wild jungle: but it seems to have been very little resorted to; and it is far from clear when, or by what means, the shrine began to be famous. At the time that the new temple and tank were erected by the famous Marathi, Rani Bhawání, no doubt their splendid appearance constituted a strong reason why larger numbers were attracted to the place. Now, no Hindu in the neighbourhood, of any pretensions to earnestness in his religion, neglects to visit the temple occasionally. Pilgrims, also, from a distance find their way to it. Throughout the day worshippers may be seen performing their devotions in the presence of the idol, while, every Tuesday, a *melá* or fair is held in its honour; and, on the Tuesdays of one month of the year, namely, the month of Sáwan, these *melás* are attended by an enormous multitude of people, who fill the road and spacious gardens adjacent to the temple.

Connected with the Durgá shrine is what may, with as much appropriateness as is often attached to the word, be called the 'institution' of monkeys. These creatures,—all living deities, gods, and goddesses,—literally swarm upon the private houses, and about the streets and bazars, in a wide circuit around the temple. They are of all sizes and ages, of all tempers and peculiarities, and, I venture to say, represent, in their aggregation, all the trickery and cunning of which monkeyhood is capable. I was told that they number one hundred thousand; but this, of course, is a great exaggeration. But that they amount to several thousand is indisputable. The presence of such a host of mischievous and destructive animals, scampering over the tops of houses, and wherever their fancy leads them, sitting on walls, and on a hundred places from which they may watch their opportunity for thieving and perpetrating divers other kinds of evil on the property of their human fellow-creatures, is nothing less than a calamity to the natives. Yet, as they think otherwise, and regard the monkey-race as of greater sanctity than themselves,—investing them, indeed, with the attributes of divinity,—there is no help for them. To kill one rascally monkey might produce a disturbance; and to kill many would certainly excite the whole city to rebellion. The civil authorities, therefore, are wise in not interfering in the matter, but suffer the natives, in this instance, to reap the fruits of their superstitions and delusions. The monkeys are fed with various kinds of grain, distributed by the worshippers, who regard the patronizing of these chattering, pilfering, incorrigible deities as a highly religious and meritorious act.

Before describing the temple, I will briefly narrate the mythic history of the goddess Durgá, as given in the *Kásí-khaṇḍa*. The story runs, that there was, once, a famous demon named Durg, son of another demon named Ruru, who devoted himself to the performance of ascetic rites, and so severely and successfully applied himself to their exercise, that he acquired a prodigious stock of merit, and, together with it, unbounded power. By degrees, he became superior to all the deities, who fled from his presence, and hid themselves; while Durg, entering their dominions and usurping their authority, began to transact the affairs of the world. Indra himself, the king of the gods, was obliged to surrender his sceptre to him; and, in like manner, Agni (the god of Fire), Pavana (the god of the Winds), and Jala (the god of Water) submitted to his irresistible authority. The demon put a stop to religion among men; and injustice, tyranny, and oppression spread over the earth. He treated the gods most ignominiously, and ordered them to feed his cows. These divine personages, in their distress, went, in a body, to Mahádeva, to whom they represented their miserable condition. Taking pity on them, Mahádeva commanded Gaurí, his wife, to go and kill the demon, and deliver the gods from their calamities. Thereupon Gaurí summoned the bloody goddess Mahákálí, and instructed her to slay the demon. In obedience to her instructions, Mahákálí set out to attack Durg; but Durg, hearing of her approach, called together his relatives and servants, and said to them: "Seize this woman, and take care she does not escape!" They then seized Mahákálí, and were carrying her off to the house of the demon; but, on the way, in her anger, she darted fire from her mouth, and burnt them all to ashes. On witnessing this mishap, Durg gathered together a larger number of his adherents, and sent them to recapture the goddess. But these fared no better than their predecessors, and were destroyed in a similar manner. The demon was now exceedingly annoyed, and assembled an immense army, numbering several millions of persons, and sent it against the goddess. Daunted by such a host, Mahákálí fled, and ascended to heaven in the form of a balloon, followed by the army, which soared up to the skies in pursuit of her. After a time the army descended to the earth again, and encamped on Bindhyáchal; but Mahákálí kept on her way, until she came to Gaurí, to whom she narrated the circumstances of her journey, adding that a vast army was on its way to capture her. On receiving this intelligence, Gaurí became incarnate in a body, possessing a thousand arms, of such gigantic dimensions, that it reached from earth to heaven. When Durg beheld her, he was smitten with her beauty, and declared to his people, that whoever amongst them should capture her should sit on the throne of Indra.

Excited by the prospect of obtaining such a high distinction, several regiments of the army made a rush upon Gaurí, with so great an uproar, that the four elephants which supported the earth on their backs became terrified, and fled, in dismay, to Bindhyáchal. Gaurí was delighted at seeing them, and, in her own defence, immediately created an army of gods and instruments of warfare. A large number of the enemy were slain through the power and activity of the goddess; and Durg himself, smarting under the loss he had sustained, now took part in the conflict. Holding in his hands a trident, a sword, a bow, and arrows, he came on with irresistible impetuosity, and, approaching Gaurí, inflicted upon her a heavy blow. The goddess fainted, but, presently recovering herself, arose and ordered the gods to engage with the foe. The battle between the gods and the demons now became general, during which Durg and Gaurí fought together, and, fighting, ascended to heaven and descended to the earth again. On reaching the earth, the demon seized a stone, and threw it at the goddess, who, on its coming near, breathed a curse upon it, and reduced it to powder. He then laid hold of an entire mountain, and, raising it up, hurled it at Gaurí; but she crumbled it, also, to powder, and, with her weapon, struck the demon, who, uttering a loud cry, fell to the ground. The merciless goddess then cut off the head of Durg; and, all the enemies being slain, the battle was most satisfactorily ended. The gods now approached Gaurí, and began to extol her for her valour and exploits, and showered flowers from heaven on the earth below. The celestial *danseuses*, musicians, and minstrels,—Apsarases, Gandharvas, and Kinnaras,—were summoned, and, together with the gods, Munis, and Ṛishis, joined in rendering praise to Gaurí. Gratified with the honour paid to her, the goddess gave utterance to these words: "Whoever shall repeat what has been written in my praise shall be delivered from pain and fear; and I will make myself present, when invoked with eulogies that name me. I will, also, change my appellation to Durgá, by which, in future, I wish to be addressed, because I have slain the demon Durg." Having said this, she vanished; and order was everywhere re-established.

Such is the history of this Hindu deity, which, for wildness and marvel, is not surpassed by the legendary stories connected with the Middle Ages. Let us look at the temple where the goddess holds her court. This is situated in the midst of a quadrangle surrounded by high walls. The main entrance is on the western side, opposite the high road. In front of the doorway, and contiguous to the road, is a building, called the *Naubat-khánú*, in which a large kettle-drum is beaten three times a day, in honour of the goddess. The upper part of this building is open on its four sides, the effect of which is, that the sound proceeding from the drum is obstructed as little as possible. On either side of the *Naubat-khánú*, but more retired from the road, and nearer the wall of the quadrangle, are two small temples, and, in the space between them, two stone pillars. The first of these is about ten feet in height, with a basement of a foot more, and is surmounted by a large figure of a lion. The other is about two feet in height, and is used as an altar for sacrifices. Near it is a wooden post, to which the victim is bound. On its being slaughtered, the head is laid on the altar, and offered to Durgá.

Passing through the narrow doorway into the interior of the enclosure, the first objects that meet the eye are two sculptured lions, one on either side of the pathway, with their faces directed towards the chief entrance to the temple, leading through the porch straight to the goddess. They are in a couching posture, and are intended for the use of Durgá, whenever she wishes to ride out for an airing. Immediately on the left of the lions are two small shrines, one of which is dedicated to Gaṇeś, whose figure, in bass-relief, juts out from the inner wall; and the other is dedicated to Mahádeva, the emblem of which deity, in white marble, stands on the floor of the shrine, while a diminutive figure of a bull, also of marble, kneels in front. To their right is another shrine, in honour of Mahádeva. On the sides of the enclosure, extending all round it, is a platform or terrace, built into the four walls, and covered in with a roof: it furnishes room for accommodating large numbers of persons, and protecting them from the sun and rain. Here I saw a painted devotee, absorbed in meditation, seated before a few leaves of a Sanskrit book. His right hand was in a sock, and held a *málá* or rosary, which, concealed from observation, it revolved; and, as he muttered his *mantras*, he counted the beads unceasingly. Upon this platform is a curious little building, with an iron grating in front, looking like a cage or den for the abode of some wild beast, but which is none other than the residence of the golden-faced goddess Bágeśwarí. A short distance from this shrine is an immodest figure of a woman, in bass-relief.

Between the platform and the temple, which, together with its porch, occupies most of the remaining space of the quadrangle, a broad path runs, separating the former from the latter. In this path, on the south side, is a stone scaffolding, from the arch of which a bell is suspended, the gift of a Raja of Nepal; and on either side of the arch is a small figure of a lion. The temple and the porch, although united together, forming one edifice, are, in reality, two distinct buildings, and were erected at two different periods. The temple was erected by Rani Bhawání, as before mentioned, during the last century; while the porch was erected by a Subahdar, or superior commissioned native officer, a few years ago.

The porch stands upon twelve elaborately-carved pillars, the designs of which are fantastic, yet not without taste. All the pillars are similarly carved. Their base rests upon a floor raised about four feet from the ground; and they are surmounted by a dome, with cupolas at each corner, connected together by a breast-work. The inner part of the dome is embellished with a variety of colours; but the painting, in several places, has suffered injury. From the centre of the dome a large bell is suspended, which, it is reported, was presented to the temple, by a European magistrate of Mirzapore, about forty years ago. This tale, incredible as its sounds, and the truth of which I am not prepared to vouch for, is commonly believed by the people.

The temple is built after the orthodox model of Hindu temples, but not with that excessive display of minute carving and sculpture, representing monstrous and indecent figures, which may be seen on many Hindu edifices of more modern times. Yet its carving is not scanty. The cornices, indeed, of the doors, situated on each of the four sides, are so covered with carving, as to be liable, to some extent, to the remark just applied to more recent buildings. But the upper part of the temple, notwithstanding the multitude of small cupolas surrounding the steeple and rising up to its very apex, exhibits a simplicity of design which every one must behold with pleasure and admiration. Each cupola terminates in a gilded point; and the steeple has a gilded trident crowning its summit. The cornices of the doors above spoken of have the peculiarity of a double arch,—an inner and an outer. Over the outer arch are figures of men, in bass-relief, each seated on a bird, and holding a kind of guitar in his hands; while the second or inner arch is ornamented with figures of Durgá and other deities. The cornices of the door, at the main entrance to the temple leading through the porch, exhibit designs of a different character from the rest. Figures of men riding on lions are carved upon the face of the outer arch; and of Gaṇeś and two women, upon the face of the inner.

In the interior of the temple is a small shrine, the residence of the goddess, painted over with bright glaring colours. The idol within is covered with tinselled cloth, and has a face of brass, or of silver, or of other kind of metal, according to the whim of the priests, who keep a stock of masks on hand, which fit on the head of the image. It is also decorated with a garland, rising like horns above its head; and with several necklaces of gold coins hanging low down as far as the chest. A small lamp burns inside the shrine; and immediately in front of the latter is a silver bath sunk into the ground. Flowers are strewn about, the offerings of the worshippers, and, being permitted to decay, emit an effluvium in the highest degree pernicious to all who approach the place.

On the north side of the outer wall of the quadrangle is one of those noble tanks which abound in northern India. It is within the jurisdiction of the temple, and, so far, may be regarded as sacred; but its waters are not held in special estimation for religious purposes, although they are of great domestic utility to the neighbourhood.

A short distance to the east of Durgá Kuṇḍ, in the

direction of the river, is Kurukshetr Táláo, which is a tank constructed by Rani Bhawání, in commemoration of the battle fought at Kurukshetr, an account of which is found in the *Mahábhárata.* The tank is square, and is built with stone stairs, leading down to the water. It is famous as a place of pilgrimage at the time of a solar eclipse, on which occasion vast crowds of people bathe in the water, with the view of frustrating the efforts of the voracious demon, who persists in temporarily swallowing the moon. On its western side is a temple built by the same lady.

In this Mahalla, which is called Bhadainí, to the north-east of Kurukshetr Táláo, is the Lolárik Kúán or well. This sacred well has a double mouth, or entrance, the water being in one reservoir, communicating with the two shafts or mouths from below. At the time of my visit, it was about twenty feet deep, and the height of the shafts above the water, about fifty feet. Each shaft is of stone, and is surrounded by a parapet; and, between the two parapets, a path runs, broad enough for walking purposes. The two shafts differ, both in form and size. That to the east is round, and is some forty or forty-five feet in circumference. The shaft to the west is in the form of a parallelogram, and is three hundred feet, or upwards, in circumference. On three of its sides are broad stairs, leading down to the water. Descending one of these stairs, you come to the water below, which flows beneath a high arch, connecting together the two shafts. The entire well, as it now exists, was the work of three persons, namely, Rani Ahalyá Bai, a Raja of Behár, and Amrit Rao; but it is uncertain by whom the original well was built. In a niche on the stairs is a disk of the sun, which is so much worn, that it was with some difficulty that, by the fading light of the waning day, I could distinguish the carving upon it. This sacred object is worshipped on the day devoted to the sun, that is, our Sunday. On a platform, about half-way down, is a figure of the god Gaṇeś, in a standing posture, which gives a very ludicrous appearance to his protuberant abdomen, and his elephant-head. By his side is a mutilated figure,—not, I am satisfied, of Hindu origin,—with a head-dress rising to an apex, having a knob standing out in front. The temples are bound by a fillet; and around the neck is a double necklace fastened by a clasp. Several other sculptures on the walls of the south stairs arrested my attention, as being very different from modern works of Hindu art, both in design and in execution. They are partly bass-reliefs of figures cut on separate stones and inserted into the walls. They must, therefore, have been brought from some other building, of a date anterior to the erection of the walls now containing them. The temple of Bhadreśwar stands on the south side of the wall, and displays a large emblem of Śiva.

CHAPTER XIV.

TEMPLE of the Maharaja of Benares at Rámnagar.—Raja Cheit Singh's Tank.—Virtue of Pilgrimage to the Rámnagar side of Benares.—Temple of Vedavyás.—The Panch-kosí Road or Sacred Boundary of Benares.—Pilgrimage of the Panch-kosí.—Sanitary condition of Benares.—Improvements suggested.

AT a distance of a mile from the Fort of Rámnagar, the residence of the Maharaja of Benares, is a handsome temple, situated on the eastern side of a capacious tank. Its foundations were laid, and the finest portions of its tower was erected, about one hundred years ago, by Raja Cheit Singh; but it was completed by the present Raja. The temple, including the platform on which it rests, is fully one hundred feet high. Each of its four sides, from the base to a height of thirty-five or forty feet, is crowded with elaborately-carved figures, in bass-relief. These are, in some places, broken, but, generally speaking, are in a good state of preservation. They are in five rows, six being in a row; so that each side of the tower contains thirty figures, and the four sides, one hundred and twenty. As no expense has been spared in the execution of this prodigious work, it may be regarded as fairly representing what Hindu genius, in modern times, can accomplish in the art of sculpture, and should be visited and studied as such. The lowermost row is filled with elephants, and the next, in succession, with lions, each of which stands on two small elephants. The lions have very spare bodies, and, in this and other respects, are grotesquely made; showing that the sculptors had no living model before them, and drew liberally on their own imaginations. The three upper rows exhibit divers figures of deities, incarnations, and other sacred objects. The three goddesses of the Ganges, the Jumna, and the Saraswatí have, each, a separate niche. Kṛishṇa, too, has his place; but he is not alone, for two of his favourite *gopís* or milk-maids are close by. Indra (the king of the gods), Brahmá, Vishṇu, and Mahádeva or Śiva (the three deities of the Hindu triad), Kuber (the god of wealth), Bhairo (the Divine Magistrate of Benares), the hero Rám and his wife Sítá, Hanumán (the monkey-god), Gaṇeś, Baldeo (brother of Kṛishṇa), etc., are, each, honoured with a statue. Here, too, is Vayu, or the wind; Súrya, or the sun; Agni, or fire; and Chandramá, or the moon; the latter having rays of glory darting from her head, and being seated in a carriage drawn by two deer. A number of sacred personages, Ṛishis, are also represented, such as Nárad and Gajendramoksh, and, likewise, the thousand-armed Arjuna or Kártavírya, whom Paraśuráma fought and killed. In the centre of the uppermost row, on the south side, is a figure of the goddess Durgá, wife of Mahádeva; and, in a similar position, on the east side, is a figure of the bloody goddess Mahákálí, who thirsts continually for human victims. In a niche on the north side a strange feat of Kṛishṇa is depicted. This versatile deity, it is said, on one occasion diverted the homage and adoration due to Indra to himself, at which Indra became exceedingly indignant, and determined to punish the worshippers of Kṛishṇa who had so dishonoured him and defrauded him of his rights. Gathering together the clouds of heaven, he commenced pouring down upon the earth a prodigious flood of water, with the object of drowning the people; but Kṛishṇa, lifting up the mountain Govardhan, held it over the country like an umbrella, balanced on his little finger, so that, over an extent of one hundred and sixty miles, no rain fell, and the people were preserved in safety. In the sculpture, Kṛishṇa is seen standing with his hand held up, supporting the mountain on the extremity of his little finger, while cattle are grazing in perfect security underneath.

On each of the four sides of the tower are two gilded faces, surrounded by a halo, one above the other, emblematic of the Sun; and, on the apex of the tower, is a circular, flat, gilded object, intended to serve the purpose of a glory to the head of Durgá in the shrine below. On the platform facing three of the entrances to the temple are three figures in marble, one of which, namely, that opposite the south door, consists of a Nandi, or bull, designed for the service of Mahádeva. A second is opposite the north door, and is a Garuḍ, a being in the form of a man, with wings behind the shoulders. The countenance is pleasing, and has been executed with much taste. The statue is surrounded by an iron palisade tipped with small brass knobs.

In front of the main entrance is the third figure,

which is that of a lion, intended as the Váhan or riding animal of Durgá. Over the entrance itself are peacocks, in bass-relief, standing with their heads towards each other. The door is not large, but is ribbed and massive, and is covered with brass; so that, viewing it from the front, it has the appearance of being made entirely of that metal.

The interior of the temple, like most Hindu shrines, is confined and gloomy. Directly opposite the door stands the goddess Durgá. Her body is of marble, covered with gold, and is arrayed in a yellow dress partially concealed by a scarf. The image is in a small shrine, in front of which is a table; and on the table lie various vessels used at the hour of sacrifice. It is over this table, and before the face of the idol, that the sacred fire is waved. To the left is another table, of smaller dimensions, which, when I saw it, was completely covered with white blossoms of flowers. Near by, in a niche in the wall, are two idols, representing Kṛishṇa and his wife Rádhá. To the right of Durgá is her five-headed husband S'iva.

The tank and a garden in the neighbourhood were also the work of Raja Cheit Singh. The former is surrounded by a spacious ghát, the stairs of which are built of stone. On occasion of the natives of Benares proceeding on pilgrimage to this spot, they are accustomed to bathe in the tank; and sometimes large crowds may be seen assembled on the stairs. But so extensive are the gháts, that hundreds of persons might dress and undress upon them, without incommoding one another. The tank is a square, at each corner of which is a temple. The pilgrims who come to bathe, therefore, pass and repass at least one temple.

The object of the pilgrimage to Rámnagar is somewhat amusing. It is said that Vedavyás, the compiler of the Vedas, once paid a visit to Rámnagar, intending to proceed to Benares; but, on reaching this place, and beholding the city in the distance, his soul was so ravished with delight, that he did not desire to enter the city itself. Remaining at Rámnagar, he signalized his visit by the institution of a pilgrimage, which should conduce to the welfare of its inhabitants and of all others in danger of future degradation. The sanctity of Rámnagar, it appears, was never equal to that of Benares; and, while all persons who died in the latter place, perforce, it is believed, obtained, after death, happiness and heaven, all those, on the contrary, who died in the former, had the misfortune to enter upon another life in the degraded and miserable condition of an ass. It was, consequently, the custom, report says, in the age of Vedavyás, and is still, for persons residing on the Rámnagar side of the river, which is called *maga*, when taken seriously ill, to repair to the Benares side, in order, if death should come, to die there, and so escape an asinine condition in the next birth. Vedavyás, however, taking pity on the *maga* land, established at Rámnagar a *tírth* or place of pilgrimage, to be honoured in the month of Mágh (January-February), promising, that whoever attended it should be delivered from the danger of becoming an ass after death. Not only do the people of Rámnagar perform this pilgrimage, but great multitudes from Benares, likewise, resort thither, that they may make their own deliverance from asshood doubly sure. Pilgrims continually arrive during the whole of the month; but Mondays and Fridays are days especially preferred, and on which the assemblages are greatest.

There is a temple dedicated to Vedavyás in the Raja's fort of Rámnagar. It is situated above the parapet overlooking the river. The approach to it is by the main stairs or ghát leading up from the Ganges into the fort. Upon the stairs to the left, in a small shrine, is a richly-dressed figure of Gangá, or the goddess of the Ganges, in white marble, seated on a crocodile, and having a crown on her head. She has four hands: one of them hangs down, a second is uplifted, a third grasps a lotos, and the fourth holds a brass vessel. Proceeding to the top of the stairs, and turning to the left, you enter a court, bounded on one side by the parapet of the fort, and open to the sky. Here are several shrines. In the first, Mahádeva resides. Another rests against the trunk of a tree, and contains various small deities. Near to this shrine is a platform, on which is a temple bearing the name of Vedavyás. There is, however, no image of him inside; and the object of worship is the emblem of S'iva. On the floor of the platform is a carved disk representing the Sun; and, a short distance off, a figure of Gaṇeś.

Mention has already been made of the Panch-kosí road, which encompasses Benares. This famous road forms the boundary of the sacred domain, on the extreme east of which the city stands. Its length is about fifty miles. Commencing at the river Ganges, and quitting the city at its southern extremity, it pursues its sinuous course far into the country, though never at any point being more distant from Benares than *pánch kos*,—that is, five cos, or ten miles. It is reputed to be a very ancient road; but that it is so, I have grave doubts, the reasons for which I shall presently bring forward. The celebrated lady, Rani Bhawání, who constructed the Durgá temple and tank, also repaired the Panch-kosí, and restored some of its temples which had been destroyed by the Mohammedans; and, since her time, the road has been kept in order. There are, now, hundreds of shrines scattered along the road; so that the pilgrim, as he pursues his journey, is constantly reminded of his idols. The deities tenanting these shrines are supposed to perform an important part in preserving the stability, the purity, and the peace of Benares and of the entire enclosure. They are, in fact, watchmen appointed by the ruling monarch Bisheśwar, to keep the boundary of Benares, and to defend it against all spiritual adversaries.

The Panch-kosí is regarded as an exceedingly sacred road. While even a foot or an inch beyond its precincts is devoid of any special virtue, every inch of soil within the boundary is, in the Hindu's imagination, hallowed. It would seem, too, that every object, animate and inanimate, existing within the enclosed space participates in the general and all-pervading sanctity. The entire area is called Benares; and the religious privileges of the city are extended to every portion of it. Whoever dies in any spot of this enclosure is, the natives think, sure of happiness after death; and so wide is the application of this privilege, that it embraces, they say, even Europeans and Mohammedans, even Pariahs and other outcasts, even liars, murderers, and thieves. That no soul can perish in Benares is, thus, the charitable superstition of the Hindus.

To perform the pilgrimage of the Panch-kosí is accounted a very meritorious act. It is necessary that every good Hindu residing in the city of Benares should twice a year accomplish this pilgrimage, in order that the impurity which the soul and body have contracted during the year may be obliterated; for it is held to be impossible even to reside in such a holy city as Benares, without contracting some defilement. Not only the inhabitants of Benares, but also multitudes of persons from various parts of India, traverse the road, and seek to obtain the blessing which, they are told, such a pious act ensures. It is customary for a large number of pilgrims to travel together on this journey. Before setting out each morning, they must bathe in a tank or stream, and, on terminating their march each day, must perform the same rite. They do not permit themselves the luxury of shoes; nor do they relieve the fatigue of the journey by the assistance of either horse, or ass, or camel, or elephant, or of any carriage, or cart, or vehicle whatever. Anxious to secure a full measure of merit, they cannot afford that it should be lessened by the appliances and arts of civilized life. All, therefore, men, women, and children, rich and poor, princes and peasants, travel on foot. The only exception to this stringent rule is in the case of the sick and infirm; and it is questionable if even they will obtain such a full meed of merit as the rest. On the way; the pilgrims must not eat *pawn*, of which all natives are passionately fond; and they must take great care that the Benares side of the road is not defiled. They must not quarrel, or give one another bad language; must not receive any present, and must not give aṇy food, or water, or anything else even to a friend, or take any such things from him. This last requirement has been dictated by a spirit of selfishness; for the pilgrim is so intent on the acquisition of merit, that he cannot bring himself to share it with any one,—though it be even his dearest friend. He will render no assistance to his neighbour to enter the gates of heaven, unless he can do so without loss to himself. While striving to enter within the sacred gates himself, he will suffer his fainting, foot-sore brother to die upon the road. Such is the hard selfishness of Hinduism. Indeed, selfishness is the very root of Hinduism, is its sap and life, is its branches, and blossoms, and fruit.

Starting from the Maṇikarṇiká Ghát, the pilgrim keeps along the banks of the Ganges until he arrives at the Así Sangam and Así Ghát, where a petty stream flows into the great river. From this spot he proceeds to a temple of Jagannáth close by, and thence on to the village of Kandhawa, where he stays for the remainder of the day, having performed a journey of six miles. The second day's march is to the village of Dhúpchaṇḍí, ten miles further on, where he worships the tutelary goddess of that name. On the third day he arrives at Rámeśwar, after a long walk of fourteen miles. The fourth day brings him to Śivapur, where he visits the famous shrine of the Pánch Páṇḍav, or five brothers who were all married to one woman.

12

On this day he travels eight miles, and, on the fifth day, six more, namely, to the village of Kapildhárá, where he worships the god Mahádeva. The sixth and last stage is from Kapildhárá to the Barna Sangam, and thence to Maṇikarṇiká Ghát, from which he first set out, which is also six miles in length. He has thus completed, in six days, a march of nearly fifty miles, about six of which,—namely, the space between the Barna Sangam and Así Sangam, the two extremities of Benares,—are along the banks of the Ganges. All the way from Kapildhárá to Maṇikarṇiká Ghát, the pilgrim scatters on the ground grains of barley, which he carries in a bag made for the purpose: this curious custom is in honour of Śiva. On reaching the ghát, he bathes in the river, makes his offering of money to the priests in attendance, and then goes to the temple of Śákhi-vináyak, or the witness-bearing Gaṇeś,—in order that the fact of his pilgrimage may be duly attested by that deity,—and thence to his home. A few grains of barley are reserved for an oblation to the idol Yava-vináyak, or Barley-Gaṇeś, whose temple rises immediately above the Maṇikarṇiká Ghát.

With the exception of the temple of Kardameśwar at Kandhawa, which is of considerable antiquity, and is the finest specimen of ancient Hindu architecture in this part of India, no temple along the road can, in my opinion, date further back than two hundred and fifty years. There may be a few of about this age; but I should say that more than five hundred out of the six hundred temples, which I compute to be now standing there, have been erected since the English came into possession of India. There are some remains of old sculptures to be found on the road and in its vicinity; but they are few in number. It is exceedingly remarkable that the traces of its antiquity, so far as the buildings skirting it furnish proof, are so slender, especially when we remember that the Hindus believe it to be of high antiquity.

Moreover, the road is, for the most part throughout its whole extent, ornamented by a double row of trees, one on either side. Many of them have massive trunks, and present a noble appearance. Some of the trunks measure from twelve to seventeen feet in girth. Most of the trees are mango; and many of those of large size are of this kind. Undoubtedly, such trees may fairly be regarded as not of recent planting: nevertheless, I do not see that they can lay claim to a greater age than that of the earliest built temples found on the road,—excepting, of course, the temple of Kardarmeśwar,—namely, about two hundred and fifty years. But it is not improbable that many of the trees were planted by the Hindu lady before-mentioned, who repaired the Panchkosí road, on the decline of the Mohammedan power.

None of the five tanks and *dharmsálás* on this road exhibit any signs of antiquity. It is said that a tank at Bhímchaṇḍí has, somewhere about it, an inscription, written upwards of four hundred years ago. If this be true,—and here I am very sceptical,—it would be only good testimony that this individual tank was of that age: taken simply by itself, it would afford no proof of the antiquity of the road. On the northern division of the road, towards Kapildhárá, certain indisputable marks and signs of age are apparent; but these, I hold, are not connected with the Panchkosí road, but rather with Sárnáth and other Buddhist sites in this neighbourhood.

Again, roads which have been trodden for many centuries, not to say thousands of years, are commonly much worn, and, occasionally, sink far below the adjacent soil. The limestone soil of Benares and the surrounding country is no exception to this rule. The old Ghazeepore road, which crosses the Panchkosí to the west of Kapildhárá, is, in one place, several feet below the fields on either side; which circumstance is valid proof of its being, to say the least, somewhat ancient. But the Panchkosí is, throughout, on a level with the land through which it winds its way, or nearly so. If the road were traversed by only a few persons yearly, this argument would not be very strong; but, seeing that innumerable pilgrims pass along it in the course of the year, it is, in my opinion, almost physically impossible that it should be of ancient date. Upon the whole, I am inclined to the belief, that, previously to the repair of the road by Rani Bhawání, there was a narrow path only, which the Hindus, dreading the vengeance of the Mohammedans, occasionally traversed in small numbers; but for how long this path had been a pilgrim's walk, it is impossible to conjecture. From the very great scarcity of old remains, however, it is my firm belief that it can lay no claim whatever to antiquity, properly so called; and the probability is, that it was originated by some zealous devotee, who conceived the novel idea of honouring the sacred city by describing an immense circuit round it, which he, first of all, trod himself, and which, doubtless to his surprise, was afterwards trodden by other persons, until, gradually, the custom was established,—an idea no more novel and strange than others which the Hindus every day put in practice.

It ought to be remembered with gratitude, by the Hindus of Benares and Northern India generally, that the British Government of India, instead of pursuing the destructive and prohibitive policy of the Mohammedan rulers, has taken the Panchkosí road under its own charge, and, in a spirit of beneficence deserving of the highest praise, defrays the expenses of its annual repairs. It would be a happy circumstance if Benares itself received the same proportion of attention as this road around it. Threaded with narrow streets, above which rise the many-storied edifices for which the city is famous, it is, without doubt, a problem of considerable difficulty, how to preserve the health of its teeming population. But, when we reflect on the foul wells and tanks in some parts of the city, whose water is of deadly influence, and the vapour from which fills the air with fever-fraught and cholera-breeding miasma; when we consider the loathsome and disgusting state of the popular temples, owing to the rapid decomposition of the offerings, from the intense heat of the sun; when we call to mind the filthy condition of nearly all the by-streets, due to stagnant cesspools, accumulated refuse, and dead bodies of animals; and when, in addition, we remember how utterly regardless of these matters, and incompetent to correct them, is the police force scattered over the city, the difficulty becomes almost overwhelming. The importance, however, of cleansing the city cannot be overestimated. And it is because it is at once so immensely important as well as difficult, that the undertaking should not be left in the hands of one man, though he should be the ablest and most energetic in all India. The Magistrate of Benares, and his assistants, have a multitude of duties to perform, besides watching over the interests of the city; and, therefore, they are totally unable, and, I believe, must feel themselves so, to originate and carry out all those schemes of utility which are required. What is needed in Benares is the establishment of a municipal corporation, similar to that which exists in various other cities of India. Such a body would accomplish great results in promoting, in various ways, the social welfare of the people. I am satisfied that there is no city in the country where such a corporation is more urgently required, and where its establishment would be more beneficial. In other respects, too, besides those mentioned, I regard the present time as peculiarly favourable for carrying out this project. The staff of Government officials in Benares, just now, is well adapted for aiding in the promotion of the objects of a municipality. Men of industry and enterprise, as some of them are, would find ample scope for their talents. Europeans of ability, unconnected with the Government, and, also, natives of influence, fitted to render useful assistance, might readily be found. With men like the Maharaja of Vizianagram and Raja Deo Narain Singh, late members of the Legislative Council of India, and other natives of this stamp, united with well-selected Europeans, not all Government officers,—men of observation, and capable of deviating, if need be, from old stereotyped forms and beaten tracks, and striking out a path for themselves,—the prosecuting of wholesome sanitary reforms, the completing of effectual drainage, the opening out and widening of thoroughfares for the free admission of air, and the purifying of the religious edifices, should be a labour undertaken heartily, and prosecuted with enthusiasm. Under the auspices of a corporation thus constituted, we should soon see a thorough transformation of the city; but, at the same time, we are perfectly sure that it is only by such a body that the radical changes, so imperatively demanded in this region of palaces and filth, in this hot-bed of periodical disease, can be effected. It is my earnest hope, that, in these days of progress, the time-honoured city of which I have been writing will not be left in the rear, as, in some respects, it now undoubtedly is, but will soon be ranked amongst the foremost cities in the land, in regard to all measures tending to advance the prosperity and happiness of the native community.

CHAPTER XV.

BARNA Sangam or Confluence of the Barna and Ganges. — A'dkeśav Temple.—Barna Ghát.—Ráj Ghát Fort: its use in 1857.—Remains of Buddhist Monastery.—Tank of Bhairo.—*Lát* or Pillar of Siva.—Ancient Pillar.—Account of Disturbance in Benares when the pillar was thrown down.—The Ghazeepore Road.—Ancient Bridge over the Barna.

BARNA Sangam, so called from the confluence of the river Barna with the Ganges, is a highly venerated spot. To bathe in the uniting waters is regarded as a very meritorious act, sufficient to wash away the transgressions of a life-time. This Sangam is one of the five celebrated places of pilgrimage on the banks of the Ganges at Benares, and is, consequently, visited by the crowds of pilgrims which, at certain seasons, pour into the city. It also occupies an important place, as intimated in the preceding chapter, in the pilgrimage of the Panchkosí road. The pilgrims, having issued from the city at the Así Sangam, return to it by the Barna Sangam; the former being its southern, and the latter its north-eastern, boundary. Here they halt, to perform the ceremonies prescribed for so sacred a place. Above the steep bank are four temples, which the Government has forbidden to be used. During the rebellion, they were in the hands of a man of a seditious and turbulent spirit, and were, consequently, seized by the authorities and closed. Subsequently, however, they were permitted to be reopened for religious purposes; but they have been again closed, though from what cause I am in ignorance. These temples were all erected by the Diwan of the Maharaja Scindia, about one hundred years ago. The largest of them is dedicated to A'dkeśav or Vishṇu, a statue of which deity, dressed in gay robes, with a crown on its head, stands in the interior of the shrine. In the same chamber is another image, that of the Sun. The porch of the temple rests on ten pillars, and is situated on its eastern side. Below the porch various idols are deposited, two of which are worthy of notice. One is called Sangameś-war, or the deity presiding over the confluence of the two rivers, which is simply S'iva under another name. The other is the four-faced Brahmá-íśwar or the god Brahmá. It is remarkable that this deity,—who, although the first member of the Hindu Triad, is rarely worshipped in any part of India, on account of his incest with his own daughter Saraswatí, as stated in Hindu writings, and believed by the people,—should have found a habitation here. Perhaps the reason of this circumstance may be, that, inasmuch as both Vishṇu and S'iva were already represented in these fanes, an image of Brahmá also was added, in order to complete the Triad. This union of the three members, in any one spot, is a most unusual occurrence; for, instead of cherishing love towards one another, they are supposed to be, and are generally represented as being, exceedingly jealous of each other's glory; and the sacred writings extol and disparage each in turn.

As worshippers are prohibited from entering these temples, a small platform has been erected on the ghát below, which is decorated with a select group of deities, who receive the homage due to the gods in the temples above. Here may be seen Sangameśwar and, likewise, the sacred feet of Vishṇu. The latter are, also, found at Maṇikarṇiká Ghát. Here are, also, the Monkey-god, two small stone figures of Satís, and a curious mythological stone, on the sides of which eight incarnations are carved in bass-relief.

On the summit of the Barna Sangam Ghát, a few remains of an old fort are visible. There is no doubt that, at one time, this fort commanded the city, which was then situated much nearer this spot than it now is. The population in the neighbourhood is exceedingly scanty; and the locality itself is now so far removed from the city, that it can be regarded as only a somewhat distant suburb of Benares.

To the west of the Barna Ghát is a plateau of elevated land, nearly a mile long and four hundred yards broad, overlooking both the city and the Ganges. The river Ganges forms a defence to the entire south-east face; the river Barna constitutes a wet ditch to the north and north-east faces; while an abrupt depression of the ground to the north-west,—said to be an old bed of the same stream,—completes the natural strength of the position. The advantage of this position, in a military point of view, was perceived by the old native rulers of Benares, who erected the fort above spoken of on the eastern edge of this tract, immediately above the Barna Sangam, but was not recognized by its British governors until the year 1857, "of scarlet memory." The terrible events of that year brought out, in bold relief, the fatal absurdity of the policy which had led our military authorities to neglect the banks of the Ganges, and to place some of their largest and most important cantonments at an insecure distance from that river. On the 4th of June, 1857, the mutiny broke out at Benares, and, through the good providence of God, was speedily quelled, although, in the action that was fought, one hundred and eighty gallant British soldiers had to contend with two regiments of native infantry and one of cavalry. After the battle, the position of the European residents,—who were all cooped up in one large building, known as the Old Mint,—and of the few English soldiers who protected them, was one of extreme peril; inasmuch as the military lines, including the Mint, were at a distance of at least three miles from the Ganges, with the city lying between; and it seemed a probable contingency that the routed sepoys, rallying again, would return to Benares, and, having excited to revolt its disaffected inhabitants, would come, in overwhelming numbers, upon the small and isolated party of Europeans, and cut off from them all means of escape, and all hope of successful resistance. This contingency, apparently so likely at the time, fortunately was not realized. The insecurity of the position held by the authorities was, however, soon discerned; and, at an early stage of the rebellion, measures were taken for fortifying the elevated land in the rear of the Barna Ghát and in the neighbourhood of the old native fort. Embankments were thrown up with incredible speed; and a citadel was soon completed, capable of making a stout resistance to a numerous enemy. The fortress was gradually strengthened, so that it may be regarded as having been, until abandoned, one of the strongest and most extensive in India. The heights overlook the entire city, which lies completely at the mercy of the force in occupation of them.

Several objects of interest to the antiquary are enclosed within the falls of the new fort. A spacious tomb, built by Lál Khán, a Mohammedan servant of a former Raja of Benares, is standing here. Passing through the western gate of the fort, you presently come to the building, which is situated a short distance off the road, on the right hand side. It occupies the centre of an extensive quadrangle, which is ornamented with four towers, one at each corner. The tomb itself consists of a massive tower, rising high above the rest, and is crowned with a dome, from the middle of which a spire emerges, pointing to the heavens. A large portion of its outer surface is still bright with the colours, chiefly blue, with which it was originally embellished. The colouring plaster, when minutely examined, has a glassy appearance, not unlike porcelain; and, although it has been for years exposed to a burning sun and to the periodic rains, yet it is questionable whether the colours have lost, from this cause, any of their freshness. The decay of the underlying masonry has, in some places, been a source of injury to the external plaster, by causing it to crumble away; but, where it has been preserved, the colours are strong and vivid. Within the building are three tombs, and on the platform outside are four more.

A few steps from the outer wall of the fort is a long building, sustained by a quadruple row of stone columns. On examination, it is evident that the building, although now a continuous whole, may formerly have consisted of two detached parts. One proof of this is, that the pillars of one portion are all uniform, while those of the other are very different in character, and that the roof of the first division is lower than the roof of the second. All the pillars are carved; and some of them, namely, those in the loftier room, which are of a variety of patterns, are most elaborately sculptured. As specimens of native art, they occupy a high position: indeed, I know of nothing superior to them among genuine native productions. They exhibit a refinement of taste, and yet a correctness and beauty of execution, that are rarely to be met with in India, except in ancient sculpture. The favourite lotos-plant, with its flower, its seed-pod, its stalk, and long flowing leaves, which have an exquisite effect in representing the tracery known as the scroll-pattern, and the Brahmani duck in various attitudes, are some of the prominent objects carved upon the pillars.

It is because this style of architecture has not been produced in India in later days, that we must assign this fine colonnade to an ancient epoch. Nor are we in doubt as to the period to which it should be referred. Its similarity to the later Buddhist architecture of the opening centuries of the Christian era is amply sufficient to solve the question of its date. In my belief, there existed, on this spot, a Buddhist monastery, of which the colonnade formed a portion of one side of its enclosure. A further description of this building is given in the twentieth chapter.

At Ráj Ghát a pontoon bridge crosses the Ganges in the dry season, but not during the rains; and along it an immense amount of traffic of all kinds passes to and from the railway station on the other side. To the south of Ráj Ghát, but at some distance off, is Praládh Ghát, stretching out a little into the stream. It is picturesquely situated, and commands a fine view of Benares and its suburbs.

To the north of the road leading from the Ráj Ghát Fort to the cantonments, at a distance of from three quarters of a mile to a mile from the former place, is the Kapilmochan Tank. It is also called Bhairo ká Táláo, or the tank of Bhairo. This is a strong and well-built structure, the stairs and foundations being of solid stone. On the high ground to the north of the tank stands a pillar, from seven to eight feet in height, and three in thickness, situated in the midst of a slightly-elevated stone *chabútra* or platform. This is the *Láṭ* or pillar of Śiva. It is representative of an ancient pillar, which formerly stood on this spot, and was thrown down by the Mohammedans, in a struggle between them and the Hindus, some sixty years ago. The original *Láṭ* was famous among the Hindu population, both for its antiquity and for its sanctity. There is some ground for supposing that the present pillar is a fragment of the ancient one; and that it, very likely, bears a portion of the carving known to have been on the original column. The probability is increased by the circumstance that it is encased in copper, and is carefully watched over by the Brahman priests. It would be interesting to examine it, and to determine the age of its carvings, or of any inscription which may be upon it.

Previously to this outbreak, the Hindus must have cherished, for a prolonged period, very bitter feelings against the Mohammedans, on account of the insult which, ever since the time of Aurungzeb, had been heaped upon their religion in this locality. The pillar was once situated in the enclosure of a Hindu temple; but that ruthless monarch destroyed the temple, and, in its place, erected a mosque, leaving the curiously carved pillar either as an ornament to the grounds, or under a wholesome dread of provoking to too great a pitch the indignation of his Hindu subjects. The Hindus, however, continued to pay divine homage to the pillar, which, although repugnant to the feelings of the Mohammedans, was, nevertheless, endured by them, especially as they were permitted to receive a portion of the offerings. The natives say, that, after the serious collision between these two great sections of the people in the city, the pillar was removed to the banks of the Ganges, and thrown into the river.

The history of this famous disturbance is singular. It occurred during the Mohurram festival, a season when the fanaticism which is inherent in the disposition of a Mohammedan reaches its boiling point. It so happened, that, in that year, the popular Hindu festival of the Holí took place at the same time. The processions of both classes of religionists were traversing the streets together; and it was, consequently, almost impossible for the violent passions of either section not to display themselves, when the processions passed one another. And so it turned out; for, on occasion of two large processions coming near each other, the one refused to give place to the other, imagining that the honour of the religion which it advocated would be sacrificed by so doing. As neither party would yield, the altercation proceeded to blows, each struggling to force a passage through the ranks of the other. The fight ended in the defeat of the Mohammedans, who, stung with resentment at the insult which had been cast upon their faith, determined to take a revenge so terrible and deep, that it should have the effect of exasperating to frenzy the entire Hindu population of the sacred city. They retired to the court-yard of Aurungzeb's mosque, in which stood the highly venerated *Láṭ* of Śiva, and, combining together, threw it to the ground.

"The Hindus had a tradition," writes the Rev. William Buyers, in his 'Recollections of Northern India,' "that the pillar was gradually sinking; it having, according to report, been, once, twice its present height; and it was also prophesied, that, when its top should become level with the ground, all nations should be of one caste. The throwing down, therefore, of this pillar was regarded as most ominous and dangerous to Hinduism. The whole Hindu population, headed by the Brahmans and devotees, rose in fury on the Mussalmans, and attacked them with every sort of weapon within their reach. One mosque was pulled down; and they determined to destroy every other in the city: but the civil authorities, with all the military force that could be collected, interposed, and, by putting guards to defend the mosques, succeeded in saving them.

"It was difficult, indeed, to trust to the native soldiers: but they did their duty well; for, though many of them were Brahmans, they kept guard manfully on the mosques, in fidelity to their military oath; though, doubtless, it would have been more agreeable to their own feelings to have joined in pulling them down. Yet they kept off the Brahmans, as well as others, at the point of the bayonet. Two Brahman soldiers, keeping guard where the pillar was lying prostrate, were overheard thus conversing on the subject: 'Ah,' said one, 'we have seen what we never thought to see—Śiva's *Laṭ* has its head level with the ground. We shall all be of one caste shortly. What will be our religion then?' 'I suppose the Christian,' answered the other; 'for, after all that has passed, I am sure we shall never become Mussulmans.'"

Although the storm was allayed through the interference of the authorities, yet the religious feelings of the Hindus, which had been so violently roused, were by no means pacified. "In the early part of the quarrel," says Mr. Buyers, "the Mussalmans, in order to be revenged on the Hindus for the defeat they had sustained, had taken a cow, and killed it on one of the holiest ghâts, and mingled its blood with the sacred water of the Gangá. This act of double sacrilege was looked on, by the Brahmans, as having destroyed the sacredness of the holy place, if not of the whole city, so that salvation in future might not be attainable by pilgrimage to Benares. They were, therefore, all in the greatest affliction; and all the Brahmans in the city, many thousands in number, went down, in deep sorrow, to the river side, naked and fasting, and with ashes on their heads, and sat down on the principal ghâts, with folded hands, and heads hanging down, to all appearance inconsolable, and refusing to enter a house or to taste food. Two or three days' abstinance, however, tired them; and a hint was given to the magistrates and other public men, that a visit of condolence and some expression of sympathy would comfort them, and give them some excuse for returning to their usual course of life. Accordingly, the British functionaries went to the principal ghát, and expressed their sorrow for the distress in which they saw them, but reasoned with them on the absurdity of punishing themselves for an act in which they had no share, and which they had done all they could to prevent or avenge. This prevailed; and, after much bitter weeping, it was resolved that '*Gangá was Gangá still*,' and that a succession of costly offerings from the laity of Benares,—the usual Brahmanical remedy for all evils,—might wipe out the stain which their religion had received, and that the advice of the judges was the best and most reasonable. Mr. Bird (the chief English official in Benares), who was one of the ambassadors on this occasion, said that 'the scene was very impressive, and even awful. The gaunt, squalid figures of the devotees, their visible and, apparently, unaffected anguish and dismay, the screams and outcries of the women who surrounded them, and the great numbers thus assembled, altogether constituted a spectacle of woe such as few cities but Benares could supply.' "

Formerly, a large annual *melá* or fair used to be held on this venerated spot; but, of late years, the place has been well-nigh abandoned, so that even the *melá* fails to attract more than a few dozens of people.

By the side of the Kapilmochan Tank a narrow road branches off from the high road, at right angles to it, and runs on to the river Barna, which it crosses, and thence winds, through the country, to the city of Ghazeepore. Judging from the depth to which it occasionally sinks, as compared with the fields on either side, it must be of considerable antiquity. The road is traversed by large numbers of people, and may be regarded as one of the chief outlets of the city in this direction. In the dry season a dam is thrown up across the Barna, over which passengers are permitted to pass, on the payment of a small toll; in the rains the river becomes swollen and deep, and, consequently, the traffic of the road is conveyed over by means of a ferry. In olden times a spacious bridge, erected by the Mohammedan rulers of the country, spanned the river at this place, but fell into decay, and, eventually, into utter ruin. Its foundations are still visible in the bed of the stream; but they are very limited in extent. A few years ago most of the stones of the ruined bridge were taken away, and utilized for the erection of the present Barna bridge, connecting the civil with the military lines. It has seemed to my mind a somewhat inconsiderate policy, on the part of the local authorities, that, while collecting a revenue from the ferry and the dam, they have never projected a new bridge, but have left the entire northern boundary of the city, for the space of between three and four miles, without any proper and adequate means of communication with the country beyond the Barna. Further up the river there is the Iron Bridge, and also that already alluded to; but these are too far off to be of any real benefit to the inhabitants of the city on the one side of the Barna, and of the numerous villages on the other side, throughout the whole of the tract to which I am referring, except by their making a considerable detour; and this, on account of the great distance to be traversed, is, I fear, in the case of many of them, impracticable.

CHAPTER XVI.

Śiválá Ghát.—The Old Fort.—Raja Cheit Singh: History of his Insurrection and of the Proceedings of Warren Hastings in Connexion therewith.

Śiválá Ghát is interesting on account of its connexion with the insurrection at Benares in the time of Warren Hastings, the downfall of Raja Cheit Singh, the former Raja of Benares, and the destruction of his family, which followed that event. When Cheit Singh rebelled against the British Government, he was residing in a strong fort built upon the banks of the Ganges, above the Śivála Ghát. Warren Hastings was, at the time, living in the garden house of Mádhodás, situated in the Ausánganj Mahalla, nearly three miles off, on the western side of the city. The history of this famous insurrection is briefly as follows.

Raja Cheit Singh, although a great noble, exercising considerable power and authority throughout his extensive domains,—in virtue of which he might, perhaps, be regarded as possessing a jurisdiction similar to that of many European princes,—yet was not, in truth, a reigning monarch, or even a great tributary chief. He had no authority beyond what he derived from the East

India Company; and his vast estates did not pay tribute, but a fixed annual rent, to the British Government. Warren Hastings says, "that his father, Balwant Singh, derived the degree of independence which he possessed during the latter part of his life from the protection and intervention of our Government. His son, Cheit Singh, obtained from our influence, exerted by myself, the first legal title that his family ever possessed of property in the land of which he, till then, was only the Aumil, and of which he became the acknowledged Zemindar by a Sannad granted to him by the Nabob Shujah-ud-Dowlah (king of Oude, whose dominions, in those days, extended as far as Benares), at my instance, in the month of September, 1773. On the succession of the Nabob Assof-ud-Dowlah, the rights of sovereignty which were held by him over the Zemindary were transferred, by treaty, to the Company. Those rights were indisputably his, and became, by his alienation of them, as indisputably the Company's; and every obligation and obedience which is due from a Zemindar to the superior magistrate, by the constitution of Hindustan, became as much the right of the Company from Cheit Singh as it had been due to his former sovereign, with the additional ties of gratitude for the superior advantages which he was allowed to possess with his new relation. The unexampled lenity of our Government in relinquishing to him the free and uncontrolled rule of his Zemindary, subject to a limited annual fine, and the royalties of the Mint, administration of justice and police, ought to have operated as an additional claim on his fidelity, but evidently served to stimulate his ambition, and, perhaps, to excite in his mind an opinion that he possessed an inherent right of self-dependency."[1]

Such being the nature of the relation subsisting between the Raja and the Indian government, it was only just and right, that, at a time of national peril, he should be called upon to contribute his quota of men and money towards the defence of his own estates and of the country in general. "On the first intelligence of the war with France, in July, 1778, it was resolved, in Council, that Raja Cheit Singh should be required to contribute an extraordinary subsidy for the expense which this new exigency had imposed on our Government; and the sum was limited to five lacks of rupees for the current year. After many excuses and protestations of inability, he, at length, consented, with a very ill grace, to the payment, and, with a much worse, discharged it. The next year the same demand was repeated; and he attempted, in like manner, to elude it, affecting to borrow money in small sums, and to sell his plate and jewels to raise it: nor was it paid at last, till he had reduced the Board to the extremity of ordering two battalions of sepoys to the neighbourhood of Ramnagar, and quartering them upon him, with their pay charged to his account, until the whole payment was completed."[2]

Fearing the anger of the Governor-General, the Raja, in the early part of the following year, despatched his confidential manager, Lálá Sadánand, to him "to solicit," says Warren Hastings, "my forgivenesss of his past

[1] Warren Hastings's Insurrection in Benares, pp. 8, 9.

[2] Insurrection in Benares, p. 3.

conduct, and to give me assurances, confirmed by oath, of his future submission to the orders of my government, and compliance with my advice. I accepted his excuses, and promised him an oblivion of all that had passed exceptionable in his conduct, and my future protection, and every good office in my power, so long as he adhered to his professions; requiring only, as the pledge of their sincerity, that he would immediately notify his ready and unreserved consent to the demand which would be made upon him—this being the period for it—of the subsidy for the current year, and that he would use no delay in discharging it." The Lálá "vowed the fullest obedience on the part of his master; the demand was accordingly made; and the Raja answered it with a liberal and unreserved declaration of his acquiescence." Notwithstanding these protestations of obedience, the Raja failed to act up to them. The whole payment of the money was due in July; but "it was not until the month of October, nor until the same constraint was practised, to compel his obedience, as had been used in the preceding year, by an order for the advance of two battalions of sepoys for that purpose, that the balance of the subsidy, which was two lacks and a half of rupees, was discharged. In the meantime, the Resident received an order from the Board to remit the money, as he received it, by bills, to the Paymaster of Lieutenant-Colonel Carnac's detachment; but these, from the lateness of the receipts, were not sent until the detachment had suffered the extremity of distress from the want of money, and very great desertions; all which calamities I charge to Raja Cheit Singh's account; as it is certain that my reliance on his faith, and his breach of it, were the principal causes that no other provisions had been made for the detachment, and that it suffered much want in consequence."[1]

Such was the first serious charge brought against the Raja. The second was, in principle, the same. I again quote the words of Warren Hastings. "On the second of the month of November, 1780, a resolution passed the Board, that a letter should be written to the Nabob Vizier, advising him to require from the Nabob Fyz-Oolla Khán the number of troops stipulated by treaty, expressed, as it was then understood, to be 5000 horse; and that the like demand should be made on Raja Cheit Singh for all the cavalry in his pay which he could spare for our service. At that time we stood in need of every aid that could be devised, to repel the multiplied dangers which surrounded us. The Raja was supposed to maintain a very large and extensive standing force; and the strength of his cavalry alone was estimated at two thousand. I had formerly experienced their utility, in the war with the Seneasses, in which they were successfully employed, and liberally rewarded. The demand was formally made, both in a letter from myself, and, in person, by the Resident, Mr. Fowke, in the easy and indefinite terms mentioned above. His manners were evasive, pleading (as I recollect, for I am not in possession of them,) scantiness of the establishment, its employment in enforcing the collections, and the danger of these failing, if the detachment were withdrawn. At length, a more peremptory order was sent to him,

[1] Insurrection in Benares, pp. 3, 4, 5.

and repeated by the present Resident, Mr. Markham. The number required was 2,000, and afterwards reduced to the demand of 1,500, and, lastly, to 1,000, but with no more success. He offered 250, but furnished none."[1]

It was not to be imagined that such acts of contumacy, disrespect, and implicit rebellion, should be left unnoticed. The honour and reputation of the Indian Government demanded that the Raja should be called on to explain his extraordinary conduct. Warren Hastings regarded these instances of disobedience as "evidences of a deliberate and systematic conduct, aiming at the total subversion of the authority of the Company, and the erection of his own independency on its ruins." "This," he adds, "had been long and generally imputed to him. It was reported that he had inherited a vast mass of *wealth* from his father, Balwant Singh, which he had secured in the two strong fortresses of Bidjeygur and Lutteefpoor, and made yearly additions to it; that he kept up a large military establishment, both of cavalry, of disciplined and irregular infantry, and of artillery; that he had the above and many other fortresses, of strong construction and in good repair, and constantly well-stored and garrisoned; that his aumils and tenants were encouraged and habituated to treat English passengers with inhospitality and with enmity; that he maintained a correspondence with the Mahrattas, and other Powers who either were, or might eventually become, the enemies of our state; and, if the disaffected Zemindars of Fyzabad and Behar were not included in the report, which I do not recollect, we have

[1] Insurrection in Benares, pp. 6, 7.

had woful proof that there was equal room to have suspected the like intercourse between them; and, lastly, that he was collecting, or had prepared, every provision for open revolt, waiting only for a proper season to declare it, which was supposed to depend either on the arrival of a French armament, or a Mahratta invasion."[1]

The Governor General determined, therefore, that some measures should be taken with the Raja, in order to bring him to his senses. Moreover, he says: "I was resolved to draw from his guilt the means of relief to the Company's distresses, and to exact a penalty which, I was convinced, he was able to bear, from a fund which, I was also convinced, he had destined for purposes of the most dangerous tendency to the Company's dominion. In a word, I had determined to make him pay largely for his pardon, or to exact a severe vengeance for his past delinquency." Opportunity was, first of all, given to the Raja to clear himself; and Warren Hastings, on his arrival in Benares, in the month of August, 1781, sent a letter to him, setting forth the leading charges against him, to which he requested an immediate reply. The answer which the Raja returned was regarded as "not only unsatisfactory in substance, but offensive in style; and less a vindication of himself than," says Warren Hastings, "a recrimination on me. It expresses no concern for the causes of complaint contained in my letter, or desire to atone for them; nor the smallest intention to pursue a different line of conduct. An answer couched nearly in terms of defiance to requisitions of so serious a

[1] Insurrection in Benares, pp. 7, 8.

nature, I could not but consider as a strong indication of that spirit of independency which the Raja has for some years past assumed, and of which, indeed, I had early observed other manifest symptoms, both before and from the instant of my arrival."

On the receipt of this communication, the Governor General ordered the Resident, Mr. Markham, to proceed, on the following morning, to the fort at Sivála Ghát, and there arrest the Raja. In obedience to his instructions, the Resident, accompanied by his usual guard, visited the Raja, who submitted, without opposition, to the arrest. Shortly after, two companies of grenadier sepoys arrived, under the command of three lieutenants, when Mr. Markham returned to the Governor General, to report the success of his enterprise. In the course of the day, three letters were sent by the Raja to Warren Hastings, two of which were expressive of much anxiety and terror. Seeing the apprehension and alarm which had seized hold of his mind, the Governor General wrote a note to Cheit Singh, wishing him to keep calm, and not to allow himself to be unduly distressed, or to imagine that any evil would befall him. The Raja's third letter was in answer to this, and was expressive of his gratitude for the gentle tone of the Governor General's communication.

The fort in which Cheit Singh was confined must, originally, have been a very strong place, capable of making a strong resistance, in case of an attack. It stands upon the banks of the Ganges, and, as seen from the river, has an appearance of great solidity.

Its high walls and buttresses are built with such compactness and strength, that, even now, not a trace of decay is noticeable in them; and they possess, moreover, all the freshness of new-built structures. In the direction of the city the fort is almost contiguous to a multitude of houses, the interval being but slight. The interior of the fort is spacious, and is sufficient to accommodate a large body of men. The two companies of sepoys who had charge of the Raja were quartered within the walls, a circumstance which, seeing that they were in possession of the fort, would have mattered little, had they had sufficient ammunition with which to defend themselves. Strange to say, these troops had been dispatched through a hostile city, on a most perilous errand, without ammunition. It is impossible to comprehend the cause of such astounding and culpable neglect. There is reason for believing that the Raja's followers were acquainted with this circumstance, and, consequently, hastily formed their plans for surprising the garrison and rescuing the Raja. In the afternoon, intelligence reached the Governor General, that large bodies of armed men were crossing the river from Rámnagar, another fort belonging to Cheit Singh, situated on the opposite side of the river, but lower down. The apartments which the Raja was at this time occupying opened on a small square, in which the troops were stationed. Another detachment of sepoys was dispatched "with ammunition, to reinforce and support the first party. When the latter arrived at the Raja's house, they found it surrounded, and all the avenues blockaded by a multitude of armed men, who opposed their passage. The minds of this tumultuous assembly becoming soon inflamed, some of them began to fire upon the sepoys within the square; and, immediately, as if this had been the concerted signal, made an instantaneous and fierce attack on the sepoys, who, wanting their accustomed means of defence, were capable of making but a feeble resistance, and fell an easy sacrifice to the superior numbers of their assailants, who cut almost every man of the unfortunate party to pieces. The officers, it is supposed, were the first victims to their fury, but not until they had, by astonishing efforts of bravery, and undismayed amidst the imminent dangers which surrounded them, involved a much superior number of their enemies in their fate. In the midst of this confusion, the Raja found means to escape through a wicket which opened to the river; and, the banks being exceedingly steep in that place, he let himself down, by turbans tied together, into a boat, which was waiting for him, and conveyed him to the opposite shore. Those who had effected his escape followed him across the river, in the same tumultuous manner in which they had assembled, leaving the party of our sepoys which had arrived, in possession of the house. On the first intelligence of this commotion, I had directed Major Popham to repair immediately to his camp, which was about two miles from the Resident's, and at the same distance from the Raja's house, and to march instantly, with the remainder of his detachment, to the support of the party. The order was executed with all possible expedition; but Major Popham arrived too late, and had the mortification to be a spectator of the effects of a massacre which he could neither prevent nor revenge."[1]

In this massacre no less than two hundred and five persons were either killed or wounded. On the upper part of the northern wall of the fortress are five small windows, or wickets, in a row, from one of which,—but which one I was unable to learn,—Raja Cheit Singh escaped. In the dry season the wall stands at some distance from the bed of the river; but in the rains the stream reaches the wall, and rises to a considerable height above its foundations. As it was the middle of the rainy season when the Raja escaped, he could have found no difficulty whatever in dropping down from the wicket into a boat below. On the west side of the small square, which was occupied by the unfortunate troops, the pinnacles of eleven temples are seen. These were, doubtless, frequented by Cheit Singh's family, but are now employed as storehouses by the Mohammedans residing in the fort. Temples, also, are found in other places in the interior of the fort; but in none of them, I believe, is any religious service ever performed. The entire building is the property of the Government, and is inhabited by a branch of the old Taimur family, the head of which was the late king of Delhi. These Delhi princes have resided in Benares for years past, and are permitted to occupy the extensive range of buildings formerly known as Cheit Singh's fort. In the recent rebellion they remained faithful to the British Govern-

[1] Insurrection in Benares, pp. 24, 25.

ment, and have, consequently, been saved from the ruin which has involved the other branches of the family.

The situation of Warren Hastings, at the time of the flight of Cheit Singh, was perilous to the last degree. He had, as before remarked, made Mádhodás' garden his head-quarters. This was a quadrangle surrounded by high walls, and containing several separate buildings, which are still standing, but in a dilapidated state. The garden is in the suburbs of the city, on its western side, and is encompassed by houses on all sides. It was never intended for defensive purposes; and the walls which surround it could never have been able to resist a determined attack made by a numerous foe. Warren Hastings says: "If Cheit Singh's people, after they had effected his rescue, had proceeded to my quarters, at Mahadew Dass's garden, instead of crowding after him in a tumultuous manner, as they did, in his passage over the river, it is most probable that my blood, and that of about thirty English gentlemen of my party, would have been added to the recent carnage; for they were above two thousand in number, furious and daring from the easy success of their last attempt; nor could I assemble more than fifty regular and armed sepoys for my whole defence." It is a wonder that the inhabitants of the city did not rise and invest the garden; for they might easily have done so, and have slain every man in it. The Governor General remained in this garden for several days; but his position, instead of improving, became more critical. The Raja had, first of all, entered his fort at Rámnagar, but, subsequently, quitted it, and proceeded to another fort, at

Latífpúr, leaving a strong force behind him. Unfortunately, the troops sent from Chunar against the fortress of Rámnagar became prematurely engaged with the enemy, and, after a loss of one hundred and seven killed and seventy-two wounded, were obliged to beat a retreat.

This was a most disastrous circumstance at such a time, for it damaged greatly the already waning prestige of the British arms in these parts. The enemy were rendered enthusiastic and daring by it, and began to assume the offensive. Intelligence reached Warren Hastings of a plan they had formed to cross the river on the night of the 20th of August, and to attack him at his quarters, in Mádhodás's garden. He thus describes the difficulties in which he was placed:—"Successive notices," he says, "were brought to me, by various channels, of preparations making at Rámnagar for an assault on my quarters, which stood in the midst of the suburbs of Benares, and consisted of many detached buildings within one large enclosure, surrounded by houses and trees, which intercepted every other prospect. The whole force which I had left amounted to about four hundred and fifty men. The reports of an intended assault, which was fixed for that night, grew stronger, as the day advanced; the boats on the other side of the river were seen to be in motion; and, besides the moral certainty of the real existence of such a design, the obvious advantages which it presented to the enemy, who had nothing left to fear, and nothing else to do, precluded all hesitation but on the choice of expedients for defeating it. There were but two, which were, to wait the danger and try the chance of repelling it, or to retreat to a place of greater security, or of equal advantage for the encounter. The confined state of the place, of which any description will be insufficient to convey an adequate idea, rendered the first plan impracticable. We had not a force sufficient to guard all the defences of that place, nor a store for the provisions of a day, even of that small number. The only arguments for it were the disgrace of a flight, and the consideration of our wounded sepoys, whom it might leave at the discretion of a merciless enemy. The former consideration yielded to the superior might of necessity; the latter, to the impossibility of protecting the wounded men in either case, as they were quartered at a distance of near a mile from Mahadew Dass's garden; nor would it have been possible, in their condition, and in the multiplicity of pressing exigencies which the resolution to remain would have created, to remove them. Yet these considerations held me suspended during the whole course of the day. In the evening it became necessary to come to a final determination, as the delay of a few hours might now preclude every option." After consulting with several officers of the army who were there with him, the Governor General concluded that the safest and wisest policy would be for himself and the entire European community in Benares to retire from the city to the fort of Chunar. "My resolution," he says, "was taken and declared, and orders given to form our little corps, that we might have time to gain the open country before the enemy, having notice of the design, could cross and attack us at the disadvantage of the streets, lanes, and broken ground, which we had to pass before we could reach it. These orders were issued between seven and eight o'clock; and, by eight, the line was in motion, having been much retarded and impeded by an incredible tumult of servants, palanquins, and baggage of every denomination, which, for a time, threatened a total destruction to our march. Fortunately, the enormous mass took the wrong road, which left the right with a free and undisturbed passage for the sepoys."[1] On the following morning all the party arrived safely at Chunar.

The evacuation of Benares by the English, as was anticipated, did not fail to exercise an immediate influence on the surrounding country. Half Oude was in insurrection; and many of the Zemindars of Behar were disaffected. Had not a strong blow been quickly struck, or had Warren Hastings been less sagacious and firm, England would speedily have lost her hold of all the provinces lying to the north-west of Bengal Proper. But his dauntless spirit was fully equal to the emergency; and, by the end of September, he had defeated the Raja's troops, had captured several of his forts, and had returned to his old quarters in Mádhodás's garden at Benares. The excitement of the people in this and the neighbouring provinces subsided even more rapidly than it had arisen. "The allegiance of the whole country," he enthusiastically remarks, "was restored as completely, in the course of a few hours, from a state of universal revolt to its proper channel, as if it

[1] Insurrection in Benares, p. 32.

had never departed from it." Raja Cheit Singh, having rebelled against the Indian Government, and, having been guilty of the "deliberate murder of our soldiers, and even defenceless passengers" who had the misfortune to fall into his hands, was declared to have forfeited his right to the estates he formerly possessed. These estates, with the title of Raja, were presented to his nephew, Babu Mahipnarain, grandson of Raja Balwant Singh. This Raja's daughter was wife of Babu Durgbijay Singh, from whom the present Maharaja is descended.

CHAPTER XVII.

Hindu and Mohammedan Melás or Religious Festivals held periodically in Benares.

Festivals, or *melás*, as they are commonly called, are very numerous in all parts of India, and present a peculiar phase of the social life of the people, such as is rarely found in civilized countries. They are more or less connected with religion; and their origin can be, in every case, traced to certain religious ceremonies performed, or said to have been performed, in some sacred locality, as on the banks of a river, or near a holy well or tank, once famous for the exploits of their deified heroes or gods. At the same time, many of them have a secular end, in addition to their religious character, and are held as much for amusement and trade as for graver purposes. They are, in fact, fairs; and, in some instances, they are of prodigious extent.

The word *melá* signifies a concourse or assemblage of persons, and is derived from the Sanskrit root *mil*, meaning 'to meet,' 'to congregate.' A *melá* is of two kinds: that at which religion and amusement are combined, and that which is simply and solely devoted to religion. To the former the people go gaily dressed; but they are present at the latter in their ordinary costume. The first kind of *melá* may be divided into two classes, namely, that which is of a moral tendency, and is frequented by persons of respectability, and that which is notoriously immoral, and visited by only the loose and licentious. The *melá* of the second order, although professedly purely religious, must, on account of the opportunities for vice which it occasionally furnishes, be regarded as immoral, so far as its necessary connexion with vice is concerned. For instance, at the Panch-Gangá Melá, in the month of Kártik, men and women bathe promiscuously in the Ganges. The Mohammedans also have their *melás*, but to a limited extent as compared with the Hindu population.

I shall now give a list of the Hindu and Mohammedan *melás* held in Benares, with a few circumstances of interest connected with each of them. The great Mohurram Festival of the Mohammedans, not being peculiar to Benares or even to India, I shall omit altogether.

1. The Navarátri Melá, held at Durgá Kuṇḍ during the first nine days of the month of Chait. Hindus, both male and female, visit the temple of Durgá from about 3 o'clock in the morning. On the 7th and 8th days, the crowd of votaries increases to upwards of ten thousand. At this festival thousands of sheep and goats are offered in sacrifice. The worshippers visit not only this shrine, but also the temples of Annpúrṇá, Sankaṭá, and Bágeśwarí.

2. The Gau-gaur Melá, held at Rájmandira Ghát, on the 3rd day of Chait. This festival is celebrated by Márwáḍís and Deswálís (people from the territory of

Jeypore). In the evening, persons of both sexes assemble at the ghát; and some put off into the stream, in boats, in order to witness the procession of a Hindu idol.

3. The Rám-naumí Melá, held at the Rám Ghát, on the 9th day of Chait. In the early morning, Hindus of the higher and middle classes, male and female, bathe together at the ghát, and worship Rám in the neighbouring temple. Respectable women, on these occasions, are apt to be molested by evil-disposed persons who loiter about the spot.

4. The Narsiṁh Chaudas Melá, held in the Bará Gaṇeś Mahalla, on the 14th day of Baisákh. This *melá* is in honour of Narsiṁh, the fourth incarnation of Vishṇu. The people fast during the day, and, in the evening, assemble in this Mahalla or Ward, to witness the dramatic performance of the destruction or tearing to pieces of Hiraṇyakaśipu by Narsiṁh.

5. The Gází-miyáṅ Melá, held at the Gází Miyáṅ Dargáh, Bakaríyá Kuṇḍ, on the 1st Sunday in Jeṭh. This is a Mohammedan festival, celebrated in honour of the nephew of the celebrated Sultán Mahmúd of Ghizni. This monarch sent his brother-in-law, Sálár Sáhú, on a mission into India. On the journey, his wife, Satar-i-Mualla, gave birth to a son, in the city of Ajmere, A.D. 1002. This child was called Sálár Masáúd; and, being unfortunately killed in battle with the Hindus, in his ninteenth year, was buried in Baraitch, in Oudh, where the battle had been fought. As he was considered a martyr to the Mohammedan faith, after his death, he was spoken of as Sultán-us-Shuhadá, chief of

Martyrs; and Sultán Gází, chief of knights of religion. In the neighbourhood of Delhi, he is also known by the appellation of Pír A'lim, Saint A'lim. Pilgrimages are made to his tomb every year. In Benares, thousands of persons of the lower classes of native society, Hindus and Mohammedans of both sexes, resort to the Dargáh of Gází Miyán, the latter word being added to the name of Gází, as an epithet of respect. There multitudes of singers, called *dafális*, are seated under hundreds of standards erected for the occasion, and sing the exploits of the martyr. Their songs produce a singular effect upon the female listeners; as some of them spread out their hair, and turn their heads in a violent manner, so as to appear to be under the influence of a supernatural power. Whatever words are uttered while they are in this state, are received as an oracular message. This festival is one of the most immoral held in Benares. Indeed, the flagrant licentiousness practised at Bakaríyá Kuṇḍ, close by, is a scandal to the city, and demands the interference of the magistrate. The festival terminates with the flying of kites. In the morning, the people assemble, for this purpose, in the vicinity of the Dargáh; and, in the evening, at Maṛhiyá Ghát, on the banks of the Barna.

6. The Gangá-Saptamí Melá, held on the banks of the Ganges, on the 7th day of Jeṭh. This day is regarded, by Hindus, as the birthday of the goddess of the Ganges, who is said to have sprung out of the thigh of Jahnu Ṛishi. Formerly, the idol representing the goddess was simply worshipped; but, of late years, a *melá* has been held, accompanied with

the *nách* or dancing. At night thousands of persons assemble to take part in the festivities.

7. The Dasahrá Melá, held on the banks of the Ganges, on the 10th day of Jeṭh, light fortnight; on which day the birth of the river Gangá or Ganges is believed to have occured. Hindus, both male and female, bathe in the river, and give alms to the Brahmans. A curious custom prevails amongst the young girls of the middle classes, who, on this day, float their *guriyás* or dolls on the river, and, for the next four months, refrain, not only from amusing themselves with them, but also from the use of all playthings.

8. The Nirjalá Ekádasí Melá, held on the banks of the Ganges, on the 11th day of Jeṭh. Tradition affirms that Bhím, one of the five Pándav brothers, whose wonderful story is told in the *Mahábhárata*, resolved to fast on this day, but, after mid-day, fainted from hunger and thirst; whereupon his friends threw him into the water, to bring him to his senses. Ever since this event the Hindus have observed the day by bathing in the Ganges in the evening. After ablution, their bodies are besmeared with *chandan* or powdered sandalwood. Hence, the day is called *Chandan Ekádasí.* Formerly, at this festival, residents of different wards of the city used to swim across the Ganges, and engage in sham fights; but the custom has been discontinued.

9. The Asnán Játrá Melá, held at Así Ghát, at the temple of Jagannáth, on the 15th day of Jeṭh. The image of Jagannáth is bathed on this day, and towards evening is exhibited to his votaries, on the terrace of the temple. This *melá* is less frequented than in former times.

10. The Rath-Játrá Melá, held in the garden of Pandit Beni Rám, on the 2nd, 3rd, and 4th days of Asárh. The idol of Jagannáth is brought out of the temple at Así Ghát, and placed upon a *rath* or car,—a peculiar vehicle, with a large number of wheels,—for three successive days, in imitation of the grand festival that takes place at the temple of Jagannáth, in Orissa. Throngs of people of all classes attend this *melá;* and on the third day as many as thirty thousand persons are supposed to be present.

11. The Bataspaníkhshá Melá, held at Chaukhá Ghát, on the 15th day of Asárh. On this day Hindus worship their Gurus or spiritual teachers; hence it is called Guru-púrṇimá. In earlier days astrologers were accustomed to meet at the ghát on the evening of this day, for the purpose of ascertaining the direction of the wind, and of prophesying, in accordance therewith, respecting the nature of the approaching harvest, rainy season, and so forth. This folly, however, has been abandoned, thanks to Christianity and education.

12. The S'ankudhárá Melá, held at the S'ankudhárá Tank, which is also called the Dwáraká-tírth or place of pilgrimage. According to the *Kásí-khaṇḍa*, it is esteemed a sacred act to bathe in this tank on this day. Formerly, the native aristocacy used to assemble here, in the garden of Champat Rai Amín, in order to witness the *nách* or dancing; but this custom seems to have been discontinued. Indeed, the *melá* itself is now in a state of decline.

13. The Bṛiddhkál Melá, held in the Bṛiddhkál Ma-

halla or ward, near the temple of the same name, every Sunday in the month of Sáwan. In one of the numerous courts of the temple is a well in which is a mineral spring, an account of which, written by Mr. James Prinsep, is found in the *Asiatic Researches*. The reason assigned by the Hindus for the medicinal virtues of the well is curious. It is said that Dhanwantari, a great Hindu physician of antiquity, threw his medicine bag into the spring; hence the healing virtues which it is believed to have acquired. The water is used by the natives both for bathing and drinking, as a remedy for diseases of all kinds, but especially for those affecting the skin. Near the well is a reservoir, a few feet deep, of dirty and refuse water, called Amṛit Kuṇḍ or Well of Immortality. This is also held to be of great virtue in removing cutaneous diseases of a contagious character, and likewise leprosy. Sick persons, first of all, bathe in the filthy water of this reservoir, and afterwards wash their bodies with the water of the well.

14. The Durgá Melá, held at Durgá Kuṇḍ or Tank, every Tuesday in Sáwan. Durgá Kuṇḍ and the temple being in the suburbs of the city, with many spacious gardens in their vicinity, the people avail themselves of this *melá*, which occurs at the commencement of the rainy season, to visit the gardens and enjoy themselves. Upwards of thirty thousand persons are present on the last Tuesday of the month.

15. The Fátimá Melá, held at the Dargáh of Fátimá, every Thursday in Sáwan. The Mohammedans have instituted this festival in imitation of the Hindus.

Dancing girls, from the city, appear in their gay dresses and brilliant jewels; and, consequently, the place is, for the most part, the resort of persons of voluptuous habits. Indeed, persons of respectable character will take care not to be found there.

16. The Nág-Panchamí Melá, held at Nág Kúáṅ or Serpent's Well, on the fifth day of Sáwan. This well is spoken of, in Hindu writings, as Kárkotak Nág Tírth or Place of Pilgrimage. Hindus of all ranks, and of both sexes, attend the *melá*, and bathe in the well, returning quickly to their homes; and only persons of loose character prolong their stay. As snakes increase in this season, and as Nág is regarded as the serpent-god, the people worship him as a security against snake-bites. It is common to purchase idols representing this deity, and to carry them home for worship. In the evening of the day, cowherds, or people of the Ahír caste, assemble together in various places, for wrestling and other sports.

17. The Kajrí Melá, held at S'ankudhárá, and also at Ís'war-gangí, on the 3rd day of Bhádoṅ. This festival is said to have originated with a Raja of Kantit, in the district of Mirzapore, who established it for the benefit of women, that they might have a *melá* especially their own. There is a song called Kajrí, which is commonly sung during the months of Sáwan and Bhádoṅ. At this *melá* women fast, and bathe in groups, in places of reputed sanctity. Gangs of Gunahrís, female singers of a very low and abandoned character, visit S'ankudhárá and Ís'war-gangí, singing Kajrí songs to the bathers. Men of the same vicious tastes also

resort to the same places, and listen to the songs, and pay the Gunahrís money. People of reputation do not go to this *melá*.

18. The Ḍhelá Chauth Melá, held at Bará Gaṇeś, on the 4th day of Bhádoṅ. The Hindus fast on this day, in honour of the god Gaṇeś, and visit his temple in crowds. The origin of the *melá* is as follows. It is a current belief, among the natives, that whoever, on the evening of this day, looks up at the moon, will assuredly be charged with a false accusation in the course of the year; and the only way to be delivered from this prospective ignominy is for the person who has, unfortunately, looked at the moon, to be abused and in some way dishonoured on this day. It was, at one time, the custom for people in this predicament to invite anybody they could procure to throw *ḍhelá* or stones at their houses. Vagabonds of the city used to take advantage of this custom, by amusing themselves with throwing large stones at people's houses; but this has been partially, though not entirely, stopped by the police.

19. The Lolárik Chhaṭh Melá, held at the Lolárik Well, near Así Sangam, on the 6th day of Bhádoṅ. Hindus of both sexes bathe in the well on this day, in honour of the Sun. The Gunahrís visit this place, as at the Kajrí *melá*; and, hence, this festival is rather a concourse of dissolute persons.

20. The Báwan-dwádasí Melá, held at Chitrkoṭ and Barna Sangam, on the 12th day of Bhádoṅ. Hindus, male and female, resort to the confluence of the Barna and the Ganges in the morning; and in the evening,

those of the male sex go to Chitrkoṭ, to witness the dramatic performance of the Báwan Avatár or Dwarf Incarnation of Vishṇu.

21. The Anant Chaudas Melá, held at Rámnagar, on the 14th day of Bhádoṅ. This is a private fast day. On this day the great festival of the Rám Lílá begins at Rámnagar.

22. The Surayá Melá, held at Lakshmí Kuṇḍ or Tank, from the 8th of Bhádoṅ Sudi to the 8th day of the waning moon of Kúár, and kept up, therefore, for sixteen days. Hindus, especially females, bathe in Lakshmí Kuṇḍ, and visit the temple of Lakshmí, goddess of wealth. On the last day of the *melá* thousands throng the temple from morning to night.

23. The Rám Lílá Melá, held at Chitrkoṭ, and in many other places, from the 8th day of the waning moon of Kúár to the 15th day of Kuár Sudi. This festival consists of a public dramatic exhibition of the exploits of Rám. Chitrkoṭ is the most ancient place in the city in which it is held; but various wealthy natives, and, especially, the Maharaja of Benares, gratify themselves, and, at the same time, indulge the populace, by giving similar entertainments at their own expense. At one, and, perhaps, more of these places, the *Rámáyaṇa*, which gives a long and detailed account of Rám's achievements, is publicly read from the beginning to the end. Figures of Rám, his friends, and adversaries, dressed up fantastically, take part in the exhibition, and are made to fight together, until the enemies of Rám are mutilated and dishonoured, and, at length, utterly destroyed. The festival of the Rám Lílá is,

perhaps, the most popular and most numerously attended of any held in Benares. There is a great deal of barbaric pomp and oriental splendour connected with it; and native gentlemen vie with each other in the amount of tinsel and tawdry they can display. On that day of the festival, — namely, the 10th day of Kúár Sudi, on which the Dasahrá or Bijai Dasamí *melá* is held at Chaukhá Ghát, when Rám fights with Rávaṇa, and the latter is killed,—an immense crowd, estimated at upwards of thirty thousand persons, is present. On leaving for their homes, the people carry away, as spoils from Lanká, of which island Rávaṇa was formerly the king, a small quantity of earth, picked up at Chaukhá Ghát, deeming it to be gold, of which, in common belief, the island was entirely composed. The Sami tree is worshipped on this day; and it is considered a good omen to catch sight of a *nílkaṇṭh* or blue jay.

24. The Durgá Melá, held by the Bengalis of Benares from the 1st to the 3rd day of Kúár Sudi. During these days, large numbers of the Bengali population make idols of the goddess Durgá, and then worship them. On the day called Dasamí, there is a procession of idols at the Daśáśamedh Ghát, in the presence of thousands of persons, which are all, at length, thrown in the Ganges by their Bengali masters.

25. The Dhan Teras Melá, held at Ṭhaṭherí Bazar and Chaukhambhá, on the 13th day of the waning moon of Kártik. On this day the people, especially bankers, worship Dhan or Wealth, at night. In the shops of the Ṭhaṭherí Bazar, or the bazar in which metal pots and pans are sold, there is a great display of vessels of

brass, copper, and other metals. Moreover, the shops are illuminated. In the bazar of Chaukhambhá, the shopkeepers make an exhibition of earthen images. It is customary, on this day, for the richer classes in the city to purchase metal vessels in the Ṭhaṭherí Bazar.

26. The Anark-Chaudas Melá, held at Mír Ghát, and in the Bhadainí Ward, in the month of Kártik, on the 14th day of the decline of the moon. On this night, the Monkey-god, Hanumán, is believed to have been born. About three o'clock on the following morning, Hindus rub scented oil and other perfumes on their bodies, and bathe in warm water, with certain religious ceremonies, which they imagine to be a preservative from disease during the coming year. At sunrise, newly clad in their winter clothing, they proceed to the shrines of Hanumán, at the two places above referred to.

27. The Díwalí Melá, held throughout the city, on the 15th day of the waning moon in Kártik. This is a day of great and general rejoicing with the Hindus, in which the Mohammedans, also, to some extent, participate. The whole city is illuminated; and even the poorest man lights his little *chirág* or tiny lamp, and places it before his door. The wells, and temples, and idols, and, indeed, every spot of any interest at all to the natives, is decorated with one or more of these lamps. Sweetmeats and parched grain are distributed amongst friends, and are given to the poor. The festival is in honour of Lakshmí, the goddess of wealth. During the night of the Díwálí, it is the custom with all the people, high and low, and of every caste, to gamble;

and many persons who will not gamble at any other time will do so at this season. The custom has a most demoralizing and vicious influence on the minds of the people generally.

28. The Yamadwitíyá (vulgarly, Jamditíyá) Melá, held at Jam Ghát, on the 2nd day of Kártik, light fortnight. This festival has reference to the mutual attachment of Yama and his sister Yamí; and, accordingly, brothers, on this day, receive from their sisters the *tilak* or religious symbol affixed to the forehead, and join in their entertainments, hoping thereby to escape the miseries of hell. They first bathe in the Ganges at Jam Ghát, and then dine at the houses of their sisters, giving them presents in return. To bathe in the river Jumna on this day is, also, believed to have the same effect of delivering from future punishment.

29. The Kártik Púrṇimá Melá, held at the Panch Gangá Ghát, on the last day of Kártik. During the whole of this month it is regarded as specially meritorious to bathe at this ghát every morning at sunrise. On the last day multitudes bathe here; and, in the evening, the ghát is illuminated. Formerly pugilistic combats used to take place; but they have now ceased.

30. The Barná Piyála Melá, held at Chaukhá Ghát and S'ivapur, on the 1st Tuesday or Saturday of Aghan. People of the lower castes resort to Chaukhá Ghát, and there offer wine or sherbet, mixed with *bháng*,—a highly intoxicating drug much eaten by the Brahmans, —in honour of Kalká and Sahjá, the former being a Brahman woman, and the latter a *chamáyin*, or woman of

the sweeper caste. They then proceed to the village of Śivapur, and spend the day in revelry, returning home on the following morning.

31. The Panchkosí Melá, held at Śivapur on the 7th and 8th of the declining moon in Aghan. The pilgrimage along the Panchkosí road, or sacred boundary of Benares, occupies five days. On the fourth day, when the procession reaches Śivapur, people from the city go out to meet the pilgrims at this place, and unite with them in merry-making.

32. The Loṭá-bhanṭá Melá, held at Piśáchmochan, on the 14th day of Aghan. Many persons from the city and from the neighbouring villages, of both sexes, bathe together in the Piśáchmochan Tank, in the morning. Afterwards they remain there for some hours, make bread or cakes, which they cook and eat with roasted Bhanṭá or the egg-plant, which abounds at this season. By way of ridicule, the *melá* was originally called *Roṭá-bhanṭá*, in allusion to the bread (*roṭí*) and *bhanṭá* which are eaten there; but the name has latterly been changed to *Loṭá-bhanṭá*, in allusion, I suppose, to the *loṭá* or drinking vessel used on the occasion. Persons of respectability visit the Tank on the 14th of the light fortnight of the month Pús, and again on the 14th of the waning moon of the same month, for the performance of religious ceremonies.

33. The Nagarpradakshaṇá Melá, held at Chaukhá Ghát and Barhiyá Tank, on the 15th day of Aghan. This consists of a pilgrimage round the city, performed in two days, on the first of which the pilgrims stay at Chaukhá Ghát. Formerly a set of licentious vagabonds

used to perform the Kṛishṇa Lílá here, but the abominable practice is now discontinued.

34. The Gaṇeś Chauth Melá, held at Bará Gaṇeś, on the 4th day of the declining moon in Mágh. The temple of Bará Gaṇeś, the god of learning, is visited on this day. It is customary for *vidyárthís* or young students of Sanskrit, to stand in different parts of the temple from sunrise to sunset, until the rising of the moon, under the belief that praying there in this posture will make them learned.

35. The Vedavyás Melá, held at the Fort and in the Tank at Rámnagar, on every Monday of Mágh. The temple of Vedavyás, the celebrated compiler of the Vedas, is situated within the Maharaja of Benares' Fort at Rámnagar. On this day Hindus from the city worship the idol in the temple, and then bathe in the Tank. The crowd of votaries is greatest on the last Monday of the month.

36. The S'iva-rátrí Melá, held at the Bisheśwar and Baijnáth Temples, on the 14th day of the declining moon in Phágun. This is a general fast-day in honour of S'iva, the chief god of the city. The temples referred to are much crowded with worshippers during the day.

37. The Holí Melá, held throughout the city, from the 11th to the 15th day of Phágun. This festival is chiefly noted for obscene representations, and the use of abusive language. No woman can venture into the streets, on these days, without being exposed to insult. All classes join in it; and, as the grossly indecent festival is immensely popular in the city, it is very difficult for the Government to interfere beyond

the suppression of licentious pictures, and, to some extent, the general giving of abuse. Still, I think that public morality loudly demands active and even stringent measures on the part of the Government; and I am satisfied that they would meet with the approval of all right-minded natives. On the Púrṇimá, or last day of the month, the people burn the Holiká, or piles of wood, in their respective wards, the expense being raised by subscription. No regular *melá* is held in any one place; but in every ward there is much festivity and merry-making. Many wear coloured clothes, and discharge red water on passers-by.

38. The Dharaddí Melá, held at Daśáśamedh and Chausathí, on the first day of the waning moon in Chait. On this day the people cast upon each other the ashes of the Holiká pile burnt on the previous day, and then wash themselves, and change their coloured clothes. Crowds of people, with obscene shows, come in the evening, from opposite directions, to the Daśáśamedh Ghát, where multitudes of natives of all ranks, some on the banks, and others in boats on the river, assemble to witness the immoral spectacle. On returning from the ghát, the people visit the shrine of Chausathí Deví or goddess.

39. The Búrwa-Mangal Melá, held on the river Ganges, the Tuesday after the Holí Festival. Formerly it was customary for Hindus to visit the temple of Durgá on the first Tuesday following the Holí; but Raja Cheit Singh added to this *melá* what is called the Búrwá Mangal. On this occasion, a very considerable portion of the inhabitants of the city spend

the night on the river, in large boats, some of which are beautifully decorated, where dancing and singing go on for hours. The scene is exceedingly picturesque; and its effect is much heightened by the brilliant lights on the large boats. The festival continues till the evening of Wednesday, and was originally called Buddhuwá Mangal (Budh, Wednesday), but is now corrupted into Búrwa Mangal.

40. The Dangal Melá, held at the temple of Jagannáth and at Rámnagar, on the Thursday following the Búrwa Mangal. This, too, is a singing and dancing festival. Singing parties proceed to the temple, accompanied by crowds of listeners; and boats, laden with people, attended by singing and dancing girls, row about the river, proceeding as far as Rámnagar. This *melá* is of recent date.

CHAPTER XVIII.

THE Buddhist Ruins at Sárnáth—Their Antiquity.—Summary of the Narratives of Fa Hian and Hiouen Thsang, respecting the buildings formerly existing at Sárnáth and in its neighbourhood.—Points of agreement in the Narratives.—Modern Explorers of the Ruins.—Extent and Nature of the Remains.—The Great Tower—Description of it by Major-General Cunningham, and Account of his Excavations. —Age of Buddhist Topes or Towers.—Remains of a Buddhist Monastery—Mr. Thomas's Account of them.—Discovery of large numbers of Statues and Bass-reliefs.—Excavated Chamber.—Foundation of an Ancient Tower—Major-General Cunningham's Description of it.—The Chaukandí Tower.—The I'śipattana Hall, or Abode of Buddhist Devotees.—Remains of Vihára or Temple-monastery.—Small Building, containing Sixty Sculptures.—The Seal Chaityas.—The Buddhist Formula.—S'ákya Muni, the historical Buddha—His visit to Benares.—Spread of Buddhism from Benares.—Decline of Buddhism in India.—Destruction of Buddhist Structures at Sárnáth, by fire.—Fall of Buddhism.

THESE ruins have, for years, excited much interest in the public mind, both on account of their antiquity and of their connexion with the Buddhist religion. The latest of them date, perhaps, from about the sixth or seventh century of the present era; while the earliest may belong to a period several hundred years prior to that. Indeed, it is a historical fact, which admits of no question, that there were buildings in existence on this spot in the first ages of Buddhism; and, although we can hardly suppose that remains of any of them are still to be found, nevertheless, it is not improbable that portions of edifices erected previously to the Christian era,—such as foundations, walls, and sculptured stones, in a more or less fragmentary state,—are amongst the relics which have been preserved down to our own times.

Two Chinese pilgrims, Fa Hian and Hiouen Thsang, have thrown considerable light on the condition of Sárnáth during the later period of Buddhism. The former visited India in the beginning of the fifth century, A.D.; and the latter, towards the middle of the seventh. These keen and sagacious observers have left records of their travels in India, of the utmost importance to the historian and antiquarian. Their narratives are, for the most part, plain matter-of-fact productions, free from the haze and uncertainty of Hindu writings; and, wherever they have been tested by extraneous evidence, have been found to be, to a large extent, singularly correct. As great interest attaches to the accounts which they furnish respecting Sárnáth and Benares at those epochs, I have given them entire, in appendices to this work. That of Fa Hian I have extracted from "The Pilgrimage of Fa Hian," translated by Mr. J. W. Laidlay, from the French edition of the "Foe Koue Ki" of MM. Remusat, Klaproth, and Landresse. This is very brief; but the narrative of Hiouen Thsang, on the contrary, is in detail. This I have myself translated from the "Mémoires de Hiouen Thsang," the French version of the original Chinese work, executed by the celebrated Sinologist M. Stanislas Julien.

Before describing the Buddhist ruins at Sárnáth, I will give a short summary of the buildings existing at the two periods referred to, according to the representations of those distinguished travellers. Fa Hian says, that, "to the north-west of the town (Benares), at the distance of ten *li* (less than two miles), you come to the temple situated in the Deer-park of the Immortal." He also makes mention of a chapel, which, perhaps, was a small shrine; and of four towers, erected on spots celebrated in the life of Buddha, one being that where he delivered his first discourse on the new religion of Buddhism he was then founding. He states, in addition, that there were two *seng kia lan*, or monasteries, inhabited by ecclesiastics.[1]

Hiouen Thsang, first of all, furnishes a brief account of the kingdom of Varáṇasí, or Benares, as it existed in his day, which was, he says, four thousand *li*, or about six hundred and sixty-seven miles, in circumference. It possessed thirty Buddhist monasteries, to which three thousand religious persons, or monks, were attached; and a hundred Hindu temples, with ten thousand heretics, priests, devotees, and others connected with them. The greater portion of the population adhered to the Hindu doctrines. In the capital were twenty Hindu temples; so that the rest must have been scattered over the province: but what proportion of the Buddhist monasteries were there likewise, he does not mention. Towers, with many stories, and magnificent chapels, beautifully carved and richly painted, he saw in the city; and, also, a brazen statue of the

[1] See Appendix A.

Hindu deity Maheśwara, nearly a hundred feet high. To the north-east of Benares, and to the west of the Ganges,—but at what distance he neglects to say,—was a *Stupa*, or sacred tower, built by Aśoka, about a hundred feet in height; and, opposite to it, a stone column, "of blue colour, bright as a mirror."

About ten *li* (or one-third less than two miles) to the north-east of the Ganges, was the monastery of the Deer Park (now called Sárnáth), divided into eight parts, and entirely surrounded by a wall, within which were balustrades and two-storied palaces, of splendid construction, and a *Vihára*, or temple-monastery, two hundred feet in height, surmounted by a huge *An-mo-lo* (or mango), in embossed gold. The foundations and stairs were of stone. Surrounding the monument were a hundred rows of niches, made of brick, each containing a statue of Buddha, in embossed gold. In the midst of the *Vihára* was a statue of Buddha, in bronze. To the south-west of this *Vihára* was a *Stupa*, of stone, raised by Aśoka; and, in front of it, a column, seventy feet in height, erected on the spot where Buddha delivered his first discourse. Near by were seven other *Stupas*, and, also, a number of ancient stone seats, fifty paces long, and seven feet high, placed there to commemorate the site where the four last Buddhas are said to have taken exercise. A statue of Buddha, in the attitude of walking, was likewise to be seen.

Within the walls of the monastery were a multitude of sacred monuments, including several hundred *Viháras* and *Stupas*. To the west of the walls was a sacred tank, in which Buddha formerly bathed; a little to the west of that was another, in which he washed his monk's water-pot; and, a short distance to the north, was a third, in which he washed his garments. On one side of this last tank was a large square stone, which exhibited, it was believed, the marks of the threads of the *Kacháya*, or brown vestment, worn by Buddha. Not far from the tanks was a *Stupa*; and, near to that, another; and, further off still, but at no great distance, was one more, situated in the midst of a large forest.

Nearly half a mile to the south-west of the monastery was a large and lofty *Stupa*, about three hundred feet in height, resplendent with the most rare and precious objects, and surmounted by an arrow. By its side was another *Stupa*, but of small size. About half a mile to the east of the Deer Park was a *Stupa*; and, close by, a dry tank, respecting which Hiouen Thsang gives a singular legend. To the west of the tank was the *Stupa* of the Three Quadrupeds.[1]

The narratives of Fa Hian and Hiouen Thsang strikingly agree in two respects. They both state, that, alike where Buddha delivered his first discourse, and where the five hermits came forward and paid him reverence, a *Stupa* or sacred tower has been erected. It is very probable that they saw the same towers. Indeed, in regard to the first, if any reliance can be placed on the assertion of Hiouen Thsang, that the tower which existed in his day was built by Aśoka, the conjecture amounts to an established fact. This tower commemorated a most important circumstance in the history of Buddhism, and was spoken of as one

[1] See Appendix B.

of the "eight divine towers;" all of them having reference to certain leading events in the life of Buddha. It might be difficult to point decidedly to any further agreement in the two narratives; although I am inclined to the belief, that "the temple of the Deer Park," referred to in such a special manner by Fa Hian, was the *Vihára*, or temple-monastery, so particularly described and so prominently distinguished by Hiouen Thsang.

The mystery connected with these ruins, united with the indisputable fact that Buddhism once reigned paramount in India, and that Benares was long one of its principal seats, has excited the curiosity of multitudes of persons who have burned with desire to know the secrets which, it was supposed, were enshrined within them. It is no wonder, therefore, that the excavations which have been carried on at Sárnáth, at various times, have been viewed with great interest by the educated portion of Europeans in India. It is to be regretted that their superintendence has occasionally fallen into the hands of inexperienced persons — inexperienced, I mean, so far as the ability to decipher inscriptions and intelligently describe what has been from time to time discovered is concerned. The most extensive excavations which have been made were effected under the personal superintendence of Major-General Cunningham and Major Kittoe, who dug out of the ruins an immense number of statues, bass-reliefs, and other curious objects. The former alone, in 1835, found about a hundred statues and bass-reliefs, all which worth preserving were sent to the

Museum of the Asiatic Society in Calcutta. Mr. E. Thomas (late Judge of Benares), and Dr. F. Hall, also, following in the track of these great explorers, both made interesting discoveries. A considerable number of the Sárnáth relics have been deposited in the Government College of Benares, and are found both in the Museum and in the College grounds.

The ruins at Sárnáth consist of two towers,—separated by a distance of about half a mile or thereabouts,—and of the walls and foundations of buildings which, for many years, remained covered over with earth, but have been lately exhumed. Moreover, there is a vast amount of broken bricks lying thickly scattered over the plain, some of which are grooved and carved, while all are hard and well-seasoned. Here and there, too, a statue, more or less mutilated, is to be seen. Near a stream which flows to the north of the plain, is a large stone figure, the base of which is imbedded in the soil. This may have been a representation of Buddha; but it is now worshipped by the Hindus, who profess to derive great benefit from their homage to it. The figure is so mutilated, that it is difficult to say what it was originally.

The account given of the great tower by Major-General Cunningham, in his Archæological Report, printed in the Journal of the Asiatic Society of Bengal (vol. xxxii.), is so elaborate and exhaustive, and, withal, so interesting, that, although lengthy, I give the extract almost entire. He says: "The Buddhist *Stupa* called *Dhamek* is a solid round tower, ninety-three feet in diameter at base, and one hundred and ten feet in

Photographed by D. Tresham, Esq.

GREAT BUDDHIST TOWER AT SÁRNÁTH, NEAR BENARES.

height above the surrounding ruins, but one hundred and twenty-eight feet above the general level of the country. The foundation or basement, which is made of very large bricks, has a depth of twenty-eight feet below the level of the ruins, but is sunk only ten feet below the surface of the country. The lower part of the tower, to a height of forty-three feet, is built entirely of stone from one of the Chunar quarries; and, with the exception of the upper five courses, the whole of this part of the building is a solid mass of stone; and each stone, even in the very heart of the mass, is secured to its neighbours by iron cramps. The upper part of the tower is built entirely of large bricks; but, as the outer facing has long ago disappeared, there is nothing now left to show whether it was formerly cased with stone, or only plastered over, and coloured to imitate the stone-work of the lower portion. I infer, however, that it was plastered; because the existing stone-work terminates with the same course all round the building, a length of two hundred and ninety-two feet. Had the upper part been cased with stone, it is scarcely possible that the whole should have disappeared so completely that not even a single block out of so many thousands should not remain in its original position. In one part I observed some projecting bricks, which appeared very like the remains of a moulding at the base of the dome. On the top I found a small brick cap, eight feet in diameter and only four feet high. From its size, I infer that this was the ruin of the base of a small pinnacle, about ten feet square, which, most probably, once supported a stone umbrella. I infer this, because the figures of Buddha, the Teacher, are usually represented as seated under an umbrella.

"The lower part of the monument has eight projecting faces, each twenty-one feet six inches in width, with intervals of fifteen feet between them. In each of the faces, at a height of twenty-four feet above the ground, there is a semi-circular headed niche, five and a half feet in width, and the same in height. In each of the niches there is a pedestal, one foot in height, and slightly hollowed on the top, to receive the base of a statue; but the statues themselves have long disappeared, and I did not find the fragment of one, in my excavation at the base of the monument. There can be little doubt, however, that all the eight statues represented Buddha, the Preacher, in the usual form, with his hands raised before his breast, and the thumb and forefinger of the right hand placed on the little finger of the left hand, for the purpose of enforcing his argument. Judging by the dimensions of the niches, the statues must have been of life-size.

"From the level of the base of the niches, the eight projecting faces lessen in width to five feet at the top; but the diminution is not uniform, as it begins gradually at first, and increases as it approaches the top. The outline of the slope may have been, possibly, intended for a curve; but it looks much more like three sides of a large polygon. Around the niches, seven of the faces are more or less richly decorated with a profusion of flowering foliage. The carving on some of the faces has been completed; but, on others, it is little more than half finished, while the south face is altogether plain. On the unfinished faces, portions of the unexecuted ornamentation may be seen traced in outline by the chisel, which proves, that, in ancient times, the Hindus followed the same practice as at present, of adding the carving after the wall was built.

"On the western face, the same ornamentation of flowing foliage is continued below the niche; and, in the midst of it, there is a small plain tablet, which can only have been intended for a very short inscription, such, perhaps, as the name of the building. A triple band of ornament, nearly nine feet in depth below the niches, encircles all the rest of the building, both faces and recesses. The middle band, which is the broadest, is formed entirely of various geometrical figures, the main lines being deeply cut, and the intervening spaces being filled with various ornaments. On some of the faces, where the spaces between the deeply-cut lines of the ruling figures are left plain, I infer that the work is unfinished. The upper band of ornamentation, which is the narrowest, is, generally, a scroll of the lotus plant, with leaves and buds only; while the lower band, which is also a lotus scroll, contains the full-blown flowers, as well as the buds. The lotus flower is represented full to the front, on all the sides except the south south-west, where it is shown in a side view with the *Chakwa* or Brahmani goose seated upon it. This, indeed, is the only side on which any animal representations are given; which is the more remarkable, as it is one of the recesses, and not one of the projecting faces. In the middle of the ornament there is a human figure seated on a lotus flower, and holding two branches of the lotus in his hands. On each side of him there are three lotus flowers, of which the four nearer ones support pairs of Brahmani geese; while the two farther ones carry only single birds. Over the nearest pair of geese, on the right hand of the figure, there is a frog. The attitudes of the birds are all good; and even that of the human figure is easy, although formal. The lotus scroll, with

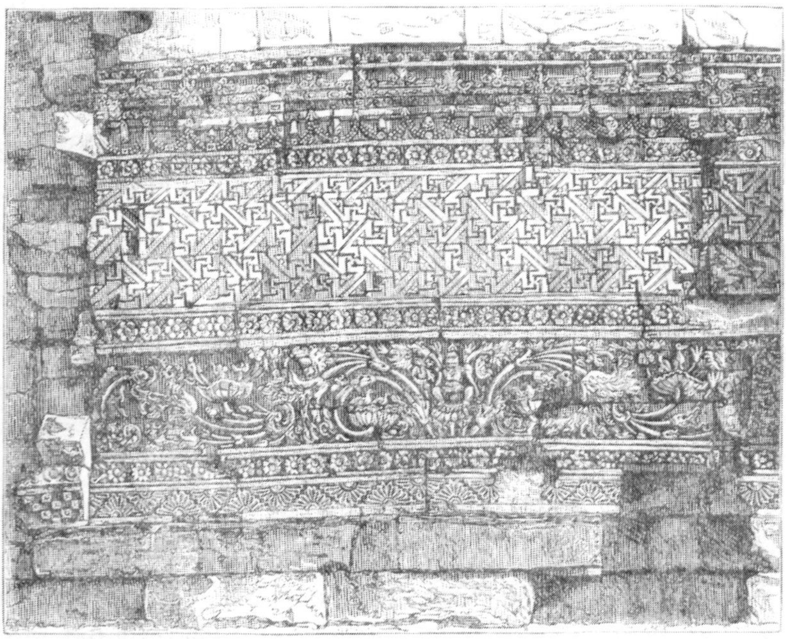

Photographed by D. Tresham, Esq.

CARVING ON THE BUDDHIST TOWER, SÁRNÁTH.—No. I.

its flowing lines of graceful stalk, mingled with tender buds, and full blown flowers, and delicate leaves, is very rich and very beautiful. Below the ornamental borders there are three plain projecting bands.

"The breadth of one projecting face and of one recess is thirty-six feet six inches, which, multiplied by eight, give two hundred and ninety-two feet as the circumference, and a trifle less than ninety-three feet as the diameter.

Photographed by D. Tresham, Esq.

CARVING ON THE BUDDHIST TOWER, SÁRNÁTH.—No. II.

"Near the top of the north-west face there are four projecting stones, placed like steps—that is, they are not immediately over each other; and above them there is a fifth stone, which is pierced with a round hole for the reception of a post, or, more probably, of a flag-staff. The lowest of these stones can only be reached by a ladder; but ladders must have been always available, if, as I suppose, it was customary, on stated occasions, to fix flags and streamers on various parts of the building, in the same manner as is now done in the Buddhist countries of Burmah and Ladâk.

16

"On the 18th January, 1835, my scaffolding was completed, and I stood on the top of the great tower. On cutting the long grass, I found two iron spikes, each eight inches long, and shaped like the head of a lance. On the following day I removed the ruined brick pinnacle, and began sinking a shaft or well, about five feet in diameter. At three feet from the top, I found a rough stone, twenty-four inches by fifteen inches by seven inches; and, on the 25th January, at a depth of ten and a half feet, I found an inscribed slab, twenty-eight inches and three-quarters long, thirteen inches broad, and four inches and three-quarters thick, which is now in the Museum of the Bengal Asiatic Society. The inscription consists of the usual Buddhist formula or profession of faith, beginning with the words, "*Ye Dharmmâ hetu prabhavâ*," etc., of which translations have been given by Mill, Hodgson, Wilson, and Burnouf. The following is Hodgson's translation, which has received the approval of Burnouf:—"Of all things proceeding from cause, their causes hath the *Tathâgata* (Buddha) explained. The Great Sramana (Buddha) hath likewise explained the causes of the cessation of existence." The letters of this inscription, which are all beautifully cut, appear to me to be of a somewhat earlier date than the Tibetan alphabet, which is known to have been obtained from India in the middle of the seventh century. I would, therefore, assign the inscription, and, consequently, the completion of the monument, to the sixth century.

"On the 22nd January I began to excavate a horizontal gallery on the level of the top of the stone-work;

and, on the 14th of February, at a distance of forty-four feet, the gallery joined the shaft, which had been sunk from above. As I now found that the upper course of stone was only a facing, I sank the gallery itself down to the level of the stone-work, and continued it right through to the opposite side. I thus discovered, that the mass of the inner stone-work was only thirty-three feet in height, while the outer stone-work was forty-three feet. In the middle, however, there was a pillar of stone-work, rising six feet higher than the inner mass. This was, perhaps, used as a point from which to describe the circle with accuracy. Small galleries were also made to reach the tops of the east and west faces; but nothing was discovered by these works.

"The labour of sinking the shaft through the solid stone-work was very great, as the stones, which were large (from two to three feet in length, eighteen inches broad, and twelve inches thick), were all secured to each other by iron cramps. Each stone had, usually, eight cramps, four above, and as many below, all of which had to be cut out before it could be moved. I, therefore, sent to Chunar for regular quarry-men, to quarry out the stones; and the work occupied them for several months. At length, at a depth of one hundred and ten feet from the top of the monument, the stone gave place to brick-work, made of very large bricks. Through this the shaft was continued for a further depth of twenty-eight feet, when I reached the plain soil beneath the foundation. Lastly, a gallery was run right through the brick-work of the foundation, immediately below the stone-work, but without yielding any result."

The remark of Major-General Cunningham, that the antiquity of the Buddhist tower may be judged of from its form, is worthy of great attention; for, if his observations be just, — and, it must be confessed, few men have had the same extensive experience in exploring Buddhist remains in India,—it would be an ascertained fact, that the large tower at Sárnáth could not date from earlier, but from later, Buddhist times. The oldest kind of tower, such as those existing at Sánchí and Satdhárá, was, he says, "a simple hemisphere." The epoch of these two was, he conjectures, the middle of the sixth century B.C. "The next, in point of antiquity, are the topes (towers) around Bhilsa, which contain the relics of Aśoka's missionaries, and of the venerable Mogaliputra, who conducted the proceedings of the Third Synod. In these, which were built in the end of the third century B.C., the dome is raised a few feet above the basement, by a cylindrical plinth. The third class of topes are those represented in the Sánchí bass-reliefs, which date between 19 and 37, A.D. In these, the hemisphere is placed upon a plinth of equal height, so that the centre of the dome is the centre of the whole building. Six representations of this kind of tope occur among the Sánchí bass-reliefs. The topes in Afghanistan are, mostly, of this shape. In the latest topes,—of which Sárnáth, near Benares, is a magnificent specimen,—the plinth is equal, in height, to the diameter of the hemisphere. From these remarks it is evident that the age of almost every tope may be obtained, approximately, from its shape; the most ancient being a simple hemisphere, and the latest, a tall round tower, surmounted by a dome."[1]

To the west of the great tower, and very near to it, are the remains of an old Buddhist monastery, which retreat from it in both a northerly and southerly direction. The excavations here have established the singular fact, that this monastery was partly built upon the foundations of a former edifice. Very little is known respecting this more ancient building. The excavations have been suspended for several years, which is much to be regretted, as the interest attached to this earlier edifice is far greater than any which can possibly be attached to the later one. The excavations, though incomplete, have, nevertheless, been conducted on an extensive scale, and have brought to light some of the chambers, walls, doorways, and foundations of the later monastery, and, also, certain undeniable traces of an earlier edifice. Mr. E. Thomas, in a communication to the Bengal Asiatic Society, in the year 1854, observes, that "the excavations already completed, viewed with reference to the substance of which the covering bodies were severally composed, tends to show, that, previous to the erection of the comparatively modern building with which we are more immediately concerned, and without, at present, adverting to the lower walls, the general line of the original bank sloped from east to west; and that the later monastery was erected on the slope of the shelving bank, forming the westward face of the *Kherah*, or natural mound, to the extreme eastward of which is situated the celebrated

[1] Bhilsa Topes, pp. 177, 178.

tope, which dates from a far earlier period. The outline profile, therefore, of that portion of the accumulations, which served to fill in the higher, but unequal, line of the broken walls now exposed, formed, by subsequent deposits, a mere continuation, to the westward, of that face of the original bank; taking, however, a more gradual slope than the sides of the clean earth mound appear to have done." He also states, that, at the south-east corner of the clearings, "the modern half wall, erected upon the remains of the more ancient edifice, was evidently built into an already existing bank, consisting, at the point of contact, of a débris of broken bricks, etc." In front of the chamber, to the east, he says, "we see traces of a verandah; and, at the north-east corner, we again observe the ancient walls performing the part of foundations for their modern successors. There would seem to have been an outlet from the main square at this point, though, as far as the excavations have yet been extended in this direction, it is difficult to say where this passage led to, inasmuch as, on the east, we encounter a mere retaining wall, supporting a corner of the high bank; and, on the north, we meet with a singular elbow-shaped superficial continuation of the outer wall of the main building. What this strange angular affair may indicate, or how far it may extend into the bank, must, for the present, be allowed to pass."

These chambers constitute portions of a complete square of the monastery, the outline of which, Mr. Thomas states, has been "preserved, as far as the foundations go, to the outside of the doorway block; and the line is further continued through the thick angular wall, at which point the deep foundations cease. Passing by three ordinary chambers on the northern face, we come to one of the image-houses. The entrance is from the inner square. The brick and the stone platform may both be supposed to have formed pedestals of erect statues of Buddha. The retreated wall in the corner, between these platforms, combined with the otherwise, apparently, isolated position of the second platform chamber adjoining towards the north, would have led to the idea that the wall had been pierced for the purpose of communication between one chamber and the other; but, as far as the standing walls admit of a decision on the point, there certainly was no doorway at this spot, whatever means of oral or ocular communication may have existed in the screen at a higher level. Such portion of the western face of the monastery as has yet been exposed seems to have consisted of cells. These bear less traces of fire than those on the opposite side of the square; but, on the other hand, a much smaller proportion of their walls remains standing, seeming as if this side of the building,—situated, as it was, on the more exposed slope of the bank,—was less early inhumed. Indeed, as far as can be seen, the south-west corner has been almost entirely swept away; its surviving portions having been covered in, at a much later period, by the gradual operation of the manufacture of pottery, etc., whose kilns, for the supply of successive generations, have been pushed on in this direction, to meet the prevailing wind. At this corner we again find traces of the verandah of the court;

and the centre chamber, on the southern aspect, brings us to the shrine. All that now remains is the square elaborately-corniced block in the centre of the chamber, which formed the *Sinhásan*, or throne, for the seated figure of Buddha. The wall to the rear of the statue has been completely destroyed; but the original opening in front of the *Sinhásan* is seen to have been enlarged beyond the breadth of the other doorways, probably to afford a free view of the object of worship, without necessitating too near an approach on the part of the ordinary votaries."[1]

It has been already remarked, that the excavations have brought to light a large number of statues and bass-reliefs: they amount, in fact, to some hundreds, many of which are representations of Buddha. These figures were, for the most part, discovered in two places, one of which, now that the mound containing them has been removed, is almost on a level with the surface of the ground, and exhibits several circular bases of brick, on which, probably, stone pillars formerly stood. Amongst them, occupying a central position, is one much larger and more elevated than the rest, which, it is supposed, constituted the foundation of the *Sinhásan* or throne of a gigantic statue of Buddha. The other place is an excavated chamber, in which a large number of images and other ancient remains were discovered. As it is, next to the great tower, perhaps the most remarkable and curious structure here, I shall proceed more particularly to describe it.

The chamber is circular in form, and is depressed

[1] Bengal Asiatic Journal, for 1854, p. 473.

about twelve feet below the surrounding soil. It is fifty-seven feet four inches in diameter, measured three feet from the floor, and is five hundred and twenty feet to the west of the large tower. Its enclosing wall is sixteen feet and a half thick, and is composed, throughout, —with a single exception, which will presently be explained,—of large Buddhist bricks, placed horizontally, in layers one upon another, and, in no single instance, placed vertically; the outermost layer abutting on the adjacent soil. For about two thirds of the distance from the summit to the base, the wall is concave; the rate of curvature being in the proportion of one inch to every five inches and one-third of perpendicular height. Beneath the lowest stratum of bricks in the concave portion is an indurated deposit of small nodes of limestone, six inches in depth; and below it, again, a thin layer of powdered brick, one inch and a half in thickness. From this point to the floor the wall is perpendicular; and the upper portion is ornamented with a cornice and moulding.

The lower division of the wall, when compared with the upper, has a very striking appearance. Its bricks are better burnt, and are larger, some of them being eighteen inches in length, nearly thirteen in breadth, and quite three in thickness; whereas not one in the upper section can be found of such dimensions. Moreover, it has an aspect of higher antiquity; and it is difficult to reject the idea that it belongs to a prior era. If this conjecture be true, it must have been a portion of an earlier building, contemporaneous, it may be, with the old edifice lately referred to, a few remains of whose walls have been discovered, forming part of the foundations of the more modern structure, the ruins of which, still visible, have just now been described. Major-General Cunningham's account of his excavations here, and of the views he entertains of the nature of the original buildings situated on this spot, I must transcribe, for the completeness of the narrative. It is strange, however, that he has not remarked the characteristics in the construction and antiquity of the existing wall of the chamber referred to. He writes as follows:—

"This is the ruin of the large brick *stupa* (or tower), which was excavated by Babu Jagat Singh, the Dewán of Raja Chait Singh of Benares, for the purpose of obtaining bricks for the erection of Jagatganj. In January, 1794, his workmen found, at a depth of twenty-seven feet, two vessels of stone and marble, one inside the other. The inner vessel, according to Jonathan Duncan's account (Asiatic Researches, vol. v., p. 131), contained a few human bones, some decayed pearls, gold leaves, and other jewels of no value. In the 'same place' under-ground, and on the 'same occasion' with the discovery of the urns, there was found a statue of Buddha, bearing an inscription dated in *Samvat* 1083, or A.D. 1026. An imperfect translation of this inscription was given by Wilford, accompanied by some remarks, in which he applies the statements of the record to the great tower of Dhamek, instead of to the building in which it was actually discovered.

"At my suggestion, Major Kittoe made a search for this statue amongst the plundered stones of Jagatganj, where it was found, broken and mutilated. The inscription, however, was still legible; and the remains of the figure are sufficient to show that the statue was a representation of Buddha the preacher, and not of Buddha the ascetic. Major Kittoe sent me a transcript of the inscription in modern Nágarí, which I strongly suspect to have been *Brahmanized* by his Benares *Pandits*. In its modern Nágarí form, as translated for me, it records that '*Mahi Pála*, Raja of *Gauḍa* (or Bengal), having worshipped the lotus-like feet of Srí *Dharmaráśi* ('heap of light,' Buddha), caused to be erected in Káśí hundreds of *Íśána* and *Chitraghaṇṭá*. Srí *Sthira Pála* and his younger brother Srí *Vasanta Pála*, having restored religion, raised this tower with an inner chamber and eight large niches.' I strongly suspect that the word *Íśána*, which is a name of Siva, has been obtained by Brahmanical modification of the original. Wilford read *Bhúpála* instead of 'Íśána'; but I am unable to offer any conjecture as to the true reading, as I know not where the original is now deposited. Major Kittoe's fac-simile of the inscription is, perhaps, amongst those deposited by him in the Asiatic Society's Museum.

"My reasons for fixing on the large round hole, five hundred and twenty feet to the west of the great tower, as the site of the *stupa* excavated by Jagat Singh, are the following:—In 1835, when I was engaged in opening the great tower itself, I made repeated enquiries regarding the scenes of Jagat Singh's discovery. Every one had heard of the finding of a stone box, which contained bones, and jewels, and gold; but every one professed ignorance of the locality. At length, an old man named Sangkar, an inhabitant of the neighbouring village of Singhpur, came forward and informed me that, when he was a boy, he had been employed in the excavations made by Jagat Singh, and that he knew all about the discovery of the jewels, etc. According to his account, the discovery consisted of two boxes, the outer one being a large round box of common stone, and the inner one a cylindrical box of green marble, about fifteen inches in height, and five or six inches in diameter. The contents of the inner box were forty to forty-six pearls, fourteen rubies, eight silver and nine gold earrings (*karṇ phúl*), and three pieces of human arm-bone. The marble box was taken to the Bará Sáhib (Jonathan Duncan); but the stone box was left undisturbed in its original position. As the last statement evidently afforded a ready means of testing the man's veracity, I enquired if he could point out the spot where the box was left. To this question he replied, without any hesitation, in the affirmative; and I at once engaged him to dig up the box. We proceeded together to the site of the present circular hole, which was then a low uneven mound in the centre of a hollow, and, after marking out a small space about four feet in diameter, he began to work. Before sunset he had reached the stone box, at a depth of twelve feet, and at less than two feet from the middle of the well which he had sunk. The box was a large circular block of common Chunar sandstone, pierced with a rough cylindrical chamber in the centre, and covered with a flat slab as a lid. I presented this box, along with about sixty statues, to the Bengal Asiatic Society;

and it is now in their Museum, where I lately recognized it.

"The discovery of the stone box was the most complete and convincing proof that I could wish for of the man's veracity; and I at once felt satisfied that the relics and the inscribed figure of Buddha found by Jagat Singh's workmen had been discovered on this spot, and, consequently, that they could not possibly have any connexion with the great tower of *Dhamek*. My next object was to ascertain the nature of the building in which the box was deposited. As I had found the box standing on solid brick-work, I began to clear away the rubbish, expecting to find a square chamber similar to those which had been discovered in the topes of Afghanistan. My excavations, however, very soon showed, that, if any chamber had once existed, it must have been demolished by Jagat Singh's workmen. Sangkar then described that the box was found in a small square hole, or chamber, only just large enough to hold it. I cleared out the whole of the rubbish, until I reached the thick circular wall which still exists. I then found that the relic-box had been deposited inside a solid brick hemispherical *stupa*, forty-nine feet in diameter at the level of the deposit; and that this had been covered by a casing wall of brick, sixteen feet and a half in thickness: the total diameter at this level was, therefore, eighty-two feet. The solid brick-work of the interior had only been partially excavated by Jagat Singh's workmen; nearly one-half of the mass, to a height of six feet above the stone box, being then untouched. I made some excavations round the outer wall, to ascertain its thickness; but I left the brickwork undisturbed.

"About eighteen years afterwards, the excavation of this *stupa* was continued by Major Kittoe and Mr. Thomas, until the whole of the inner mass had been removed, and the foundations of the outer casing exposed. The inner diameter is given, by Mr. Thomas, as forty-nine feet six inches; the slight excess over my measurement being due to the thickness of a base moulding of the original *stupa*. I have again carefully examined the remains of this monument; and I am quite satisfied that, in its original state, it was an ancient hemispherical *stupa*, forty-nine feet in diameter at base, and about thirty-five or forty feet in height, including the usual pinnacle. Afterwards, when, as I suppose, the upper portion had become ruinous, it was repaired by the addition of a casing wall, sixteen feet and a half in thickness. The diameter of the renewed edifice thus became eighty-two feet, while the height, inclusive of a pinnacle, could not have been less than fifty feet. On a review of all the facts connected with this ruin, I incline to the opinion, that the inner hemisphere was an ancient relic *stupa* (or tower), and that, this having become ruinous, it was repaired, and an outer casing added by the brothers Sthira Pála and Vasanta Pála, in A.D. 1026."[1]

There can be no doubt that great spoliation has been perpetrated on this ruin. Excavations have been carried on to such an extent, that all the central portion of the bricks, originally at the base of the ancient tower,

[1] Cunningham's Archæological Report, pp. 104-7.

has been entirely removed; so that, now, only the bare retaining walls remain, and the cavity looks like a chamber, as I have designated it. Thus it comes to pass, in this instance, that the repeated exploration of an ancient and most singular structure means almost its utter destruction. The wall, or casing, as Major-General Cunningham describes it, is, most certainly, of two eras. The upper portion may be of a comparatively modern date, and may have been added by Sthira Pála and his brother, in the eleventh century A.D.; but the lower portion is much older.

From the narrative of Hiouen Thsang, it is evident, that, formerly, there were many towers at Sárnáth, of which two only are now visible. One of these, the Dhamek tower, has been described. The other is two thousand five hundred feet to the south of it, and was once called Chaukandí, but is now called Lorí-kí-kúdan, or Lorí's Leap, in consequence of a Hindu of the name of Lorí having leaped from its summit, and killed himself. There is a mound of solid brickwork, seventy-four feet in height, on the top of which is an octagonal building, twenty-three feet eight inches high, erected to commemorate the ascent of the mound by the Emperor Humáyún, son of the great Baber, who succeeded to the throne on the death of his father, A.D. 1531. Extensive excavations have been made into the mound, but no relic-chamber has been discovered in it; and it is supposed, therefore, that, unlike the tower erected above the chamber just described, it was not a relic-tower at all. Now, as Hiouen Thsang places a magnificent *Stupa*, about three hundred feet high, at the distance of half a mile or so to the south-west of the monastery, and as this is the distance of the Chaukandí mound from the Dhamek, with its neighbouring monastery, and almost its exact position in regard to the latter, there is exceedingly good ground for the supposition that the two edifices are identical.

Now, it should be remembered, that Sárnáth was famous, amongst the Buddhists, not so much for its religious edifices, solely appropriated to the worship of Buddha, as for its being the spot where Śákya first "turned the wheel of Law." The original building which he frequented may have become decayed in the lapse of time; but it is only natural to suppose, that, as the fame of the Ísipattana hall, or abode of saints, was very great throughout the entire Buddhist world, the utmost care was taken to preserve the original structure as long as it stood, and on its decay, of that erected in its room. It appears to me, therefore, highly probable, that a building, representing the original Ísipattana hall, which Buddha visited on first delivering the Law, was in existence both when Fa Hian and Hiouen Thsang visited Sárnáth.

Other excavations conducted by Major-General Cunningham are of considerable interest. Observing a piece of terraced floor, which he had ordered to be cleared for the purpose of pitching his tent upon it, he found that it terminated on what appeared to be the edge of a small tank, thirteen feet nine inches square. "Continuing the work," he says, "I found the bases of pillars, in pairs, surrounding the square. Amongst the rubbish inside the square, I found an elaborately sculptured bass-relief, in grey sandstone, representing the *Nirváṇa* of Buddha. The stone had been broken into four pieces, of which one was missing; but the remaining three pieces are now in the Calcutta Museum. This sculpture I consider particularly interesting, as the subject is treated in a novel and striking manner. In the ordinary representations of the death-bed scene, the spectators are confined to a few attendants, who hold umbrellas over the body, or reverentially touch the feet. But, in the present sculpture, besides the usual attendants, there are the *Navagraha* or "Nine Planets," in one line, and, in a lower line, the *Ashṭa Śakti*, or "eight female energies," a series of goddesses apparently belonging to one of the later forms of Buddhism.

"Further excavation showed that the small pillared tank, or court-yard, was the centre of a large building, sixty-eight feet square, of which the outer walls were four feet and a half thick. My exploration was not completed to the eastward; as the walls of the building in that direction had been entirely removed by some previous excavation, with the exception of detached portions of the foundation, sufficient to show that it corresponded exactly with the western half of the building. The central square was, apparently, surrounded by an open verandah, which gave access to ranges of five small rooms or cells on each of the four sides of the building. In all the cells I found pieces of charred wood, with nails still sticking in some of them; and, in the middle cell, on the western side, I found a small store of unhusked rice, only partially burnt. In a few places I found what appeared to be pieces of terraced roofing; and, in one place, a large heap of charcoal. On the south side the central room was lost by previous excavations; but on the north side I found a room entirely open towards the verandah, as if it was a hall, or place of general meeting for the resident monks. Inside this room there was the base or pedestal of what I believe to have been a small votive *Stupa*, the top of which probably reached to the roof, and took the place of a pillar. A small drain led under ground from the north-west corner of the central square to the outside of the building on the north, for the purpose, as I conclude, of carrying off the rain-water.

"The building which I have just described would appear to have been a Vihára, or 'Chapel Monastery,' that is, a monastery with a chapel or temple, forming an integral part of the building. From the thickness of the outer wall, I infer that this edifice was not less than three or four stories in height, and that it may have accommodated about fifty monks. The entrance was, probably, on the south side; and I think that there must have been a statue of Buddha in the northern verandah. The bass-relief which I found in the central square almost certainly formed one of the middle architraves of the court.

"Continuing my excavations on the high ground to the westward, I came upon the remains of a building of a totally different description. The walls of the edifice were three feet thick throughout; and I found the plaster still adhering to the inner walls of what I will call the verandahs, with borders of painted flowers,

quite fresh and vivid. The mass of the building consisted of a square of thirty-four feet, with a small porch on each of the four sides. The building was divided into three parts, from west to east; and the central part was again subdivided into three small rooms. I think it probable that these three rooms were the shrines of the Buddhist Triad, Dharmma, Buddha, and Sangha; and that the walls of the two long rooms or verandahs, to the north and south, were covered with statues and bass-reliefs. The entrance verandah of one of the *vihára* caves at Kánheri, in Salsette, is adorned in a similar manner; and, even in the present day, the inner walls of the temples, both in Ladak and in Burmah, are covered with figures of Buddha. This, also, we know from Hiouen Thsang's account, was the style of the walls of the great *vihára* in the Deer Park at this very place; and a similar style of ornamentation prevailed both at Buddha Gayá and at Nálanda. Outside the walls, also, I found a great number—about fifty or sixty—of deeply-carved large stones, which had once formed part of a magnificent frieze, with a bold projecting cornice. The face of the frieze was ornamented with small figures of Buddha, seated, at intervals, in peculiar-shaped niches, which I have traced from the rock-hewn caves of Dhamnár, in Málwa, to the picturesque but fantastic Kyoungs of Burmah. A few of these stones may now be seen in the grounds of the Sanskrit College at Benares. As I found no traces of burnt wood, I am inclined to believe that the roof of the building was pyramidal, and that the general appearance of the edifice must have been strikingly similar to that of the great temple of Brambanan, depicted in the second volume of Raffles's 'Java.'"

I have before observed, that, for the most part, the statues discovered in these ruins were found in two places. One of them was the chamber, above which stood the relic-tower, an account of which has been already given. The other was a small building, ten feet square, which contained about sixty statues and bass-reliefs. Of this curious discovery, Major-General Cunningham, in his report, says:—"I was informed by Sangkar, Rájbhar of Singhpur, the same man who had pointed out to me the position of the relic box in Jagat Singh's *stupa*, that, whilst he was engaged in digging materials for Jagatganj, the workmen had come upon a very large number of statues, all collected together in a small building. The walls were pulled down, and the bricks were carried away; but the statues were left untouched, in their original position. I at once commenced an excavation on the spot pointed out by Sangkar, which was only a few feet to the north of the temple just described. At a depth of two feet below the surface, I found about sixty statues and bass-reliefs, in an upright position, all packed closely together within a small space of less than ten feet square. The walls of the building in which they had been thus deposited had been removed, as stated by Sangkar; but the remains of the foundation showed a small place of only eleven feet square outside. I made a selection of the more perfect figures, which, together with the bass-reliefs, I presented to the Asiatic Society. A sketch of the principal bass-relief, which represents the four great events in the career of S'ákya Muni, has been published as Plate I. of M. Foucaux's translation of the Tibetan history of Buddha. A second bass-relief represents the same four scenes, but on a smaller scale. A third bass-relief, which gives only three scenes, omitting the *Nirváṇa*, has a short inscription below, in two lines, which records the sculpture to have been the gift of Hari Gupta. The characters of this inscription, which are of the later Gupta type, show that this piece of sculpture is certainly as old as the third or fourth century. Some of the seated figures were in excellent preservation, and, more particularly, one of Buddha, the teacher, which was in perfect condition, and coloured of a warm red hue. The remaining statues, upwards of forty in number, together with most of the other carved stones which I had collected, and which I left lying on the ground, were afterwards carted away by the late Mr. Davidson, and thrown into the Barna river, under the bridge, to check the cutting away of the bed between the arches.

"As the room in which I found all these sculptures was only a small detached building, and as it was quite close to the large temple which I have just described, I conclude that the whole of the sculptures must have belonged to the temple, and that they were secreted in the place where I discovered them, during a time of persecution, when the monks were obliged to abandon their monasteries and take refuge in Nepal. This conclusion is partly borne out by the fact, that I found no statues within the walls of the temple itself. To the north of the temple, at a distance of twenty-six feet, my excavations uncovered a large single block of stone, six feet in length, by three feet in height, and the same in thickness. The stone had been carefully squared, and was hollowed out underneath, forming a small chamber, four feet in length, by two feet in breadth, and the same in height. This large stone has, also, disappeared, which is the more to be regretted, as I think it highly probable that it was the celebrated stone, described by Hiouen Thsang, on which Buddha had spread out his *kasháya* to dry, after washing it in the neighbouring tank. Certain marks on the stone appeared to the Buddhists to represent the thread lines of the web of Buddha's cloth, as 'distinctly as if they had been chiselled.' Devout Buddhists offered their homage before the stone daily; but, whenever heretics or wicked men crowded round the stone in a contemptuous manner, then the dragon (*Nága*) of the neighbouring tank let loose upon them a storm of wind and rain."

One of the most curious and interesting relics found at Sárnáth is the *chaitya*, a small vessel made of baked clay, flat below, and ending in a blunt point above. When the bottom is knocked off, a seal-inscription, in a circular form, and, originally, made separately from the vessel itself, is displayed within, exhibiting the celebrated religious formula of the Buddhists, the translation of which has already been given. These words comprise the Buddhist confession of faith, which, it seems, every Buddhist is well aware of, and is able to repeat. "Nothing can be more complete, or more fundamental," remarks Mr. Hodgson, "than this doctrine. It asserts that Buddha hath revealed the causes of (animate) mundane existence, as well as the causes of its complete cessation; implying, by the latter, translation to the eternal quiescence of Nirvṛitti, which is the grand object of all Buddha vows."

Several hundreds of these *chaityas* have been discovered. Mr. Thomas states, that "the entire number of these diminutive prayer-temples seem to have been placed as votive offerings in one and the same position, to the right front of the chief figure of Buddha. Whether, however, this was the appropriate spot, so far removed from the statue, for the deposit of the pilgrims' offering, or whether, when once dedicated at the shrine itself, the officiating priest considered this site of sufficient proximity for absent worshippers' leavings, may be a question; but the little varying uniformity of the character and execution of the legends contained within the *chaityas* would seem to indicate that they were manufactured on the premises, or, at all events, that the ruling hierarchy had a beneficial interest in the trade, and, possibly, went so far as to make the site above indicated a location for sale and delivery, at an opportune pitch of devotional excitement on the part of the confiding votary. Besides the three varieties of inclusive *chaityas*, there were found specimens of a more primitive form, of the same manufacture, in which the entire mould of clay seemed to have been prepared at one and the same operation, and after the external outline had been received. The impression was made by forcing the engraved seal into the soft clay, from the base of the *chaitya*. In this case the inscription remained comparatively unprotected; but the manipulative process was more simple, and, possibly, more assuring to the mass, who were then enabled to see the writing that was to aid their act of worship."[1] A plan was adopted, too, by means of flat clay cakes, on which *chaityas* were represented, offering as many as twenty of these sacred objects at one and the same time.

It has already been observed that the city of Benares was associated with the early history of Buddhism, and was formerly one of the chief seats of that religion, and that it was in Benares that the religion first developed itself, and whence the streams proceeded which, by degrees, flowed over India, Ceylon, Burmah, China, and Tibet. Some of its distinguishing doctrines and principles had, indeed, been cherished in India long before Buddhism, as a historical religion, sprang into existence; but, as a definite and distinctive creed, holding itself aloof from Hinduism, and claiming an individuality of its own, the religion must date from the lifetime of him who gave it historical reality. This is no other than Buddha himself, or Śákya Muni, who, some say, was born in the sixth century before Christ, and died B.C. 477. This wonderful personage was the son of the Raja of Kapila, a small territory, probably in the neighbourhood of Goruckpore, upwards of a hundred miles to the north of Benares. Until his twenty-ninth year, Śákya paid no special attention to religion, but passed his time in the pursuit of pleasure. At this age, however, his habits changed; and, becoming an ascetic, he practised the austere rites which were then

[1] Bengal Asiatic Journal, for 1854, pp. 474, 475.

in vogue. But it was chiefly by meditation that he is said to have gained that mysterious knowledge which he afterwards preached, and the possession of which raised him, as he imagined, to the rank of Deity, and constituted him the visible representation and embodiment of the Supreme. When he was thirty-five years of age, he is said to have become Buddha, on attaining which condition, he proceeded to Benares, and there made himself known in his new character. Here his ministry commenced, which continued for upwards of forty-five years, during which period he visited a multitude of places, and gathered to himself a great number of followers. "At his death," says Major-General Cunningham, "his doctrines had been firmly established; and the divinity of his mission was fully recognized by the eager claims preferred, by kings and rulers, for relics of their divine teacher . . . . In the short space of forty-five years, this wonderful man succeeded in establishing his own peculiar doctrines over the fairest districts of the Ganges—from the Delta to the neighbourhood of Agra and Cawnpore."

Buddhism continued to advance in India, with steady step, until the reign of Aśoka, grandson of Chandra Gupta, in the third century B.C., when, through his conversion, it received a prodigious impulse. Aśoka showed his zeal for Buddhism by erecting, in various places in his dominions, spacious *Vihâras* or temple-monasteries, enormous topes or towers, and massive stone pillars, on which his edicts for the propagation of the faith were inscribed. Similar edicts were, likewise, engraven on rocks in various parts of the country.

In his reign, Buddhist missionaries were sent to distant places in India, and to countries out of India, for the purpose of making converts to Buddhism. Among them was his celebrated son, Mahendra, who, together with his sister, Sangamitrá, had the honour of preaching the Buddhist doctrines to the inhabitants of Ceylon, and of being chief instruments in their conversion. With the era of Aśoka, commenced the palmy days of Buddhism in India, which then became the popular and paramount religion, and continued to remain so for several hundred years. The history of this period is, to a great extent, involved in obscurity; but the evidence that exists, while fragmentary and confused, is decidedly in favour of the general prevalence of the Buddhist, and of the depression and weakness of the Brahmanical, faith. Much, though not all, of this evidence is gathered from coins and inscriptions. Even in the fifth century of our era, when the Chinese pilgrim, Fa Hian, travelled through Northern India, the national religion was Buddhism. "At the time of Fa Hian's visit, Buddhism was the prevailing religion of the Punjab and of Northern India, from Mathurá to the mouth of the Ganges. Between the Punjab and Mathurá,—that is, in Brahmávarta Proper,—the law of Buddha was not held in honour. But this was the original seat and stronghold of the Brahmans and their religion; and its exception, by Fa Hian, is one amongst the many proofs of the pilgrim's accuracy. Everywhere else, Buddhism was honoured and flourishing; the kings were firmly attached to the law, and showed their reverence for the ascetics by taking off their tiaras before them. But at Shachi and at Shewei in Oudh, the heretical Brahmans had attempted to destroy a sacred nettle and some holy topes. The very attempt shows the increasing power of the Brahmans, and their confident hope of ultimate success."[1] In the seventh century, when Hiouen Thsang visited India, Buddhism was losing its influence, and was being supplanted by its powerful rival.

Although Buddhism was in this age declining very sensibly, yet it still retained considerable vigour. The existence of so many sacred monuments at Sárnáth is strong evidence of this; especially as their number seems to have been greatly increased since the visit of the previous traveller, Fa Hian. It is always a work of time for ideas which have been inwoven into the national life of a people to undergo complete expulsion, and for other ideas to be introduced in their room. Religious ideas are, of all ideas, the most tenacious and powerful; and, when once a set of dogmas, no matter how false and erroneous, has taken possession of a nation, those dogmas will never relax their hold of the popular mind, until after a long conflict with ideas which are more cogent than themselves; and, although, through exhaustion, they are compelled to give place to them, they will, as they retire, nevertheless, fight every inch of the way, and continue the contest even when reduced to absolute weakness. Thus, it took several centuries for Buddhism to expire in India. It is possible that the erection of so many sacred edifices at Sárnáth and in its neighbourhood, between the periods of Fa Hian and

[1] Bhilsa Topes, p. 156.

Hiouen Thsang, was an effort not unlike that of a drowning man making desperate struggles to prolong his existence, and actually devising some plan whereby his existence is temporarily prolonged. But, at length, the moment of dissolution arrived. Its adversary, Brahmanism, became too strong for it, and, eventually, crushed it for ever. Its extinction occurred in the eleventh or twelfth century, when, says Major-General Cunningham, "the last votaries of Buddha were expelled from the continent of India. Numbers of images, concealed by the departing monks, are found buried near Sárnáth; and heaps of ashes still lie scattered amidst the ruins, to show that the monasteries were destroyed by fire." And, in a note, he adds: "I wrote this passage from my own knowledge, as I made many excavations around Sárnáth in 1835-36. Major Kittoe has since (1851) most fully confirmed my opinion by his more extended excavations in the same neighbourhood. He writes to me: 'All has been sacked and burned—priests, temples, idols, all together; for, in some places, bones, iron, wood, and stone are found in huge masses: and this has happened more than once.'"[1]

Mr. Thomas gives us further information. "The chambers on the eastern side of the square were found filled in with a strange medley of uncooked food, hastily abandoned on their floors—pottery of every-day life, nodes of brass, produced, apparently, by the melting-down of the cooking vessels in common use. Above these, again, were the remnants of the charred timbers of the roof, with iron nails still remaining

[1] Bhilsa Topes, pp. 166, 167.

in them; above which, again, appeared broken bricks, mixed with earth and rubbish, to the height of the extant wall, some six feet from the original flooring. Every item bore evidence of a complete conflagration; and so intense seems to have been the heat, that, in portions of the wall still standing, the clay, which formed the substitute for lime in building the brick-work, is baked to a similar consistency with the bricks themselves. In short, all existing indications lead to a necessary inference, that the destruction of the building, by whomsoever caused, was effected by fire applied by the hand of an exterminating adversary, rather than by any ordinary accidental conflagration. Had the latter been the cause of the results now observed, it is scarcely to be supposed that so well-peopled a convent, so time-hallowed a shrine, should have been so hastily and completely abandoned."[1] Food, also, was found in several places; and Major Kittoe made the singular discovery of "the remains of ready-made wheaten cakes, in the small recess in the chamber towards the north-east angle of the square." On the floor of a cell, likewise, a "large quantity of rice was found, together with portions of wheat and other grain, part of which was spread out, or, possibly, scattered at the moment of the destructive inroad that was brought to a climax in the conflagration of the monastery." Again, Mr. Thomas says: "In the cells to the eastward were found, among other things, considerable masses of brass, melted up into nodules and irregular lumps, as chance gave them a receptacle amid the general ruin. Here, also,

[1] Bengal Asiatic Journal for 1854, p. 472.

were seen, broken or whole, the pottery vessels of every day requirement; and the iron nails which connected the cross rafters, still fixed in the larger beams that had escaped complete combustion. Among other bits of iron-work, there remained a well-fashioned ring-bolt, that might pass muster at the present day. Of matters of domestic utility, I must not omit to mention a clay *chirágh* or lamp, of the pointed wick-holder description, which, though it has retained its position in that form in other parts of India, is now superseded, in local use, by the ordinary small circular saucers of baked clay." [1]

Thus perished Buddhism in India, where it had reigned, as the dominant religious power, for, at least, seven hundred years, and had exerted an influence of gradually diminishing strength during several hundred years more.

[1] Bengal Asiatic Journal for 1854, p 476.

CHAPTER XIX.

ANCIENT Buddhist Ruins at Bakaríyá Kuṇḍ.—Remains of old Wall.—Carved Stones and Ancient Pillars.—Remains of small Buddhist Temple.—Remains of larger Temple.—Traces of Buddhist Monastery.

A STRICT investigation instituted in places where Buddhism was once famous and powerful would, in most cases, bring to light certain relics which it has left behind. New discoveries of Buddhist remains are continually being made in various parts of Northern India, every instance of which is a fresh illustration of our conviction, that Buddhism has left numerous footprints of itself in all places where it eminently flourished. Seeing that it existed in Benares during many centuries, and was the dominant faith professed there,—casting into the shade the elder creed, and asserting proudly its triumph over it,—it is highly interesting to inquire what Buddhist remains are yet traceable in the city, whereby its historical position, as one of the chief seats of Buddhism, may be tested. Strange to say, until very recently, few or no remains, in the city proper, had been discovered; but the reason of this was, I believe, that they had never been carefully sought after. The extensive ruins at Sárnáth, described in the previous chapter, are, at least, three miles distant from the present city.

Now, while the hope of finding any buildings of the early Buddhist period in Benares might be pronounced too sanguine, yet, on the other hand, he would betray a singular ignorance of the massiveness and durability of Buddhist architecture, who should venture to assert that it was otherwise than exceedingly likely that portions of buildings of the later Buddhist period were still existing, waiting to be discovered. Even as late as the seventh century, A.D., when Hinduism had regained much of its old prestige and influence, there were, as we have already seen, in the city and kingdom of Benares, according to the testimony of Hiouen Thsang, upwards of thirty Buddhist monasteries,—to most or all of which temples were, probably, attached,—and, with them, about three thousand priests and disciples were associated. It cannot be, for an instant, supposed that these monasteries, which were, unquestionably, built of strong material, have all been swept away with the lapse of ages, and have "left not a wreck behind." Several of these were, doubtless, situated at Sárnáth and in its immediate neighbourhood. Indeed, the existence of the Sárnáth ruins, which are, mostly, of the later Buddhist period, is a strong argument for believing that portions, more or less considerable, of some, perhaps of most, of the remaining edifices, are still discoverable. We must not imagine, that, in any instance, they are existing in their original integrity; but, on the contrary, that, where they exist at all, they have been appropriated by Hindus and Mohammedans, and, principally, by the latter, for their own purposes; and that, therefore, they have become blended with other buildings, from which they must be disentangled. The use of numerous pillars in the cloisters of Buddhist monasteries, which were frequently of uniform patterns, greatly aids the identification of the remains of this ancient period.

A careful examination of Benares will reveal those portions of the city which contain buildings, or parts of buildings, or sculptured stones, or other objects, of undeniable antiquity. Such ancient remains are, for the most part, I believe, to be found only in the northern division of the city, and among the narrow streets on its eastern border, running parallel with the Ganges, in a narrow band, as far as the Mán-Mandil Observatory.

Under the conviction that Buddhist remains were to be met with in Benares, I commenced a search for some of them in the course of the year 1863. On the very first day of the search, the ruins at Bakaríyá Kuṇḍ were discovered, which I shall now proceed to describe.

I would here acknowledge my deep obligations to my friend and fellow-labourer, Charles Horne, Esq., C.S., late Judge of Benares, and now Judge of Mynpoory, N.W.P., a gentleman to whom I am greatly indebted for much valuable information in these researches, and with whom I was associated in the preparation of two papers on "Ancient Remains found in Benares," which were presented to the Asiatic Society of Bengal, and published in their Journal, and are now, with a few necessary alterations and corrections, introduced into this volume, forming this and the succeeding chapter.

These ruins are situated at the north-west corner of the city, in the Alipore Mahalla, and are visible from the Ráj Ghát road, leading from the cantonments to the Ganges. The path conducting to the tank, or Kuṇḍ, leaves the main road a short distance to the west of the 420th mile-stone. The tank commonly known as Bakaríyá Kuṇḍ is about three hundred yards distant from this road; and upon the summit of its banks the ruins are, in the main, to be found. In the hot season very little water remains in the Kuṇḍ; but, during the rains, it contains a considerable body of water. It is about five hundred and fifty feet in length, and two hundred and seventy-five in breadth.

On approaching the tank, you pass along the foot of a high mound, on its northern side, on the top of which lie several blocks of stone. Proceeding to the western bank, you perceive a massive breastwork, formed by large stones, bearing upon them various mason-marks,—some of which are similar to those inscribed on the stones at Sárnáth,—and sustaining a solid platform or terrace, which runs by the side of the Kuṇḍ to a great distance. This terrace is twenty feet above the tank, and supports two others of smaller dimensions, one above the other, each of which is girded by a breast-work of huge stones. The lower terrace is one hundred and thirty feet broad, two hundred and seventy feet long on its western face, and three hundred and thirty on its eastern face, overlooking the tank. It was, originally, held up by the wall of heavy stones just referred to; but this wall is, in many places, much broken down, especially towards the Kuṇḍ, the great blocks lying in disorder at its ancient base. Nevertheless, extensive portions are still standing. On the northern face, about seventy feet are visible; while the western wall, which extends two hundred and sixty-seven feet, is almost continuous throughout. The height of the terrace is uniform; but the height of the wall varies greatly, owing partly to its being in a ruinous state, and partly to the circumstance of its forming, in one place, the flank of an old edifice, where it attains a height of at least thirty feet, measured from the ground on the western side, which is on a higher level than the tank. Two small windows or doorways open through this part of the wall; and over each a single stone projects, forming its eaves. The bare appearance which the wall would here have presented to the eye is provided against by a broad moulding half-way down, a foot in width, and by a noble cornice, parallel with it, above.

Ascending the terrace, you come to the building itself, which is occupied by Musalmans, one portion being partitioned off and used as a zenana. The beams and slabs constituting the roof are, in some cases, nine feet in length; and the roof is supported by three rows of immensely thick stone columns, the capitals of which are in the form of a cross. The cornice decorating the walls is not of modern narrowness, but is twelve inches deep, and is ornamented with carvings of various elegant devices. As the building is divided into two distinct sections, and, moreover, as the spaces between the pillars are, in several instances, filled up with a mud wall, it is impossible to gain a correct idea of its original character. The outer wall, on the western side, is strengthened by a huge buttress of stone, fourteen feet wide and fifteen feet high.

With pillars, breastwork, and buttress, of such prodigious strength, it seems not improbable that, formerly, there were several stories above this lower one; but this point is merely conjectural, and is not easy to be decided. Moreover, it is not unlikely that other structures once existed along the border of the terrace, throughout a considerable portion of its extent, not only on its western, but also on its northern and eastern, sides.

Directly in front of the building just described are two other extensive elevations of the ground, or terraces, one over the other, as already stated. The lower elevation is eighty-six feet long by sixty-two and a half feet broad, and about four feet in height. The upper is forty-eight and a half feet by twenty-four feet, and is crowned with an ornamental cornice, which runs, in an unbroken band, throughout a large portion of the circuit of the terrace; but this may, possibly, be of a comparatively modern date, the Mohammedans having selected this spot for a mausoleum, and, in many cases, adopted the prevailing forms of ancient ornamentation. The breastworks of the two terraces, by which the enclosed soil is sustained, although they have been, evidently, at times, extensively repaired, appear as ancient as the neighbouring building.

Beyond the two upper terraces is another raised terrace, which, in all likelihood, was originally connected with one of them; but is now isolated from them. On this, possibly, stood a Buddhist shrine, connected, by a cloister, with a building on the main terrace. A short distance further on, also, are remains of the foundations of what was, probably, another; but the traces of this are almost obliterated.

On the eastern side of the Kuṇḍ is a mound,—two hundred and twenty feet long by ninety feet broad, running parallel with it,—which might be taken for a mud embankment thrown up from the tank, were it not for the circumstance that layers of large Buddhist bricks, lying *in situ*, crop out from its side, and that upon its summit and slopes are numerous blocks of sculptured stones, symbols of bygone glory. One brick measured twenty inches in length; and the bricks of an entire layer were three inches and three quarters in thickness. Among the stones was an enormous segment of a *kalas*, or jagged circular stone found on the pinnacles of temples. The original *kalas*, of which this segment is exactly the fourth part, was not less than nine feet in diameter, and of proportionate thickness, and must have belonged to a temple of superior strength and dimensions. Several small *kalases* are lying not far from this segment. Eight of these were counted at one time. Excavations into the mound would, probably, throw some light on the buildings formerly standing here.

To the east of the mound is a small round structure, called Jogí-bír, on the site of which, we were informed, a devotee buried himself alive. It is made of earth; but on the top is a hollow circular stone, the exterior surface of which is divided into sixteen equal sections, each of which exhibits the sculpture of a man, with one leg turned up, and the hands apparently grasping a garland, which encinctures and connects together all the figures. The stone is in a reversed position. A portion of one similar to it, found at the foot of a tree, was afterwards removed, and forms one of a group of sculptured stones taken from Bakaríyá Kuṇḍ, and photographed. Both these stones were, probably, capitals of highly-enriched columns.

To the south of the tank is a ghát, or broad flight of steps, the stones of which are scattered about in great disorder; so that, looking at it from a distance, it has the appearance of an utter ruin. And such it really is. But it is, nevertheless, a comparatively modern structure; for the stones of which it is composed, judging from the elaborate and finished carvings on many of them, have been contributions from fallen edifices in the neighbourhood.

At the south-west corner of the tank is a water-course, depressed considerably below the ground on either side. It is not improbable that, formerly, this was the main source of water-supply to the tank. To the south of this water-course, overhanging the Kuṇḍ, is a huge breastwork of stone, on the top of which is a spacious courtyard, with a Mohammedan Dargáh, or place of prayer. By reason of the carved stones used in the foundations, the underlying mortar, and the evident frequent repairs, it is difficult to say whether any portion of this breastwork, or of the buttress jutting out at its base, is really ancient, although some portions seem to be so. The buttress is continuous with the stone ghát, and merges into it.

To the east of the Dargáh is a small mosque, thirty-seven feet long by nineteen feet and a half broad, open to the east, and supported by three rows of pillars, five in each row. The pillars in the second row have deep scroll carvings on their sides, with ornamented corners, consisting of lotos seed-pods, one on another. Each pillar is seven feet nine inches high, including the capital; and the latter is two feet six inches in length, and two feet four inches in width. The capitals of the outer pillars are somewhat larger than those of the inner, and are in the form of a cross, the extremities being rounded off; while the upper surface of each limb exhibits a convex curve, the line of which rises higher, in proportion as it recedes from the extremity. The architrave is about a foot in thickness; and on it rests the flat stone roof. Seven niches are placed, at intervals, round the three walls of the room. The entire building is of stone. The western wall, on its outer side, is strengthened by a buttress, at the base of which runs a beautifully carved band, eleven inches broad, which projects a couple of inches from the wall; and below it is a cornice, ten inches in width and seven in depth, bearing on its front a broad band of elegant carving. While the building itself can hardly be regarded as original, there can be no doubt of the antiquity of the pillars,—which belonged, probably, to some Buddhist cloister,—and of the modern character of the walls.

A few steps off is an enclosure, in the form of an irregular parallelogram; a wall being on either side, and two small buildings at its extremities. That situated on the northern extremity is, in some respects, like the mosque just described. Its carvings, however, are not all similar; and its ornamented band is of a very ancient type. There is a small building, used as a *Rauza*, or mausoleum, attached to its north-west angle, and sustained by ancient pillars and modern walls. The building is surmounted by a low cupola, of primitive construction. It is not unlikely, that, originally, there were cloisters on this bank of the Kuṇḍ, and that the three small buildings just described were, all, at one time, connected together.

The edifice at the southern extremity of the enclosure well exemplifies the old Hindu and Buddhist method of making a roof, by the imposition of stone beams, one upon another, cross-wise and corner-wise, until they meet in the middle. The roof of this building exhibits a mass of such beams, piled upon each other, exactly like the roof of a house which children build with their little wooden bricks. A second object of interest here is a cut stone screen, which serves the purpose of a window.

Nearly a hundred and fifty feet to the east of the last-mentioned buildings is another, which has, evidently, been erected from old materials, and is of doubtful antiquity. It has four pillars, two outer and two inner, exclusive of others imbedded in the walls, and has five recesses on its three sides. The carvings have been, to some extent, obliterated by the whitewash with which the mosque is besmeared.

Still further eastwards, at a distance of seventy-five feet, is a terrace, walled round by a stone breast-work, forty-eight feet long by thirty-six feet broad, on which stand four profusely carved columns, supporting an ancient roof, the remains probably of a *Chaitya* or

Buddhist temple, or of its innermost shrine. Its position is exactly opposite the Buddhist temple to the west, still to be described, from which it is distant five hundred and fifty feet. The columns are seven feet seven inches in height, including the base, and are elaborately ornamented; in which respect they differ from the pillars of the other temple, which, in large measure, are destitute of ornamentation. The four sides of the base display an elegant carving of a vase with flowers drooping low over the brim,—a device always found, in these parts, in Buddhist shrine-pillars. The well-known representation of a face with a floreated scroll streaming forth from the mouth, eyes, and moustache, is repeated four times on each column; and above it runs a band of beads, each of which is nearly an inch in diameter. An arc of the sun's disk rests upon this band; and, higher up, the column becomes octagonal. It then becomes quadrilateral again; and on each side is a chaste design, exceedingly well executed, of an overflowing vase. The pillar is crowned with a capital, beneath which is a broad double moulding. The cornice above the architrave is, also, beautifully cut. But the ceiling of this shrine, consisting of overlapping stones, built as before described, is, perhaps, its most striking feature. Each stone is richly carved, and was, originally, coloured; while representations of suns and lotoses are depicted upon them in bold relief. Taking it altogether, this little remnant of antiquity is, as a work of art, a striking proof of the delicacy in taste and expertness in chiselling of the architects of those times, and also of the degeneracy of their successors.

This *Chaitya* seems to have been the eastern extremity of the range of ancient buildings under notice. Leaving it, the boundary line took a southerly direction, and, probably, included several buildings of the same character as those on the northern side; but only very faint traces of their foundations are, at most, visible. The boundary line, however, on its southern side, takes in a remarkable structure, consisting of a massive stone breastwork, one hundred and thirty feet long, ninety feet wide, and five feet four inches high, sustaining a terrace now used as a Mohammedan burial-ground. The breastwork is, in some places, in decay; yet, to a great extent, it is in good condition. Its stones, especially where exposed in the foundations, have mason-marks upon them; and some as many as three symbols in a row. It is surmounted by a cornice, six inches deep. Ascending the terrace, no buildings besides Mohammedan tombs are visible; but it is probable that an extensive Buddhist edifice stood on this spacious area. On the western side, exactly in the centre, is a projecting buttress, originally the Sinhásan or throne of Buddha, round which the moulding also runs. On this spot may have stood a gigantic figure of Buddha, visible to every one entering the court; for such we hold it to have been originally. Indeed, the large terraces which have been described may, all, have been cloistered courts, where disciples and devotees congregated for religious purposes. An inspection of the Atállah and Jama mosques at Jaunpore, formerly Buddhist monasteries, confirms this view.

The most remarkable of these ruins still remains. This

Photographed by D. Tresham, Esq.

ANCIENT BUDDHIST TEMPLE.—BAKARÍYÁ KUṆḌ, BENARES.

is the temple to which reference has been already made. The Mohammedans have appropriated this edifice, and capped it with a dome, and now use it as a mausoleum. It stands on forty-two pillars, all which are in good order, with the exception of one in the southern portico, which has been twisted by the falling of a large tree upon it. Formerly there were, evidently, two pillars more than there are at present, upholding the heavy entablature of the southern portico, so that the whole number of pillars was, originally, forty-four. Of these, thirty-two supported the temple proper, and four the roof of each of the northern, southern, and eastern porticos. To the west there is no portico, but simply a sort of projecting buttress or Sinhásan, on which, probably, the chief idol stood, and was, therefore, at once seen by persons coming in through the main entrance to the east. The northern and southern porticos are fifteen feet long by ten feet wide, while the eastern is only twelve feet by ten. The inner part of the temple is eighteen feet square. Round the whole of the exterior of the temple, above the capitals of the columns, and supported by their external limb, runs an eaves-stone, nearly three feet in width; and, as at the Atállah and Jama Musjids at Jaunpore, this eaves-stone has been made to imitate wood, thus confirming Mr. Fergusson's remarks, where writing about this class of structures.

Each column is eight feet and a quarter in height, of which the quadrilateral shaft between the capital and the plinth is four feet and a half. The capital is in the form of a cross, each limb consisting of two portions; the lower being bell-shaped, with an ornament in the corners. The columns in the temple proper stand two or four together; and the abacus or square stone upon them, between the capital and architrave, is thirteen inches deep, and is beautifully carved. The architrave has a rich double band sculptured upon it, which passes all round the temple, including the porticos. Above this is a flat stone, and, above the stone, a row of niches, which are, probably, of Mohammedan origin.

Viewing the temple from the outside, a practised eye soon distinguishes between the ancient portion and that added by the Mohammedans. Above the portico, all below the octagonal breastwork is, evidently, of Buddhist workmanship, and the remainder, of Mohammedan; but the Mohammedans, there is reason to suppose, availed themselves of old materials. At the termination of the breastwork at each corner rests a small *kalas*, about two-thirds of the circular disk of which is exposed, the remainder being inserted in the wall. Although so many ages have elapsed since this temple was erected, and although it has been exposed alternately to the ruthlessness of Hindu and of Mohammedan fanaticism, yet with such singular skill have its proportions been designed, and its blocks of stone been joined together, —though without cement of any kind,—that, at the present moment, in spite of its aspect of hoary antiquity, it seems almost, if not quite, as durable as on the day on which it was finished; and it is unquestionable that, if it be not barbarously damaged by vandalish hands, it will continue to stand for centuries to come. The simplicity, combined with the great strength, of its parts, and the symmetrical arrangement of the whole, give to the building, notwithstanding the general scantiness of its ornamentation, an appearance which the most fastidious must pronounce to be of no mean order of beauty. A small cloister was, originally, connected with the south-west corner of the temple, as is shown by the continuation of the ancient basement moulding, — a moulding which surrounds, indeed, all Buddhist buildings, in this quarter of India. Here was, probably, the vestry or retiring room of the officiating priests. Some of its walls are still visible.

It is greatly to be regretted that a large portion of the site of these ruins is in a disgustingly filthy state; so that none but the most ardent investigator would care to visit a place so foul and abominable.

In pronouncing upon the originality of any of the buildings which have been described in this chapter, great caution should be shown, especially as they are, all, in the hands of Mohammedans, who have utilized them for various purposes; and these are a race of people, in India, who have ever exhibited a wonderful aptitude for breaking down old Hindu edifices, and employing their materials in the erection of their own religious structures. At the same time, while, doubtless, very extensive transformations have been made in the course of ages, it is not too much to suppose that, in some few instances, portions of old buildings have escaped the general destruction, and still stand as at first erected. At any rate, as there is a vast amount of sculptured stones visible in all directions on this extensive site, whatever opinions may be formed respecting the existing buildings in which they are more or less found, there can be none regarding the antiquity of much of the material of which they are composed. We may fairly suppose that one or more of the monasteries referred to by Hiouen Thsang, together with the temples attached to them,—as in the case of the monasteries at Sárnáth,—were situated here on the banks of the Kuṇḍ. Many of the blocks of stone have one or more letters or symbols inscribed upon them, of which I made a collection of seventy. They are, chiefly, of the Gupta period, which is, therefore, in all likelihood, the date of most of the buildings to which they primarily belonged. When looking upon these remains, we cannot fail to recall the time when the ancient edifices, formerly here, were frequented by crowds of priests, monks, and disciples of the Buddhist faith. Then, probably, the tank was flanked, on three sides, by a lofty terrace of stone, while a spacious ghát, or flight of stairs, was on its southern side. Around the edges of this terrace, both southwards and westwards, ran cloisters; and to the east there must have been massive temples, capable of supporting such caps or *kalases*,—one of them nine feet in diameter,—as have been referred to in this description. It is a matter of much interest to the archæologist, to save from total oblivion these scattered traces of the past, when the Buddhists, who were long since expelled the country, were still famous, if not powerful, and, perhaps, were already engaged in that persistent struggle with the Brahmans which eventually terminated in their own utter extinction in India.

In illustration of these investigations, there were originally submitted to the Bengal Asiatic Society two plans, one representing this entire locality, and the other, the ground-floor of the Buddhist temple; and, besides, six photographic views, all which were appended, as plates, to the paper as it appeared in their Journal. Of these, one, namely, the representation of the Buddhist temple, has been reproduced in this work. It should be borne in mind that the dome is of Mohammedan construction, and that only the lower portion of the building is of Buddhist origin.

CHAPTER XX.

FURTHER Account of Ancient Remains recently discovered in Benares and its vicinity.—Meaning of the epithets 'ancient' and 'old' in relation to Benares.—Ancient Remains, No. I., in Ráj Ghát Fort.—Ancient Remains, No. II., near Ráj Ghát Fort.—Ancient Remains, No. III., Small Mosque in the Budáoṅ Mahalla.—Ancient Mound or Ridge.—Ancient Remains, No. IV., Tiliyá Nálá and Maqdam Sáhib.—Ancient Remains, No. V., Láṭ Bhairo.—Ancient Remains, No. VI., Battís Khambhá. — Ancient Remains, No. VII., Arhai Kangúra Mosque.—Hindu Temple of Kírtti Bisheśwar.—Ancient Remains, No. VIII., Chaukhambhá Mosque.—Ancient Remains, No. IX., Aurungzeb's Mosque, near Bisheśwar Temple.—Ancient Remains, No. X., A'd-Bisheśwar Temple and neighbouring Mosque.—Ancient Remains, No. XI., Stone Pillar standing in Sone ká Táláo.—Note.

FULLY satisfied, as we believe most persons are, that Benares is a city of extreme antiquity, we have endeavoured to ascertain to what portions this epithet will apply. And by the term 'old' is meant, in this chapter, not a few hundred years merely, although a city six or seven hundred years old is generally regarded as an ancient city. But it is necessary to remember that Benares lays claim to an antiquity of several thousands of years; and, undoubtedly, it is referred to in various ancient Hindu and Buddhist writings. Consequently, we are not satisfied with discovering, in it, edifices erected half a dozen centuries ago, any more than we should feel satisfied with discovering edifices of a similar date in Jerusalem, or Damascus, or Rome. The terms 'ancient' and 'old' will, therefore, not be applied here to buildings erected five hundred or even eight hundred years ago, but to those of an anterior period.

That wonderful mass of lofty houses, separated by narrow lanes, and packed together in such wild disorder,—appearing, in fact, like one immense structure of gigantic proportions,—which extends along the banks of the Ganges for more than two miles, having a circumference of at least six, and which is regarded, by all visitors of Benares, with great curiosity, although built, for the most part, of solid stone, and presenting, largely, the aspect of hoary age, has no right to the epithet of 'ancient.' Some of the buildings of which it is composed have been standing fully five hundred years; yet there are very few indeed, if any, that have not been erected since the commencement of the Mohammedan period in India. Nevertheless, speaking generally, this, together with a part of the northern boundary of Benares, is the oldest portion of the present city; while the vast expanse of buildings lying south and west beyond it, and occupying four or five times its area, is, chiefly, of recent date.

The question which we have attempted to investigate is, what is there in Benares more ancient than, say, the epoch of Mahmúd of Ġazní, who invaded India in the year of our Lord 1001? Are there any remains of the preceding Hindu, Jaina, and Buddhist periods? And is there any remnant whatever of the first Hindu period, before the rise of Buddhism,—perhaps in the sixth century B.C.,—or even before that religion became paramount, in the reign of Aśoka, B.C. 250?

When, after diligent search and careful scrutiny, we endeavoured to find proofs of the existence of Benares during these earlier periods, we soon ascertained that they were scanty, and, with a few exceptions, unimposing. The débris of ancient Benares, as was stated at the commencement of this work, may be traced in the multitude of carved stones, portions of capitals, shafts, bases, friezes, architraves, and so forth, inserted into modern buildings in the northern and north-western quarters of the city. These fragments exhibit a great diversity of style, from the severely simple to the exceedingly ornate, and are, in themselves, a sufficient proof of the former existence of buildings of styles of architecture corresponding to themselves, yet differing, in many important respects, from the styles of modern Hindu and Mohammedan structures, and coinciding with those of ancient temples and monasteries of the Gupta and pre-Gupta periods, the ruins of which still exist in various parts of India. Were these the only remains found in Benares, they could not fail to awaken much curious interest in the mind of the antiquarian; and he would, naturally, carry on a process of induction in regard to them, and would say to himself: "Here are the stones; but where are the buildings? What was their form? What their age?" And, with the help of the ruins of other places, he would be able to answer most of these questions satisfactorily, and would, to a large extent, describe the buildings to which the stones at one time belonged, and also determine the epochs of their erection. Our belief is, that the most ancient ruin yet discovered in India exhibits nothing older than some of these Benares stones, now embedded in modern walls and parapets, and scattered about in divers holes and corners of the city.

The fact that such old fragments are found in Benares, conjoined with the circumstance that an exceedingly small number of structural remains of any pretension to high antiquity are traceable in it, goes far to prove that the city has been, not once, but several times, destroyed, until,—except in rare instances, and these chiefly, though not exclusively, consisting of foundations and basement mouldings,—not one stone of the ancient city has been left upon another, and the foundations of its temples and its palaces have been torn up, so that their places are no longer known. Moreover, there is no manner of doubt, that the site of Benares has considerably shifted, and that, at one time, it came quite up to the banks of the river Barná,—which flows into the Ganges on its northern boundary, from which it is now distant nearly half a mile,—and stretched far beyond the opposite bank. Consequently, the Hindu pilgrim, who performs his wearisome journey of perhaps many hundreds of miles, with the object of reaching holy Káśí, and of dying in the city of his fathers, is labouring under a very grave delusion; for the city which he visits has been chiefly erected under Mohammedan rule, and on a spot for the most part different from that which his fathers trod; and the fanes in which he worships are not the spacious temples which his ancestors built, but either the pinched and contracted cage-like structures which Mohammedan emperors grudgingly suffered their idol-loving subjects to erect, or modern imitations of the same.

I shall now proceed to describe such ruins and remains of ancient edifices, whether Hindu or Buddhist, —those at Bakaríyá Kuṇḍ, spoken of in the preceding chapter, excepted,—as we have discovered in Benares and its immediate suburbs.

ANCIENT REMAINS, No. I.

In Ráj Ghát Fort.

These remains are in the interior of the fort at Ráj Ghát, in the outskirts of the city on its northern boundary. There is a small tongue of high land, about fifty feet above the plain below, extending to the junction of the Ganges and the Barná, which, in the mutiny, was strongly fortified, and has been styled, ever since, the Ráj Ghát Fort. There is a belief, amongst the natives, that this spot was selected, ages ago, for a similar object, by the traditional Raja Banár. It is probable that, formerly, the whole of this elevated space was built over, and that the Raja governing the city had his chief residence there. It is the natural key, not only of modern Benares, but also of the country for several miles round; and a well-equipped force in possession of it would with difficulty be approached and dispossessed. The Government has lately abandoned this grand strategical position, on the ground of its alleged unhealthiness.

A short distance to the right of the main road leading into the fort, may be seen the ancient remains which I will now describe, and which, next to the Buddhist temple at Bakaríyá Kuṇḍ, are the most complete, and certainly are the most beautiful, of any yet discovered in Benares. They consist of two cloisters, in a continuous line, each sustained by a quadruple colonnade, but differing both in height and length. The smaller cloister is sixty-six feet long, and the larger eighty-four; and, therefore, the entire façade is exactly one hundred and fifty feet in length, whilst the breadth of both is uniform, and is twenty-five feet. There are eight columns in each row, in the one room, or thirty-two in all; and, in the other, there are ten in each row, or forty in all; so that the number of stone pillars standing in the entire building is seventy-two. Those in the smaller cloister are barely nine feet high, and are all square and of a uniform pattern, a slight difference only being traceable in the capitals, which are of the old cruciform shape. There is not much ornamentation on these pillars; but the chess-board and serrated patterns are abundantly carved upon the architraves. The pillars in the larger cloister, including the capital and base, are ten feet in height; but the architraves above the capitals are of the same height as those in the smaller cloister, namely, one foot. These pillars differ greatly, both in shape and ornamentation, from those just described. Some of them are covered with profuse carving, cut deep into the stone; and, in many instances, it is so sharp and well-defined, as to wear the appearance of having been recently executed. The lotos-plant forms a conspicuous object in many of the designs, all which are striking, whilst some are chaste and elegant. The *chakwa* or Brahmani duck is represented, in divers positions, on the noble scroll-work extending along the square sides of several shafts, from the base to the capital. These scroll bass-reliefs equal some of the carvings on the Sánchi pillars in richness; and the designs are, perhaps, more free in their conception. There were, formerly, human figures, probably of a grotesque form, carved upon some of the pillars, as traces of them are still distinctly discernible; but these figures were defaced, and almost obliterated, by the Mohammedans, on taking possession of the edifice, and appropriating it to their own uses. The pillars are regularly arranged with regard to the Sinhásan or throne of Buddha; and the finest pillars are in the centre of the cloister, in the direction of its depth; and, above them, near the inner wall, the stone ceiling, in two divisions of the roof, is singularly carved, and, strange to say, is of the kind described, by Fergusson, as Jaina architecture. One of them is covered with lotos-blossoms carved in relief.

There is not the smallest doubt that these cloisters have been much altered from their original condition, and that principally by the Mohammedans, who transformed them into a mosque, for which purpose they were employed even as late as the mutiny in 1857, and were regarded with peculiar sanctity by this people. On closely examining the columns, architraves, and ceilings, it is plain, not only that there has been a good deal of shifting of places, but that new pillars, carved in recent times, have been added to the old, some of the old have been cut up for repairs, and their separated portions have been distributed amongst several pillars, and joined to them. The inner massive stone wall running along the entire length of the building is, evidently, unconnected with the original structure; as also is the present stone floor, which is a foot and upwards higher than the old. A trench having been dug on the east side, it was discovered that the bases of many of the columns were embedded deep below the modern stone pavement; while, in the front-part of the smaller cloister, at the depth of about a foot, the outer moulding of the earlier floor could be traced continuously, from one end to the other. Notwithstanding all these extensive alterations which the building has undergone from time to time, at the hands of different masters, we cannot but think that many of the columns are standing on their proper sites, and that the edifice, although greatly changed, is still, in its main features, a Buddhist structure, and formed part of an old Vihára or Temple-monastery. The cloisters were transformed into their present condition, as a mosque, some eighty years ago; and the modern pavement was then laid down.

There is reason to believe that a third cloister, corresponding to the smaller, formerly existed at the southern extremity of the larger one; and this supposition is greatly strengthened by the circumstance of a Sinhásan (already referred to) being still standing by the wall in the centre of the latter, but altered from its original form, having been used, by Mohammedan Mulláhs, as a rostrum or pulpit. The monastery, when complete, was, in all likelihood, a square, each side being, at least, the length of these three cloisters; and the chief Buddha was exactly opposite the centre of the square. What other buildings were formerly here, besides those now visible, can, of course, only be conjectured. It is probable, that, on three sides, there were cloisters; and, on the fourth, namely, that to the east, was a row of temples, the largest containing the principal figure of Buddha. That other buildings were once here is certain from the various sculptured stones found near by. We observed seven pillars, sixteen isolated capitals, and four large carved stones used for architraves, some of which support a recently erected structure attached to the smaller cloister.

The venerable ruins described above present a very remarkable appearance. In the year of the mutiny, barracks for European troops having been erected in their neighbourhood, they were converted into a spacious cooking-room or kitchen. Fires were lighted inside, on the stone floor, from one extremity to the other; and, consequently, the roof, walls, and columns were charred by the heat and blackened by the soot; so that the interior of the edifice is now most dismal and forbidding. Mr. Horne went to the expense of cleaning the building, and removing, as an experiment, the encrusted soot from some of the carvings. Fortunately, the Mohammedans, or the British Government authorities,—we know not which,—in their care for these beautiful works of art, have embedded them in mortar, from base to capital, so that many of them might be restored. The removal of the encrustations, however, will have to be accomplished with the greatest care, or else the surface stone, rendered friable by the heat to which it has been subjected, will come away with the superimposed mortar, thereby destroying the delicate edge of the carvings. We trust the Government will not grudge a few hundred rupees for the thorough cleaning of this interesting specimen of Buddhist architecture. The inner stone wall and the modern pavement should, also, be removed.

Besides these remains, there were, until quite recently, hundreds of stones lying about in the fort, bearing traces of great antiquity. In the mutiny, many of these were collected, and were utilized for the foundations of temporary barracks which were then erected. These stones may once have belonged to the monastery just described, when it existed in its integrity; but they may also have been portions of other contemporaneous buildings situated in its vicinity.

During the mutiny, Mr. Tresham, by Government order, blew up some ancient buildings standing near the monastery; and there are still the foundations of one remaining, which defied all attempts at its destruction. Mr. Horne also remembers a Buddhist temple, which was removed to afford space for barracks.

ANCIENT REMAINS, No. II.

Near Ráj Ghát Fort.

A few hundred yards due north from the old gateway leading to the Ráj Ghát Fort, is a mound, of circumscribed extent, now used as a Mohammedan burial-ground; and on its summit are the ruins of, apparently, an old Buddhist temple. They consist simply of four pillars, richly carved with scroll-work, sustaining an ancient roof. At the corners of the shafts is the ordinary ornamentation, resembling a chain of lotos seed-pods. The capitals are cruciform; and the bases are square, with embellished faces. The ceiling is very beautifully sculptured, and is composed of slabs over-lapping one another, with the centre stone crowning the whole, according to the primitive mode of Indian roof-building. This latter stone exhibits the expanded petals of a lotos-blossom; while eight out of the twelve triangular spaces, formed by the intersection of the slabs, are freely carved with the scroll-pattern. A few sculptured stones lie about the mound: amongst them is an erect figure of Buddha, with garland and armlets, much mutilated. There are, also, three stone beams, or architraves, bearing the chess-board and spear-head patterns. In the small terrace, likewise, on which the ruin stands, are inserted four carved stones, taken, doubtless, from some ancient building formerly in the neighbourhood. The occurence of three or four plain cloister pillars, of the usual form, adapted by the Mussulmans as head-stones for graves, together with the carved architraves already spoken of, would seem to indicate that a small cloister for monastic purposes must, originally, have stood upon this mound, which was then terraced, and that its stones have, by degrees, been removed, both for building Mohammedan graves and for repairs in the fort.

ANCIENT REMAINS, No. III.

Small Mosque in Budáoṅ Mahalla.

In the Budáoṅ Mahalla, near the Ráj Ghát Fort, a short distance south of the high road, there is a small mosque, —in an enclosure,—made up, to a great extent, of old remains. The building seems to have been curtailed from its original dimensions, leaving a ruined portion still standing on its southern side. The entire structure contains seventeen stone pillars, eight of which exhibit ornamental carvings, and, probably, belonged to a Buddhist chaitya or temple. There are, also, eight capitals inserted in the walls, without shafts and bases; and, besides, there are fragments of other capitals in various places. None of these old remains are *in situ*. They were brought, most probably, from some temple in the neighbourhood,—perhaps, indeed, from the mound occupied by the small ruin not far off, referred to in No. II.

Ancient Mound or Ridge running from near the mouth of the Barná into the Adampura Mahalla.

This very remarkable ridge extends for a long distance, and commences at the river Barná when at its flood. In the dry season, therefore, there is a stretch of low land lying between its extremity in that direction and the bed of the stream itself. The ridge is, manifestly, an artificial work, and was originally intended either as a wall to the ancient city, or as a rampart thrown up against it and the neighbouring fort of Ráj Ghát. The latter supposition was that held by Mr. James Prinsep, who imagined that it was cast up by the Mohammedans, in their attack upon Benares, and was specially directed against the fort. This supposition may be true, although it is difficult to perceive how it could have been of much service, whether in an attack on the fort or on the city, especially at a period when artillery was not in use. Had it reached as far as the river Ganges, we could understand how, by severing the fort from the city, it might have been a source of danger to both; but the south-western extremity is not nearer the Ganges than a third of a mile or, perhaps, more. We are inclined to think, however, that this extremity was once connected with that river, but at a time far more distant than the Mohammedan conquest of India. On the whole, it appears not unlikely that this long embankment was the old boundary of the city in this direction, in the early periods of its history, and was, possibly, employed for offensive purposes by the Mohammedans, on the extension of the city to the south and south-west, and the consequent abandonment of this means of defence by the inhabitants. The embankment may have been carried on, originally, to the Ganges, in a straight line with its present direction; or, making a short circuit, it may have entered it by Tiliyá Nálá, on the banks of which are the remains of a Buddhist ruin, which will hereafter be described. In this case, a portion of it must have been thrown down, and swept away, to make room for the growth of the city; and there is good ground for supposing that the city extended, in a narrow band, on the banks of the Ganges, about as far as the Mán-Mandil Observatory, even, perhaps, before the Christian era. Should this idea be correct, it would follow that the most ancient site of the city of Benares was comprised within the limits of this wall, stretching across from the Barná to the Ganges, marking off a tongue of land as far as the confluence of the two rivers, and including the high land of the Ráj Ghát Fort, which was, in all probability, once covered with houses. The city must then have been of small compass, as compared with its existing dimensions, unless, as we believe, and as is indisputably certain, it crossed over to the right bank of the Barná.

That both sides of the river Barná were, in former days, better inhabited than at present, is somewhat substantiated by an examination of the ground on either side. Brick débris lies scattered about among the fields on the right bank of this stream; and old coins and broken stone images are, occasionally, found by the people, or are turned up by the plough; while, on the other or Benares side, old remains occur in the fort; and, likewise, below it, on the low land already referred to, blocks of stone, some of which are carved and exhibit ancient mason-marks engraved upon them, are still to be seen. Moreover, it is stated, in the Ceylon Annals, that, formerly, the city surrounding Sárnáth was continuous with, or a part of, Benares; which, if true, must have been at a period of remote antiquity. Indeed, these records carry us back to an epoch anterior to that of the historical Buddha, or Śákya Muni, and, therefore, perhaps, prior to the sixth century B.C. Their statements must, of course, be received cautiously, and not as unadulterated authentic history. At the same time it is certain that there was a tradition amongst the Buddhists of India, conveyed thence by their missionaries to Ceylon, that, in remote ages, the city of Benares extended to Sárnáth.

In visiting this ridge, or embankment, it will be observed that the high road leading to Ráj Ghát cuts right through it; the earth of the cutting being used to raise the road above the level of the country. It is well to remark, too, that, where the road passes below the fort to the ghát, the soil has been cut away, to make room for it; so that, formerly, we may suppose, that, instead of a steep and almost precipitous wall, which the elevated land to the east of the road now exhibits, the mound of the fort, in this direction, diminished in a gradual slope, terminating, perhaps, not far from Tiliyá Nálá.

The ridge is, in one part, formed of three terraces, the uppermost being, perhaps, thirty feet above the land; upon which elevated spot is the tomb of Mírá Sáhib. In the mutiny, a large portion of the mound opposite the fort was cut away, for strategical reasons; although what is left is sufficient to prove of great service to an enemy attacking the fort.

On the south side of the ridge, in sight of Mírá Sáhib's tomb, is an Imámbára, a modern edifice, built altogether of new materials; and a few paces distant from it are two small structures, one in front of the other, which, although of recent erection, are partly composed of old materials. Each building possesses four ancient pillars of the Buddhist type; and, lying about in various places, are four pillars more, five *kalases*, two architraves, and seven bases,—one of the last being extensively carved. All these are the spoils of some ancient temple or monastery.

ANCIENT REMAINS, No. IV.

Tiliyá Nálá and Maqdam Sáhib.

We have chosen to combine these remains, and to speak of them under one head, because, although separated, and standing in different Mahallas or wards, they are near enough together to suggest the supposition, that they may have been, at one time, connected. There is, to my mind, no question that, formerly, either a Buddhist temple or monastery stood in this neighbourhood, which is very rich in old carved fragments of stone scattered about amongst the walls and foundations of dwelling-houses, and in divers other places. The ruins at Tiliyá Nálá, now forming part of a deserted mosque, were, originally, so far as I can judge, a portion of a temple; yet, seeing that the remains at Maqdam Sáhib are only a short distance off, and that sculptured stones lie everywhere about, there is some ground for the supposition, that a *Vihára* or temple-monastery was situated in this district, and that the existing remains, for the most part, belonged to it.

The ruins at Tiliyá Nálá are immediately above the *nálá* or stream, on the high ground of its left bank, a very short distance only from the point where it runs into the Ganges, and close to the main street under which the stream flows. They not only overhang the *nálá*, but there is no doubt that, at one time, they must have extended nearly, if not entirely, across its present bed. They consist of seventeen massive square columns, in three rows; namely, four double columns in the front row, four single ones in the second, and five in the third or innermost row. Between the third and fourth pillars of the last row is the Sinhásan or throne of Buddha, an immense slab of stone, nine feet three inches in length, and five feet and a half in breadth, retreating beyond the boundary-wall behind, into which all the pillars of this row are inserted. There can be no dispute that the Sinhásan was in the centre of the building; that is to say, that, as there are three pillars to the right of it, there were as many to the left, in each of the three rows, the front row being of double pillars throughout. Reconstructing the edifice as it originally stood, there were, therefore, one row of six double pillars, and two rows of six single pillars, or twenty-four pillars in all. Each capital is ornamented with the bell-pendant, to which the Buddhists were so conspicuously partial, and which was, after them, much used by the Brahmans. The double columns are surmounted by one huge capital, five feet and a half in breadth; and each capital possesses a long arm for the eaves-stone. Over the two inner rows are two domes, one of which is above the Sinhásan, and is more ornamented than the other. There must have been, originally, a third dome, to the left of the central dome, corresponding to that on the right. Outside the building there is a fine basement-moulding, which doubtless belonged to it, before it was seized and appropriated by the Mohammedans. Estimating the building as it once stood, it was quite fifty-four feet in length, and about twenty-four feet in breadth. The Mussulmans may have altered the primitive structure very considerably, in transforming it into a mosque. Some of the large stones have fallen into the *nálá* and upon its banks; and others have, probably, been used in the repairs of the bridge and of its adjoining stone wall; so that, we believe, it would not be a difficult task to find nearly all the missing pillars and capitals.

The Maqdam Sáhib is a square enclosure, in the

Gulzár Mahalla, near to Tiliyá Nálá, used by the Mohammedans as a cemetery. On its northern and western sides are cloistered pillars, with portions of ancient stone eaves overhanging their capitals, presenting, on their upper surface, imitations of wood-carving. There are twenty-five pillars on the western side, and twenty-eight, or, if all could be seen, probably thirty-two, on the northern side. Several of the pillars are carved, while some of the capitals are ornamented, and some are double. There may be seen, also, handsomely carved stone brackets, for the support of the eaves above spoken of. The eastern wall bounding the enclosure is, evidently, composed, to some extent, of cut stones of an ancient date. The entire court is one hundred feet long from east to west, and sixty feet broad from north to south.

ANCIENT REMAINS, No. V.

Láṭ Bhairo.

At the junction of the Ghazeepore road with the Ráj Ghát road, to the north of the latter, and about a short mile from the fort, is a large square tank, on the left bank of which, as on a terrace, stands the *láṭ*, or pillar, of which some mention has been made in a previous chapter. It is only a few feet high; and it is covered with copper sheeting. We endeavoured to prevail on the faqír residing here to permit us to lift up the copper cap, by removing the plaster which connects it with the flooring below, in order to gain a view of the stone pillar which it now conceals; but so great is the reputed sanctity of this object, that our efforts were entirely fruitless; and, had we persisted in them, a disturbance might have been occasioned. The original stone column, of which the concealed pillar is, doubtless, a small fragment, was about forty feet high, and, it is reported, was covered with ancient carvings, which were, most probably, inscriptions. It was stated, before, that this was thrown down by the Mohammedans, during a terrible conflict with the Hindu population, in the early part of the present century. The natives say, that the pillar was thrown into the Ganges; but, as that stream is half a mile off, or more, this must have been done piecemeal. In all likelihood, it was destroyed by fire, the action of which on sandstone soon causes it to crumble to pieces. As there is strong reason for believing that this was one of Aśoka's pillars, it would be exceedingly interesting to inspect the remaining fragment, which we may reasonably suppose to belong to the original column, and, in that case, to possess a portion of an inscription sufficient to certify its connexion with Aśoka, or with the Guptas, or with some other monarch by whom the column was erected.

It is important, in our present investigation, to know that the pillar once stood in proximity to a temple, or in its courtyard: the temple was destroyed by Aurungzeb; and, on its site, a mosque was erected, the courtyard of which enclosed the pillar. On examining the terraces where the *láṭ* stands, we see, quite distinctly, that the upper portion has been thrown up in modern times, and that the ancient level of the ground was some six or eight feet lower than what it now is, and, indeed, was flush with the soil of the Mohammedan cemetery close by, in the midst of which are a few Buddhist remains, in the shape of pillars and architraves, made up into a Mohammedan sepulchre. What this so-called temple was, admits of very little question, inasmuch as the boundary-walls of the terrace and of the neighbouring cemetery and garden exhibit a considerable variety of isolated carved remains, sufficient to afford abundant attestation to the supposition, that, formerly, a large structure stood on this site, covering, probably, the whole extent of the ground above the tank on its northern side. Some of the carvings are in excellent preservation, and are worthy of being removed to the archæological collection in the Government College grounds at Benares. There are several pillars embedded in the brickwork; and, also, a stone, seven feet in length, and one and a half in depth, which is deserving of special remark, as from its face project four magnificent bosses, each ten inches in diameter, with an elevation of two inches from the surface of the stone. These bosses must have formed part of the decoration over the main entrance.

Below the upper terrace on which the *láṭ* stands, is, as already observed, a Mohammedan cemetery, with a *Rauza*, or tomb, in the middle. This building rests upon sixteen pillars, each eight feet two inches in height, and having architraves, between their capitals, one foot two inches in thickness. Moreover, there are five pillars in the verandah to the south. Some of the pillars are ornamented with scroll-work and the lotos-plant, while their four corners are deeply indented with representations of the lotos seed-pod. One pillar has eight sides in its lowest division, and sixteen in its upper; and has, also, a band of four grinning faces connected together, and, under them, a row of beaded garlands. The pillar is crowned with a round stone, projecting two inches. A curious assemblage of thirty-two grotesque faces, with beaded garlands and tassels issuing from their mouths, runs round the edge of the stone.

It should be mentioned, that, if our conjecture, that the upper terrace has been only recently thrown up, be correct, then, on the supposition that the fragmentary pillar on its summit is part of the original pillar, which, in ancient times, stood here, it would follow that the length of the existing fragment is equal to the depth of the terrace above the foundations of the neighbouring cemetery, in addition to its elevation above the terrace, and to the extent of insertion of its lower extremity in the primitive, but now subjacent soil. In this case, it would be not less than from fourteen to sixteen feet in length.

ANCIENT REMAINS, No. VI.

Battís Khambhá.

About a third of a mile to the east of the Bakaríyá Kuṇḍ remains is a beautiful little structure, called, by the natives, Battís Khambhá, or "thirty-two pillars." It is a very picturesque object, as seen from the Ráj Ghát road, from which it is some four hundred yards distant. It consists of a dome, sustained by twenty-four square pillars, standing in pairs, at intervals, all round.

Formerly, each corner had four pillars, thus increasing the present number by eight; and then, of course, the entire number was thirty-two: but two from each corner have been removed, leaving the spaces occupied by them empty. All the upper part of the building is Mohammedan, while all the lower part is, indisputably, Buddhist, in its style of architecture. On the western side is a projection for the Sinhásan of Buddha, similar to that which is seen in the temple at Bakaríyá Kuṇḍ, and, indeed, so far as our knowledge extends, in all genuine Buddhist temples. The pillars stand upon a platform raised above the ground. The interior of the building is a Mohammedan tomb.

It is remarkable that there should be so many ancient remains lying almost in a straight line from Bakaríyá Kuṇḍ to the Ráj Ghát fort; for most of the remains hitherto referred to lie in this line. I have no doubt that formerly a large number of Buddhist buildings stood between these two boundaries; and that the foundations of some of them might be discovered, in addition to the more prominent remains already brought to notice, if a keen search were instituted. It seems evident, therefore, that there was a road here during the Buddhist period, not far distant from the line of the present one. This road was at right angles to another, proceeding from Bakaríyá Kuṇḍ in the direction of Sárnáth, which still exists. Search might be made along this road, for the foundations of ancient buildings and Buddhist relics; as there can be no doubt that constant communication was kept up by the monks of Sárnáth with Bakaríyá Kuṇḍ, in both which places there were vast monastic edifices and numerous temples.

Near this ruin, and between it and Bakaríyá Kuṇḍ, is a small building, standing by the road side, in which several pillars of an ancient type are inserted into the containing walls. They were, very probably, brought from Bakaríyá Kuṇḍ. The building has an unpretending appearance, and is kept whitewashed by the Mohammedans, its proprietors.

ANCIENT REMAINS, No. VII.

Aṛhái Kangúra Mosque.

It is not our purpose thoroughly to describe this handsome structure, one of the finest mosques in the whole city, and which is situated in the Mahalla bearing its own name. Its magnificent and lofty dome, as well as various parts of the mosque itself, unquestionably exhibit a Mohammedan style of architecture; but we have no hesitation in saying that by far the greater portion of the building, and certainly five-sixths of its materials, belong to an epoch far more distant than the Mohammedan invasion. The numerous square columns, with their cruciform capitals, and also the screens between some of them in the upper story, are of Buddhist workmanship; but we are inclined to think that both Buddhists and Hindus have made use of the same materials in different eras, and that, in fact, the mosque is a mixture of three styles, namely, Buddhist, Hindu, and Mohammedan. The first edifice was, we believe, a monastery, with, most probably, one or more temples attached; but it is hard to say whether any portion of the original building stands *in situ;* and we have not sufficiently examined it to be able to arrive at a decided opinion on this point. Our conviction, however, is, that certain leading characteristics of the first structure were perpetuated, by the Hindus, in that which they raised on the departure, or rather expulsion, of the Buddhists from Benares. It is not easy to determine accurately what this Hindu building was; but, perhaps, it is more likely to have been a *maṭh*, — that is, a monastery or religious house for Hindu ascetics, such as one sees in many parts of the land at the present day,— than a temple. In the roof of the second story of the mosque, a slab was discovered, bearing a long Sanskrit inscription, towards the end of which is the date 1248, which, regarded as Samvat, is equivalent to A.D. 1191. The inscription itself is of no particular importance, except that it abounds with references to the Hindu religion, and shows that it belonged to a building erected by a Hindu, and to a time subsequent to the Buddhist period. It alludes, also, to certain tanks, temples, and *maṭhs*, erected and embellished in and about Benares, which, of course, were all in honour of Hinduism. It is not unlikely, indeed, that these structures were erected, and that this inscription was written, with somewhat of a religio-political object, to testify to the triumph which Hinduism had then recently gained over Buddhism; for there is good ground for believing that the buildings at Sárnáth were not burnt, and that the monks were not expelled therefrom, till about the twelfth century of our era,—that is, about the period here referred to. We have obtained a copy of the inscription in Sanskrit, with a translation in Hindí, through the kindness of Babu S'iva Prasád, Joint Inspector of Schools, whose intelligence, enterprise, and extensive knowledge place him in the front rank of native gentlemen in these provinces.

We would direct especial attention to the small side-door or postern, with its massive wall, to the right of the building, which has a striking air of originality; and also to two noble capitals, of gigantic dimensions, lying in the court-yard in front of the mosque, and now converted into small cisterns, which are the largest carved capitals we have found anywhere.

HINDU TEMPLE OF KÍRTTI BISHES'WAR.

A'lamgirí Mosque.

Near the temple of Bṛiddhkál,—one of the very few Hindu temples of the earlier Mohammedan period, still standing in Benares, not appropriated by the Musulmans,—and a few paces from the well-known shrine of Ratneśwar, is a mosque, spoken of, in the neighbourhood, as the A'lamgírí Masjid, which was erected during the reign of Aurungzeb, or A'lamgír, and was designated after that Emperor. Upon it may be read the following inscription, in Arabic:—

فول و جهک شطر المسجد الحرام

سنه ۱۰۷۷ هجري

The translation of which is: "Turn your face towards the sacred mosque. 1077 Higira," or A.D. 1659.

The mosque is built, tradition states, from the materials of the Hindu temple of Kírtti Bisheśwar, and has three rows of lofty stone pillars, eight in each row; but the pillars at the extremities are not single, but three-fold. The capitals are large and massive, and are cruciform in shape. In the centre of each shaft, upon all the four sides, is the boss ornamentation, each boss being fully a foot in diameter. The pillars have a double base, a false and a true; the one consisting of the lower end of the shaft, the other, the true base, of a separate stone. Both are covered with carvings. Some of the architraves also bear upon them the boss pattern; but it is possible that these were, formerly, shafts of pillars. The inner wall of the mosque is, likewise, of stone. Viewed from behind, many of the blocks display various mason-marks inscribed upon them.

From an examination of the marks or symbols, and of the architecture represented by the remains now briefly described, there is no reason for supposing that the temple which once stood here, and which was levelled to the ground by Aurungzeb, was of great antiquity. We should be inclined to fix the date of the Hindu temple at some five or six centuries ago. It must have been a place of great sanctity; as many Hindus still visit the spot on pilgrimage, and, instead of an image,—which, we suppose, the Mohammedans would not allow them to put up,—worship the spout of a fountain, rising up in the centre of a small tank in the court-yard of the mosque. It is not improbable that the tank is the site of the old temple; but, if the temple was a large one, as is likely, it must have occupied not only a considerable portion of the present courtyard, but also some extent of ground on either side. A few persons perform their devotions in the tank daily; but the grand festival is at the *Śivarátri melá*, for one day in March, when crowds throng reverently around the sacred spout, and present *it*,—or, perhaps, regarding it as a god, they would say *him*, or *her*,—with abundant offerings; all which, down to the last rupee, are received by the Mulláh of the mosque, who thinks, we suppose, that, if he connives at the idolatry,—which, in fact, he cannot put down,—he may as well be handsomely paid for it.

In noticing the remains of the Kírtti Bisheśwar temple, we are aware that they do not come under the designation of 'old' or 'ancient,' as applied to other remains described in this chapter; and yet, as they are not without interest, we have given them a place in it.

ANCIENT REMAINS, No. VIII.

Chaukhambhá Mosque.

The long Chaukhambhá street in the city of Benares, in or near which most of the great bankers have their places of business, takes its name from four low massive pillars, of modern erection, towards its north-eastern extremity, standing in the lowermost story of a lofty building, the weight of which they entirely sustain. There is a narrow court running out of this street, terminating in a small enclosure, on the further side of which is a mosque. The entire enclosure has a very remarkable appearance, and, for the archæologist, is a place of considerable interest. The entrance is by a doorway let into a breastwork or wall formed of blocks of stone. The wall is twenty feet long, thirteen feet high, and four feet thick, and is constructed, for the most part, systematically, as is evident from the ornamentation on one stone answering to that on the stone contiguous to it. Over the doorway is an inscription, in Arabic. But, with the exception of this doorway and the castellated structure crowning the wall, there is nothing Mohammedan in its architecture.

The mosque and corridor adjoining are supported by twenty-four pillars, of which six are double. The capitals are of the simple cruciform pattern; and their outer limbs are decorated with the dwarf bell-ornamentation. To the south of this building is a staircase leading up to the roof, built of heavy stones; and along the south side of the enclosure, for about twenty-five feet, is a low stone wall, six feet in height; and, attached to it, is a peculiar ledge, three feet from the ground. It is known that a similar wall exists on the north side, also; but it is hidden from view.

Most of the pillars, probably, once formed part of an ancient edifice; but of what character, it is difficult to say. The whole of the old materials may have been brought from other places; and yet there is a peculiarity about the position of some of them, which leads us to conjecture that the original building from which they were taken stood on this spot; but, if so, it is likely that it occupied a much larger space. The wall, with the projecting bench, is very curious. The latter may have been used by priests or monks to recline upon.

ANCIENT REMAINS, No. IX.

Aurungzeb's Mosque, near Bisheśwar Temple.

The mosque built by the Emperor Aurungzeb on the foundations of what is commonly, though erroneously, regarded as the old or original Bisheśwar temple, is of interest, not for its own sake,—for, notwithstanding its lofty appearance, it is a structure without any striking beauty in its own right,—but on account of the ancient remains with which it is associated and from the materials of which it has largely been constructed. The courtyard consists of a terrace, raised some five feet above the level of the temple-quadrangle in the centre of which it is situated, occupying a large portion of the area. On walking round the quadrangle, and examining the retaining wall of the terrace, one's attention is arrested by peculiar openings, or niches, in the wall; and, in these, architraves, and capitals, and parts of pillars on which they rest are visible; though, in some places, the openings are filled with earth, almost up to the level of the capitals. Proceeding from west to east, the ground gradually declines; until, after descending four steps, and arriving opposite a large stone bull, or Nandi, the opening in the terrace becomes clear, and a portion of a cloister, such as surrounded a Buddhist monastery, comes into view, and reveals the character of the entire series. The cloister is now divided into a number of small chambers, supported by genuine Buddhist pillars, severely simple in their type, and, without doubt, of considerable antiquity. Formerly, a succession of such cloisters encompassed not less than three sides of the existing terrace, which must, consequently, date from the same epoch. It would be desirable, if the consent of the Mohammedans could be obtained, to remove the external wall, by which these cloisters have become almost completely hidden, in order to ascertain their extent and condition.

This series of cloisters formed, we conjecture, the lowermost story of a *Vihára* or Temple-Monastery which once enclosed the entire space occupied by the terrace, and rose to the height of, probably, two or three storeys above it. On the southern side stood the chief temple, which, on the suppression of Buddhism, passed into the hands of the adherents of another religion, who transformed it according to their own tastes. The mosque on this side is altogether composed of the remains of an ancient temple, of large dimensions and of very elaborate workmanship. The high pillars, moreover, on its northern face have been transferred from the same spacious building. These remains are, chiefly, Hindu; and it is unquestionable that the edifice, which was destroyed in order to make way for the mosque, was an old temple of Bisheśwar. An excellent ground-plan of this temple, prepared from a minute examination of the extant remains, was drawn by Mr. James Prinsep, and published, by him, in his "Views of Benares." The remains are, however, not entirely Hindu. Some portions, judging from the elaborate ornamentation of certain details which it was the custom of the Buddhist architects to leave plain, seem to be of Jaina origin, and to have been appropriated by the builders of the Hindu temple. If this supposition be correct, the mosque, with its terrace, exhibits a singular architectural anomaly; and, furthermore, points to no fewer than four religious communities, namely, Buddhist, Jaina, Hindu, and Mohammedan. The square terrace pillars, with their cruciform capitals, are so simple in structure, that, compared with the highly carved and decorated pillars of mediæval and later Buddhist times, they almost belong to another style, which might be called early Buddhist or Hindu, accordingly as one or other of these communities is supposed to have invented it. It is not our object to discuss the interesting and important topic, who were the first Indian sculptors and builders of permanent edifices; yet it is one that, by and by,—when materials have been sufficiently accumulated, which they have not been at present,—must be thoroughly investigated. After such investigation, the antiquity and, possibly, the origin of these terrace-pillars may be definitely ascertained.

ANCIENT REMAINS, No. X.

Ád-Bisheśwar Temple and neighbouring Mosque.

Ád-Bisheśwar is the name of a lofty temple situated a short distance from Aurungzeb's mosque just referred to, and in sight of it; and it is held, by some persons, to be the most ancient temple of this deity. Only a doubtful interpretation of its name may bear out this supposition; for the temple itself, from the pinnacle to the base, has nothing really ancient about it. On the eastern side of the enclosure, the ground takes a sudden rise of eighteen feet, forming a terrace manifestly of artificial construction. On this side there is a retaining wall of stone masonry, which is wanting on the southern side of the terrace, where there is only an earth bank. The other two sides of the terrace are covered with buildings, so as to prevent the exact determination of its boundary in these directions. On the flank contiguous to the A'd-Bisheśwar enclosure stands a mosque, erected some eighty years ago or less, but not finished, for want of money. It was built of stones found on the spot, with new Chunar slabs added. The terrace existed before, with the buttress, and is, evidently, of ancient construction.

The building is in two divisions,—each of which is twenty-three feet and a half in length,—connected together by a massive wall, five feet and a half thick, composed of large blocks of stone. This wall projects considerably beyond the building into the courtyard to the east, and has the appearance of a huge buttress; but what its object is,—seeing that the mosque, which is entirely of stone, is amply sustained by its columns and walls, and requires no such additional support,—it is hard to say. Possibly, the buttress is pierced with a staircase, that led, formerly, to an upper story which the buttress supported; and the Mohammedan architects, not caring to remove the massive prop, have retained it in the mosque. They appear, moreover, to have confined themselves chiefly to materials lying upon the spot; as, in three places, carved pillars, similar to those sustaining the centre aisle, have been adopted as architraves. There are fourteen columns in the interior of the mosque, which are peculiarly, but not extensively, carved, and are crowned with ornamented capitals. The western wall is strengthened, externally, by three rounded buttresses, which are of the Paṭhán dynasty, like those found at Jaunpore, and were built at the same period. They did not exist in the Buddhist period, and were added as much for ornament as for strength. All the mosques about old Delhi have them.

There is no doubt, in our mind, that the A'd-Bisheśwar temple stood on this site, and was destroyed by the Mohammedans, who, as usual, transferred its stones to their own mosque. The neighbouring temple bearing this name the Hindus built, with the connivance of their friends, the Mohammedans, of course for the purpose of perpetuating the worship of their old idol, A'd-Bisheśwar. Yet, while allowing that the edifice which stood on the site of the present mosque when the Mohammedans took possession of it was the temple of A'd-Bisheśwar, we are, nevertheless, equally certain, that the primitive building was of a Buddhist character. We were inclined, at one time, to imagine, that, from its proximity to the Buddhist *Vihára* (No. X.) just described, it must have been a part of that monastery; but two reasons have led us to abandon this idea. One is, that a separate terrace, of extensive dimensions, was appropriated to this structure, whatever it was, and that, between this terrace and that of No. X., the ground is depressed, corresponding to the depression of all the neighbouring soil; and the second is, that the styles of architecture of the ancient buildings, upon or around the two terraces, differ exceedingly. We are led to conjecture, therefore, that the original structure was Buddhist, but later, in date, by several hundred years than the *vihára* erected on the terrace opposite. It was, probably, a quadrangle, encompassing the four sides of the terrace. Nothing remains of it, except the massive transverse wall, with the buttress, and the lower portion of the retaining wall. The amount of stone material expended on the present comparatively small building is exorbitantly great, and furnishes a proof that an edifice of much larger dimensions formerly stood here.

ANCIENT REMAINS, No. XI.

Stone Pillar.—Sone ká Táláo.

Before closing this chapter, we would direct attention to a stone pillar, standing in the midst of a tank between the city of Benares and the Buddhist remains at Sárnáth. The tank is called Sone ká Táláo, or the Golden Tank, and is situated on the opposite side of the river Barná, near the road which branches off from the high road leading to Ghazeepore, and not far from the point of its junction with several other roads. The road is a portion of the Panchkosí, or sacred boundary of Benares. Proceeding along it for somewhat less than a mile, you arrive at the tank, which is to the right of it, and is approached by a strong and well-built ghát, on which are several Buddhist figures, brought, most probably, from Sárnáth. It is three hundred yards in length, and one hundred and forty in breadth. In the midst of it is a round pillar, eighteen feet high, and upwards of nine in circumference, composed of great blocks of stone, cut in quadrants, and put together without cement or mortar. There is no inscription on the pillar, and there are no mason-marks; so that we have been unable to assign any date, even approximately, to its erection. Its base is always, we believe, surrounded by water; yet it would be worth while to ascertain whether any inscription exists below. We probed it to its foundations, but found no face for an inscription. It is likely that the pillar has somewhat sunk, and that, formerly, the tank was less choked with mud than it is now. In appearance, therefore, the pillar was once higher than at the present time. It was, probably, surmounted, formerly, by a lion, or some other figure; and, on close examination, it is seen to bear marks of great age.

It is necessary to state that the ancient remains which have been thus described are, for the most part, unimposing in appearance. They are, however, none the less interesting on that account. Seeing that Benares is a city of undoubted antiquity, and has ever been famous throughout the long period of Hindu history, it is, perhaps, strange that it does not possess remains of buildings that existed in past ages, of a more striking character. And yet the very fact of the fragmentary nature of its ancient relics may be a strong corroborative proof of its great antiquity; especially when it is remembered that it has been the home of a large population, and the constant resort of pilgrims from all parts of the country, for thousands of years; that it has always taken a prominent part in the religious and political struggles which have visited the land; and that, consequently, it has been exposed, beyond most cities, to the wear and tear of time. I have regarded it as a matter of interest, if not of importance, to explore these remains, and to give a succinct account of some of them. Opinions may differ as to their date, origin, and interpretation; but no one, I imagine, cherishing any love for the past, will despise such research, or will characterize as vain and uninstructive the effort that has now been made to throw some light, however dim, on the outer aspects of ancient Benares. The conclusions to which we have come may be challenged; but the labour itself,—and it has been by no means slight, although the results of it are compressed into a small space,—will, I trust, be regarded with approval. If our conjectures be right, we have been able to trace out, in Benares, remains connected with several Buddhist monasteries and temples, and, also, the sites on which they stood. We cannot, indeed, actually assert that these remains belonged to any of the thirty monasteries which Hiouen Thsang affirms to have existed in the kingdom of Benares in his day; and yet there is a strong probability that the sites, if not the ruins and scattered remains, of some of them have been indicated in the foregoing pages.

In conclusion, we may remark that we are much inclined to believe that many of the ancient Buddhist monasteries and temples were on a line of road leading from Bakaríyá Kuṇḍ to the Ráj Ghát Fort, in one direction; on a second line, at right angles to this, running from Bakaríyá Kuṇḍ to Sárnáth; and, on a third, proceeding from the site of Aurungzeb's mosque, and joining one of the others, or both, possibly, at Bakaríyá Kuṇḍ; and that, hereabouts, other remains of such buildings, if found at all, will, mostly, be discovered.

Note.

Since the above was written, I have visited and examined the lands lying on the banks of the Ganges to the north-east of the river Barná. To my utter astonishment, though, I must confess, not contrary to my anticipation, I found brick and stone debris scattered over the fields for, as far as I could conjecture, five miles or thereabouts. In many places, the rubbish lies thick upon the ground, choking up the soil; and, to a large extent, the deposit can be traced continuously. Here and there small bits of sculptured stone are visible; and, occasionally, where the broken bricks and stones are in very great abundance, they have been collected into ridges or small mounds. This is especially manifest at the termination of the deposit at a spot called Patharaká Siwán, where, in ancient times, doubtless stood a large fort, of which the foundations may even now be partially traced. Although the fields beyond this point seem to be clear of rubbish, yet, further on, at Muskábád, at the distance of a mile, it recommences, and becomes as thick as in any other place. Perhaps this latter was the site of an outlying town.

But what are we to say of these remains? They lie immediately on the great river's bank, and never extend from it more than three quarters of a mile. It is, I think, very evident that, all the way from the mouth of the Barná, this bank has been, in the lapse of centuries, considerably cut away. Indeed, I believe that as much as a quarter of a mile may have fallen into the river. In all probability, therefore, the space covered by debris was much broader than it is at present. There can be no question, however, that here a great city once stood. I have no hesitation in expressing my belief that, judging from the great scantiness of ancient structural remains in the present city of Benares,—dating from even the Buddhist period, not to speak of the pre-Buddhist epoch, when, as we know from historical records, Benares was in existence,—the original city of the pre-Buddhist and early Buddhist eras, for the most part, must have occupied this site. Beyond the northern extremity of the remains of the earlier city is a series of mounds, also covered with debris, tending in a north-westerly direction, where formerly forts or towns existed. I think it not unlikely that, in a far distant age, the connexion of the primitive city of Benares with Sárnáth was along the course of these mounds. Sárnáth is spoken of, in the Ceylon records, as though it may have been a city of itself; and there is no doubt that it is referred to, in ancient documents, as a part of Benares. Now, modern Benares is nearly half a mile to the south of the Barná; whereas Sárnáth is out in the country, about three miles to the north of that stream. If we suppose, however, that Benares, in its most remote period, was mainly on the north side of the Barná, likewise; and if such supposition is corroborated by extensive remains of ancient buildings, in the shape of brick and stone debris, stretching over several miles of country, as already shown, and terminating in mounds lying in the direction of Sárnáth; the proof approaches to demonstration, that, at that early epoch, a union, more or less intimate, existed between Sárnáth and Benares, as stated by historical records. I had no opportunity to examine thoroughly the country lying between these remains and Sárnáth; but I feel satisfied that, at some point in these remains, a line of debris would be found connecting the two spots, with only a few breaks in its course,—the debris indicating the former existence of solid buildings, and being the broken relics of the same. This point must not be searched for at the southern extremity of the ancient city, but at the northern extremity; and, perhaps, the line of junction may be the line of the mounds just now referred to: but of this I am not able to speak positively.

If these observations respecting the site of the early city be correct, it must follow that the derivation of the word Benares, as the city lying between the Barná and the Así, is utterly absurd, as applied to the most ancient city. That it may be taken to explain the word, as denoting the city of modern times, even as far back as the Gupta dynasty, and, perhaps, somewhat further, is, historically, unobjectionable. But Banár-así has nothing whatever to do with the most ancient city of Benares, and, as applied to it, would be a ludicrous misnomer. It seems, indeed, probable that the Buddhists were the first people to occupy, to any extent, the southern side of the Barná; and such a notion is remarkably substantiated by the existence of various Buddhist remains there, as described in this chapter; but none of them, so far as I know, date from earlier than the Gupta period. It is, however, extremely likely that a small portion of the fragmentary remains found in this quarter belong to an epoch much anterior to this period; having been, probably, attached to buildings existing there when Benares lay chiefly on the north side of the river Barná, and had suburbs or outlying edifices on its southern side. The Panchkosí road, or sacred boundary of modern Benares,—regarded, by many natives, as of immense antiquity,—is no older than the city which it encompasses, and must also be assigned to a comparatively recent date. Many pleasant and, perhaps, hallowed associations, connected, in the minds of multitudes, with Benares, as it now stands, will be found to possess but precarious foundation, when they discover that the Benares of today is by no means identical with the Benares of their remote forefathers.

CHAPTER XXI.

SOURCE of the great wealth of Benares—Its chief articles of Commerce—Its native Bankers—Its Poor.—Increased desire for Education.—The Government or Queen's College.—Monolith in the College Grounds.—The Normal School. —The Church of England Mission.—The London Society's Mission.—The Baptist Society's Mission.— Native Schools of various classes.—The Benares Institute.—Public Buildings in the Suburbs.—Monument to Mr. Cherry.—Influential Native Gentlemen of Benares.

BENARES is a city of great wealth, yet not of great trade. Just as there are fashionable places of resort in more civilized countries, to which multitudes of persons are drawn at certain seasons of the year, so, in India, there are places that are annually visited by crowds of people, but with this difference, that they are of nearly all ranks and conditions, and their object is, mainly, of a religious character. Of this type is Benares. Myriads of Hindus come on pilgrimage, every year, to the sacred city, not a few of whom are merchants, landed proprietors, and princes. Some of these latter classes are casual visitors; others, however, possess residences of their own in the city, where trusty servants, and, perhaps, one or two members of their families, habitually dwell. Rajas and men of high social position, in all parts of India, pride themselves on having a house in Holy Káśí. For these reasons, chiefly, it has come to pass that Benares is one of the richest cities in India.

Although religion, rather than trade, forms the principal occupation of the inhabitants of Benares, still the merchants constitute a numerous and important body. A considerable trade is carried on in sugar, saltpetre, and indigo, which are produced in the district. Silks and shawls are manufactured in the city; and Benares is especially famous for its gold embroidered cloths called Kincob (*Kimḳhwáb*) and for its beautiful filigree work in gold. A large quantity of Manchester goods yearly finds a ready market here, and is sold for consumption in the neighbourhood, or is sent to other parts of the country. The most important place of trade, however, for English cotton manufactures, in the North-western Provinces of India, is the city of Mirzapore, which, at one time, was the chief emporium, not only of these Provinces, but also of a large portion of Central India. One very striking sign of general prosperity, in Northern India, and, I imagine, in the country at large, is seen in the taste, now almost universal, for white or parti-coloured British fabrics of fine texture, which, although neither so durable nor so cheap as native products, are much more elegant. No persons except the poorest are destitute of one or more raiments made of English cloth; and, in the cities and towns, no one considers himself fit for respectable society, if arrayed in cotton garments of native manufacture.

The bankers of Benares constitute an extensive fraternity. The habits of borrowing, and of plunging recklessly into debt, are lamentably prevalent in India. As multitudes are ready to borrow, it is a natural consequence that there should be many ready to lend, especially as the rate of interest is enormously high. This pernicious custom of society enriches a few, but impoverishes many, and greatly interferes with the comfort and happiness of the Hindu community generally.

While the number of persons with very small incomes in Benares is, undoubtedly, extremely large, yet, for a city of its size, I believe the number of abject poor is remarkably small. The sum needed for the support of a family there, would, in England, be regarded almost with incredulity. As labour, for the most part, is sufficiently abundant, there is no reason, therefore, why any family, the leading member of which is in health, should be in distress; yet, should he fall ill, unless other members of the family are able to work, it will, probably, be brought into difficulties, though not, at first, into misery. The friendly banker is then applied to, who, for a time at least, is usually willing to lend the family money, at high interest, expecting to be repaid when the sick person is restored to health; but, at the same time, an incubus of debt will rest upon the household for many long months, and, it may be, for years.

The desire for education, above all in the English language, is rapidly increasing, from year to year, amongst nearly all classes of natives in Benares. At one time it was a hard matter to induce parents to send their sons to the Government and Mission schools, to receive a gratuitous education; now they are eager to send them, and are also willing to pay the fees imposed in every such school. Indeed, so keenly are the natives beginning to appreciate the advantages of European knowledge, that it is found not only practicable, but even desirable, occasionally to increase the scale of fees.

The Government College in Benares, or, as it is now termed, the Queen's College, is a noble Gothic structure, of the perpendicular style, faced with Chunar free-stone. It was completed in the year 1853, at a cost of £12,690. Some have regarded it as the most imposing building yet erected by the British in India. Its architect was the late Major Kittoe, R.E., the Government Archæologist. The centre tower is seventy-five feet high; the nave, sixty feet long, thirty feet wide, and thirty-two feet high; and the transept, forty feet long, twenty feet wide, and thirty-two feet high. At each corner are smaller towers, connected by open arcades. The names of those persons who subscribed to defray the expense of certain portions of this edifice have been recorded, by the architect, on such portions, which are designated as their special gifts.

The College has had the advantage of distinguished scholars as Principals and Professors. Its late principal was Dr. Ballantyne, a gentleman of wide reputation for his acquaintance with Sanskrit literature and philosophy; and its present is R. T. H. Griffith, Esq., M.A., Boden Sanskrit Scholar, Oxford, well known for his exquisite poetical translations of Sanskrit legendary verse. Dr. Fitzedward Hall, Librarian of the India Office, and, formerly, Inspector of Schools in the Central Provinces of India, whose erudition and researches have placed him in the front rank of living Sanskrit scholars; and, also, Dr. Kern, Professor of Sanskrit in the University of Leyden, once shed a lustre on the College, as Anglo-Sanskrit Professors. Seven hundred youths receive instruction, the number having considerably increased under the able management of its present Principal. There are two distinct and separate departments in the College, namely, Sanskrit and English. The Sanskrit College was founded by the Government of India, in the year 1791, and is regarded as the Oxford of India, in respect of the cultivation of Hindu learning. The number of students in the English department has more than doubled of late years.

Within the surrounding grounds, and lying to the north of the College, is a monolith, thirty-one and a half feet high, which was discovered near Ghazeepore, and was placed there by order, and at the expense, of Mr. Thomason, late Lieutenant-Governor of the North-Western Provinces. It bears an inscription, somewhat defaced, in the Gupta character.

A short distance from Queen's College is the Normal School, established, by the Government, for the training of village schoolmasters. It is under the superintendence of D. Tresham, Esq., a gentleman of great ability and perseverance as a teacher, who has been, for many years, a faithful and very efficient servant of the Government. Every year about one hundred and twenty young men become qualified for appointments as teachers.

In Benares there are three Missions,—belonging to

the Church of England, and to the London and Baptist Missionary Societies, — which are labouring, with more or less efficient means of European and native agency, in conveying the Gospel to the inhabitants of the city and the surrounding villages. The Mission in connexion with the Church of England was established in the year 1817. It comprises four ordained and two lay missionaries, thirteen native Christian school-teachers, and six readers or catechists. There are, besides, bungalows for the resident missionaries, orphan institutions for boys and girls, a village inhabited by native Christians, a Gothic Church capable of holding between three and four hundred persons, two Normal Schools,— one for the training of native Christian young men as teachers and evangelists, the other for the training of native Christian young women as teachers of female schools, — a large College, and several girls' schools. The Normal Schools have a catholic basis, and admit pupils from all Protestant missions in the neighbourhood, who receive a good education, fitting them for employment in their several missions. The College is situated in the city, and is called Jay Náráyaṇ's College, from a native gentleman of rank (Raja Jay Náráyaṇ Ghosál), who founded it, in 1817, for the education of his poorer countrymen, and liberally endowed it. The Government also gives a large sum, annually, to its funds. In the year 1366, the college had four hundred and seventy-five students; and the number of native Christians in the mission was four hundred and thirty-seven. A new Church is now being erected in the midst of the Hindu population of the city, near to Daśáśamedh Ghát.

The Mission of the London Missionary Society was inaugurated in the year 1821, and is situated, like the Church of England Mission, in the suburbs of the city, but between it and the military cantonments. It has four missionaries, one ordained native minister, several catechists, and one hundred and six native Christians. In 1866, the mission sustained eleven schools; nine for the education of boys and young men, and two for the education of girls, numbering, in all, five hundred and seventy-nine pupils. A substantial Church, in the Grecian style, was erected about twenty years ago. The girls' school is an elegant Gothic structure, built by Major Kittoe, in the year 1852.

The Mission of the Baptist Missionary Society was founded in 1817, and was, originally, an outpost of the Serampore Mission, in connexion with that body. For many years it had no European agent, and its operations were carried on by an East Indian, a man of great simplicity and piety. Of late years, the Society has, generally, had two European missionaries residing in Benares. In 1866, the Mission possessed two missionaries, three native catechists, three candidates for the office of catechist, and two Christian teachers. The number of converts is small, as compared with the two other Missions. There is an orphanage for the support and training of native boys and girls. A handsome Church, in which Divine service is performed for the benefit of the English and East Indian residents, was erected, a few years since, in the cantonments.

Other schools, unconnected either with the Government or with missionary institutions, exist in the city.

They are of several kinds. There are, first, those which receive a Government grant, and yet are entirely under native management. Of such I believe there are not more than two or three. One, originated by several Bengalis, and called the Bengali Tolá Preparatory School, is of a very useful character. The second class consists of numerous Sanskrit schools, or small colleges, presided over by pandits, and attended only by Brahman youths; their object being simply the cultivation of Sanskrit literature. A third class embraces schools which impart a rudimentary knowledge of Hindí, together with writing and accounts: these are sadly destitute of method and proper organization. And there is a fourth, intended chiefly for Mohammedan youths, and devoted largely to the study of Persian and Arabic. The importance of educating Hindu women is beginning to be recognized by intelligent natives in Benares; and schools are springing up, for their benefit, in addition to those established by the missionaries, not to mention the private instruction imparted in some of the *zanánas*, or female apartments in the houses of native gentlemen.

One of the most hopeful and encouraging signs of the times, in a country like India,—which has, for many ages, been in a stagnant and unprogressive state,—is, that the thirst for knowledge is, year by year, greatly increasing. In some of the cities and large towns, educated natives are forming themselves into societies, with the view of investigating and discussing subjects connected with civilization and human progress. These societies, especially in Bengal, have, sometimes, a directly religious bearing, and are strongly opposed to the prevailing idolatry; but, in the North-Western Provinces, they are, usually, more cautious, and, although advocating sentiments of a liberal and enlightened character, yet, for the sake of peace, avoid religious matters. The influence of all, however, is, undoubtedly, more or less good, tending to dissipate the mists of superstition from the minds of their members. In Calcutta and some other places, a schism has arisen between educated and uneducated natives. The former, as a class, have avowedly abandoned idolatry, and, with it, all religious reverence for the sacred books of their country, and have established a new sect known as the Brahmo Somáj. Natives of intelligence and education have proceeded with greater timidity and hesitancy in the holy city of Benares, and have been careful not to assail too suddenly the prejudices of strict Hindus.

Several societies were, at one time, in existence in Benares. One of these, the most distinguished of all, styled the Benares Institute, still flourishes. It numbers more than one hundred native members, of whom some are princes and nobles of high rank, others are pandits and maulavís,—men of great learning in Sanskrit, Arabic, and Persian literature,—some are professors and teachers in colleges, others are magistrates and judges in the courts of law, while all are men of consideration and local influence. A few European residents of the station are, also, connected with the Institute. At the meetings which are held, lectures and essays are delivered on subjects of general interest and importance; and the discussions which are carried on are often most earnest and exciting. Hindus of the old school here contend with Hindus of the new school, —men of the past, determined to uphold the old systems to the last, with men of the present, determined at least to modify them, and to bring them to the test of rigid scrutiny; all which is beneficial to the mind, although, it may be, not always satisfactory in its immediate issue. The Institute has five constituent sections, each of which has a European president and one or more native secretaries. The sections are devoted to the following subjects: Education; Sociology or Social Progress; Philosophy and Literature; Science and Art, with which is associated Medical and Sanitary Improvement (in Benares); and Jurisprudence. The Institute published a volume of Transactions in the year 1865.

The foreign residents of Benares live chiefly at Secrole, an extensive suburb on the north-west side of the city. This Station is divided by the Barná river, to the south of which the greater portion of the military cantonments and buildings connected therewith are situated, and, likewise, the English Church, the Government College, the Medical Hall, the old Mint, the town residence of the Maharaja of Benares, the three Missions of the Church of England, and of the London and Baptist Societies, and the Courts of Law of the Civil and Sessions Judge, the Deputy Judge, and the Judge of Small Causes. To the north of this river are the houses of the civil officers of Government, the Courts of the Commissioner of the Division, and of the Collector and other Magistrates of the district; several bungalows, inhabited by deposed Rajas and other natives; the Wards' Institution, for the residence of sons of native noblemen, under special charge of the Government, and while pursuing their studies at Queen's College; the beautiful Public Gardens, supported by subscription; the Swimming Bath; the Jail, in which, occasionally, seventeen hundred prisoners are confined; the Lunatic Asylum, established in 1812, sheltering one hundred and ten patients; the Blind and Leper Asylum, with one hundred and thirty inmates, founded, in 1825, by Raja Kálí S'ankar Ghosál; and the Cemetery. A Hospital and four Dispensaries are situated in various parts of the city, and afford gratuitous relief to numerous patients daily.

In the cemetery is a lofty monument, erected to the memory of Mr. Cherry—formerly Political Resident at Benares—and a number of European gentlemen, who were all killed together on the 14th of January, 1799. Being seated at breakfast with Wazír Alí, the deposed Nawab of Oudh, on a signal being given, the Nawab and his servants rushed upon them, and the former stabbed Mr. Cherry with his own hand, while the rest were slain by his native attendants. The Nawab believed Mr. Cherry to be opposed to his interests, and, therefore, took this atrocious means of showing his resentment.

Benares is, and has long been, a favourite place of residence and resort for native princes. At the head of the Hindu community of the city, is the Maharaja of Benares,—descendant of the famous Raja Cheit Singh, — a person of much amiability and geniality of disposition, who, by reason of these excellent qualities, and also of the high station he occupies, commands the respect of all classes. The Maharaja of Vizianagram, K.C.S.I., late Member of the Legislative Council of India, lived there for several years. His knowledge of English, his liberal views, and his abundant generosity secured for him a position of considerable influence. Another former member of the Indian Council, Raja Deo Narain Singh, K.C.S.I., President of the Benares Institute, has won golden opinions, both from the English and native community, for the zeal he has displayed in promoting many useful projects of social and national interest. Nor must I omit to mention the popular and kind-hearted Babu Futteh Narain Singh, Vice-President of the Institute, at whose house the meetings of this society are held; and his accomplished son, Babu Aiśwarya Náráyaṇ Sinh, the Secretary of the Institute. One of the most enterprising men of the city is Babu Śiva Prasád,—of whom mention has already been made in this work,—who, by his personal labours as Joint Inspector of Schools, and by the many valuable books he has written, has done more, perhaps, for the education of the people than any other native in the North-Western Provinces of India. As a *littérateur*, the disguished Mohammedan, Saiyid Ahmad Ḳhán, is the most prominent of his coreligionists. He is the author of a Commentary, in Urdú and English, on the Sacred Scriptures, part of which has already been printed,—a work that has excited no little curiosity amongst various classes of persons. Connected with the Government College are several natives of great learning, the names of some of whom are known beyond their own country; such as Pandit Bápú Deva Śástrí, Honorary Member of the Royal Asiatic Society, and Professor of Mathematics and Astronomy in the Sanskrit College; and Babu Mathuráprasád, author of the valuable Trilingual Dictionary, in English, Urdú, and Hindí, lately published.

CHAPTER XXII.

SENTIMENTS engendered by the contemplation of the city of Benares—Its history, the history of India.—Principles of progress at work in the city.—Changes visible in native society.—The Brahmo Samáj.—Diminished study of Sanskrit.—Diminished faith in idolatry, in Benares and Northern India generally.—Influence of education on Hindu youths.—A Martin Luther for India.—Influence and spread of Christianity.—Priests of Piśách-Mochan Tank.—Literary and Religious Societies amongst the natives.—The Benares Institute—Nature of its discussions.—Lecture of Pandit Lakshmají—His account of the consequences of Hinduism.—Effect of Missions and Education on Benares, and on India.—Religious agitation in India.—What is the destiny of Idolatry, and of Christianity in India?—The Future in respect of Benares.—Remarks of the Rev. Dr. Thomson, Bishop of the Methodist Episcopal Church of the United States, on the religious and social condition and future prospects of India.

THE ancient and modern buildings of Benares and its neighbourhood, about which I have been discoursing, were constructed by a living, earnest people, who have, for the most part, passed away, but have left these remains behind them, illustrative of their power and skill, of their greatness and glory. By examining these buildings, we gain some knowledge of the people who erected them; and this is the main object we should have in view. Undoubtedly, there is a subtle mysterious pleasure awakened in the breast by the contemplation of an old ruin; but it owes all its force to the fact that the old ruin is associated with human existence in a by-gone age, with the forefathers of the present race inhabiting the earth. These sentiments, again, are modified in proportion to the extent of our knowledge of the past. For instance, if we are able to accumulate data sufficient to compare one epoch with another, we are conscious of experiencing pleasure or pain, in proportion as we find humanity progressing or degenerating. There are few sentiments more elevating to the soul than those which spring from the study of a nation which has carried on a long and desperate struggle with great systems of error and moral corruption, and has come out of the conflict triumphant, with clearer perceptions of truth and purer notions of virtue. On the other hand, there is no sentiment more depressing than that which is produced by the study of a people who have declined from bad to worse; from one abomination to another; from one system of evil to others more and more opposed to truth, to reason, and to God.

Now, in regard to the history of Benares, I cannot say that many pleasurable feelings have been engendered in my mind, as I have pondered over it. Its history is, to a great extent, the history of India; and, therefore, it is hardly fair to isolate the city from the country, and to pass judgment on it alone. Speaking, then, of this great city as representative of an immense empire, one is bound to say, that, while its career has been of long duration, it has not been of a character to awaken much of enthusiasm or admiration. It cannot be said that either the moral, or the social, or even the intellectual, condition of the people residing here is a whit better than it was upwards of two thousand years ago.

One fails to trace, throughout this vast period, any advance in those higher principles of human action, the practice of which alone makes a nation truly illustrious and great. On the contrary, the revelations of the past, brief and scattered though they be, are found to establish the fact beyond all dispute, that, at least in one distant epoch of Hindu History, more respect was paid to truth, honesty, and virtue, than is generally shown by the present inhabitants of India. Now, just as we do not admire a man who happens to be a hundred years old, unless we know that he has lived a life of integrity and uprightness, and has increased in wisdom and probity with his years, so we must withhold our admiration from a city or nation which, from a combination of certain peculiar circumstances, has drawn out an existence of wondrous length, but, in respect of its virtues and moral excellences, in respect of those higher qualities which mainly distinguish man from the brute, and by the possession of which he becomes, in a measure, assimilated to his Creator, has, for many ages, been in an unprogressive and stagnant condition. Such a nation or city may possess fine buildings, fine temples, fine gháts, and fine tanks, as Benares has done for thousands of years; but its material splendour will only augment the pervading gloom, just as the stars of heaven give intensity to the darkness of night.

These remarks are intimately connected with the object of this work, which has reference not only to the physical and external circumstances of Benares, but also to its highest moral relations. While I look with profound regret on much of the past history of India, I look forward to its coming history with strong hope and confidence. The sacred principles of progress, which have raised the western nations of the world to that high position of civilization and greatness which they at present occupy, have already reached this land, and begun to operate upon its inhabitants. These principles have both an intellectual and a spiritual aspect, tending everywhere to strengthen and expand the mind, as well as to purify the heart, and, when brought to bear upon communities and nations, regenerate them socially and religiously, by bringing them into harmony with God. They have, therefore, a divine origin, and, if properly applied, never fail to improve those who receive them, and to lift them up to Him from whom they proceed.

The great changes manifestly taking place in the material and social condition of the people of India are more than equalled by the changes being wrought in their religious sentiments and habits. What the telegraph, and railroads, and canals, and bridges, and metalled roads are accomplishing, physically, in opening up the country, and in developing its immense resources, so much, and more, Christianity and education are effecting, intellectually, in uprooting error and superstition, in imparting right notions respecting virtue and religion, and in elevating the people generally. The most conspicuous and decided illustration of this is, undoubtedly, visible in some parts of Bengal, particularly in Calcutta and other cities and towns in which the society called the Brahmo Samáj exists. This society now numbers several thousands of adherents, who are, for the most part, men of education and intelligence, and is, next to

Christianity, the most formidable assailant of idolatry in India. It is, also, professedly, a stout opponent of caste; but, in practice, its members are not so much released from its bondage as from that of idolatry; nor are they such unequivocal adversaries to its authority as to the authority of the numerous gods of the land.

In Benares and its neighbourhood, Bengalis exert but little influence, except upon their fellow-countrymen of Bengal residing there; for they are regarded, by the Hindústání population, as foreigners, although holding the same religion; and their sentiments and projects are always looked upon with suspicion. But even here the Brahmo Samáj has a branch society, which is slowly exerting an influence similar to that which the parent society exercises. Such an influence, wherever it exists, although not all that Christians desire, yet, so far as it goes, is, to a large extent, salutary. It is mixed up with error, but, nevertheless, contains many noble principles, the operation of which upon the hearts and consciences of the natives cannot fail to raise them far above the degraded social and spiritual condition in which, for ages, they have remained. Better, far better, that all India should attach itself to the Brahmo Samáj, than that its inhabitants should blindly persist in the worship of Śiva, and Kṛishṇa, and Rám, and should continue benighted by the fatal errors which such worship sanctions. But, in saying this, I am no advocate for the adoption of this religion as such. I earnestly hope that, having taken a great step in advance of gross heathenism, the members of the Brahmo Samáj will take another, still further in advance, and yet more decided, and will embrace the pure religion of Christ, in its entirety, from which nearly all that is good in their own reformed religion has been derived.

However, the signs of improvement apparent in Benares, and in the North-western provinces generally, have little or no connexion with this society, or with its adherents, but are the legitimate results of other agencies locally at work. They are of a twofold character. There is a destructive process visible, on the one hand, and a constructive process, on the other. The old fabric of Hinduism is being undermined and destroyed; and a new structure, altogether different in form and material, is being erected. These I shall speak of conjointly; because, in point of fact, they can hardly be separated. One of the principal reasons that Benares is so famous is, that it was formerly the resort of large numbers of Brahmans, who, divided into schools and colleges, pursued the study of the ancient Sanskrit writings. At one time there were many hundreds of such establishments, in which thousands of students were taught the philosophical tenets of Hinduism; and princes and nobles, in all parts of India, vied with each other in the support they rendered to the priests and pandits of Benares, and to the numerous Sanskrit colleges established in it. Enormous sums were annually given for this purpose, so that learned pandits and their disciples were alike nourished and cared for. Such munificence to teachers and pupils naturally attracted to Benares aspiring young Brahmans, from every province of India, who, receiving a thorough education in certain branches of philosophy, during their long and severe course of study, returned, eventually, to their native villages and towns, and became great local authorities on all religious topics, and the defenders and expounders of the national creed. For the most part, their support was rendered annually; but, for several years past, especially since the mutiny, the amount of that support has greatly diminished. The consequence is, that the pandits, in many instances, have abandoned the close study of Sanskrit, and, with it, the instruction of their pupils, and have largely directed their attention to other and more profitable pursuits. At the present moment, I have been given to understand that not twenty families of Brahmans in all Benares are devoted to the study of the Vedas, and that, of those which engage in this peculiar study, there is not one indigenous to Benares, but all are of the Bhaṭṭ Brahmans from Gujerát. I cannot, however, vouch for the absolute truth of this statement, although I believe it is quite true that the study of the Vedas has very much fallen off in Benares. Not only are the most ancient sacred books being neglected in Benares, but, with the exception of a few favoured works, such as the Rámáyaṇa, the Bhagavad Gítá, and certain of the Puráṇas, in which the sensuous forms of Hinduism, now the vogue in India, are depicted with oriental prodigality of imagination and intensity of extravagance, and, perhaps, with the exception, also, of works on astrology, the interest for Sanskrit literature is rapidly decaying; and it is almost a certainty, that, a few years hence, Sanskrit will be scarcely studied at all, except in the Sanskrit College. In addition to the reason already assigned for the production of this state of things, it should be remarked, that the pandits are beginning to see that various situations are open to them under British rule, which they can fill with honour and comfort to themselves; and, as they are just as desirous of worldly ease and distinction as other people, it is only natural that they should be anxious to obtain them, even at the risk of foregoing their favourite study.

Again, while it is an undoubted fact, that Hinduism is still kept up by the people generally in the temples, at the sacred wells and tanks, on the ghâts, and in the holy streams, with enthusiasm and punctiliousness, yet it is, I believe, indisputable, that there are thousands of persons, in this city alone, who are not satisfied with their rites and devotions; and, although, for the sake of appearance, they do as others do, they have no faith whatever in idolatry. Furthermore, there are some who have entirely abandoned it, except under certain circumstances, when the necessity of their position has got the better of their convictions, and who, nevertheless, have not outwardly embraced a better creed, nor have any immediate intention of doing so. As already remarked in a previous chapter, this is an age of temple-building, in Benares and in all this part of India, such as has not been known, perhaps, since the period preceding the Mohammedan rule and succeeding the decline and extinction of Buddhism in India; and yet, withal, it is an age of uneasiness, anxiety, and alarm, among all ranks of rigid Hindus. These latter know well, that they are erecting temples in vain, and that, while they are contributing to the outward splendour of their religion, its inner life is being gradually undermined and destroyed; for the thought constantly rises up in their minds, that their sons are a different race from themselves, with new and enlarged ideas, antagonistic to and destructive of those which they and their forefathers long cherished. The ground, they feel, is slipping from under them; and there is a dim prevision of consciousness in their breasts, that, one day, their temples will be forsaken, and that the huge structure of their religion will fall with a crash.

These remarks are especially true with regard to the youths brought up in the Government and Mission colleges and schools. These institutions are yearly sending forth a large number of young men, well-trained and well-educated, who understand our English books, speak and write our language, take delight in European literature and civilization, and are generally, more or less, acquainted with the Sacred Scriptures. During their course of study, they have reflected upon the facts of history, of science, and of the Christian religion, that have been brought before their attention; and they have, almost involuntarily, been led to compare them with the dogmas of their own religion, and with the practices which it either permits or enjoins. The consequence of this course of instruction and reflection is, that, after spending several years as students, when they come to go forth to the business of the world, they find themselves very different, in thought and belief, from their friends and parents at home. A few of them, as shown before, of more courage than the rest, whose hearts the grace of God has touched, honestly avow their disbelief in idolatry and belief in Christianity, and, in spite of all opposition, cast in their lot with the small but continually increasing body of native Christians. Others, —but how large a class I cannot say,—abandon their idols, yet do not become Christians. Others, again,—a considerable number, I believe, — worship idols reluctantly, from feelings of respect to their relations and acquaintances, and, if possible, solely on public occasions and at festivals. They are not yet ready to give up everything for their principles; they are not ready to sacrifice property, position, family, and friends, for what they have been brought to feel is the truth.

The fact is, all this class are beginning to be scandalized by idolatry, and somewhat ashamed of it. They know too much to be honest and conscientious idolaters. They cannot willingly prostrate themselves before an image of stone or clay. Some have deeper feelings than others; and some are too frivolous and thoughtless to distress themselves much about the matter. But, I believe, very few, indeed, of the educated class,—that is, educated on the English model, — are thorough and hearty idolaters; and I am satisfied, that there is not one who does not hold Hinduism with a lighter and looser grasp than formerly, or than would have been the case, had his mind not been expanded and benefited by the education he has received. Let it be well understood, that education de-Hinduizes the Hindu, breaks down idolatry, and inspires him with a distaste for it, and a latent desire to be free from it. Not long since, as I was conversing with an educated native gentleman in Benares, he made a remark of great significance, as showing the feeling of men of his own class, attached by association to idolatry, and yet prepared for something better, if only a movement were commenced, and if some one of courage, of force of character, and of enthusiasm, would lead the way. "We need," he said, "a Luther amongst us;" as who should say, that, under the guidance of a Martin Luther, he himself, with the rest, would break away from Hinduism; that, led by such a man, a new era of religious reformation would be inaugurated in the land; and that all who were longing for reform, who were ready to be free, but not daring to be so, would rush eagerly to his standard, from every quarter.

This brings us to the constructive process at work in this city, and in other places in the country. It was no easy task, but one of gigantic difficulty, to awaken a desire for knowledge, or for any improvement whatever, amongst a people so confident in their own creed, so satisfied with their own condition, and so profoundly unconscious of the necessity of any change in the one or in the other. Nevertheless, the task has been performed, and with astonishing quickness. And it may be affirmed, with perfect truth, that the desire for knowledge, for an advanced civilization, for a thorough conformity to some of the enlightened usages of life practised by European nations, and for the possession of nobler principles than idolatry inspires, is the most important and noticeable feature among all the changes now taking place in native society. In accomplishing this result, the liberal legislation of an upright Government, the education imparted in the Government and Missionary Schools, and the various influences, of a more or less salutary character, produced by the great material improvements which British enterprise and skill have introduced into the country, have lent their aid; but the most potent and efficacious instrument of all, it must be confessed, has been the direct and indirect teaching of Christianity in many places, the patient and persistent exhibition of its divine principles, the preaching of the Word to all classes, in the city and in the village, in the streets and in the lanes, and in all places, and at all practicable times, perseveringly and unintermittingly.

Putting together all the favourable circumstances connected with the Hindus in relation to the progress of Christianity among them, I consider that there is every reason for encouragement and hope in the future. Indeed, I feel that it is incumbent on the Church to render special thanksgiving to God for the wonderful change in the sentiments of the people generally which He has already graciously effected. To cherish doubts and fears in the prosecution of this great work, or in regard to its ultimate issue, would be significant of unbelief, and of distrust of God's all-powerful grace. It is one of the most gratifying features of the spirit of inquiry now manifest among the natives, that it has spread to the most unlikely and unpromising members of the community. I will give an illustration of this assertion. It is well known, that a large number of priests are engaged in temple and other religious services in Benares. They are a very bigoted people, and, in fact, with the pandits, are the main stay of Hinduism. Of this entire class, the most prejudiced and most strongly attached to idolatrous rites are the Gangá-putras, or sons of the Ganges, men who gain their livelihood by the offerings made by worshippers at the ghâts of the sacred stream and at certain sacred pools in the city. There is a celebrated reservoir in Benares, where some forty thousand pilgrims, from all parts of India, annually present sacrifices to their ancestors, and bathe. Not more than five or six head-priests direct the religious ceremonies of this host. And it must be borne in mind that the ceremony, once performed, need never be repeated here; so that the pilgrims are renewed every year. It has been the custom, for several years past, for this tank to be visited, occasionally, by missionaries and native evangelists from the missions in the city, for the purpose of preaching to both priests and pilgrims. In this way several of the priests became well acquainted with Christianity, and also personally attached to ourselves. But I must confess that we were greatly astonished, one day, at receiving a visit from two head-priests, accompanied by some seven or eight disciples. These had come to the mission, professedly for the purpose of confessing their belief in Christianity, and of making arrangements for publicly abandoning Hinduism and embracing the true religion. I regard the circumstance as one of incalculable significance, as indicative of the influence which the Christian religion is exerting on the people, even on that class most difficult to reach and most wedded to superstition. Nor is its significancy at all diminished by the fact that not one of these persons persisted in his determination, and that all, startled by the obstacles in the way,—not raised by the missionaries, but entirely by themselves,—after a short interval, returned to their temples, and to their idolatrous practices, as before.

On the 24th of December, 1866, a lecture was delivered before the Benares Institute by a Hindu,—not a Christian, nor a member of the Brahmo Samáj,—named Paṇḍit Lingam Lakshmají Pantlú Garu, private secretary to his Highness the Maharaja of Vizianagram, on "The Social Status of the Hindus," in which some very remarkable statements were made on a great variety of topics connected with the social usages and inner life of his fellow-countrymen. It is astonishing that a Brahman, before a company of Brahmans and others, forming the *élite* of native society in the holy city, should have had the courage to utter sentiments like the following, striking at the root of the prevalent philosophy and religion of the land. At page 27, the Pandit says:—

"Then we come to the Augean stables of our religion—the never failing source of all our misery, of all our demoralization, of all our deterioration, in short, of our ruin and fall. Our faith, as all of you are aware, is of two kinds, one idolatrous and the other monotheistic; yet both are so intermixed that it is impossible to treat of the one without touching the other. We have, indeed, a trinity, to represent the creating, the preserving, and the destroying powers; and we are charitable enough to give to each of these gods a wife. Then we have the ten incarnations of the preserving power . . . . Then we have idolized and deified everything possible; giving, at the same time, with sedulous care, a wife to each god. This is the Puranic account of our popular faith. In the superior system, which is generally called the Vedanta philosophy, there is but one self-existent, eternal Supreme Being, who is the cause of all, and into whom everything is finally absorbed. In both systems, man is not a free agent: prompted by the within-himself-seated divine power, he acts; yet, inconsistently, he enjoys the fruit of his good actions, and suffers pain for the bad ones. In the Vedanta system, heaven and hell are not *formally* recognized. In both, our souls pass through many bodies, not only human, but also those of all sorts of animals,—nay, even through different parts of inanimate creation. We cannot blame our ancestors for building such a system of theology for us; but, as intelligent and rational beings, it behoves us to examine whether our present religious ideas are consonant with reason, and whether they are calculated to give us happiness both here and hereafter. Idolatry is denounced by our own texts; it is, indeed, intended for small intellects. If we attribute to God the creation of this world; if we endow Him with the qualities of omnipotence, omnipresence, and omniscience; if we call Him the regulator of every mundane thing, how can we, without inconsistency, represent Him as a small idol? Is it not the greatest insult that we can offer to the Almighty, by representing Him in any shape? Can we represent him? . . . . The shape in which we worship Mahádeva is most revolting to all who have any sense of decency and personal respect left in them. Not to say that we regard the numerous idols as monuments of some bygone powers, and no more; this would be something reasonable, at least. On the contrary, we regard every idol we worship as the *self-existent, eternal, Supreme Being, who is the cause of everything, and into whom everything is finally absorbed.*

"Purity of personal character is nothing to many of us: the Gangá (Ganges) and our idols help us to heaven! But, sir, we are not free agents; what we do, we do prompted by the divine essence implanted in us. Yet we enjoy the fruits of our good acts, and suffer punishment for our sins! Our souls pass through a series of births, according to our actions, over which we have no control! If we do everything prompted by the implanted divine essence, and if unreasonably God punishes us for our sins, and rewards our merits, all by carrying our souls through a series of corporeal existences, then what need have we of a God? Does not this throw us into the dark abyss of atheism? We do nothing of our own accord, not even the act of worshipping our favourite idols! All this nonsense is the fruit of endless and superstitious priestcraft under which we groan."

Although, in the actual prosecution of Missionary labour, not only in Benares, but also in other places in India, there are many difficulties and discouragements to encounter, both in the opposition of idolaters, and in the not infrequent inconsistency of native Christians, yet the results are most extensive and extraordinary. Considering the small amount of money which has been expended, the limited means which have been employed, and the brief space of time which has elapsed since the Missionary enterprise was inaugurated in the sacred city, and bearing in mind, likewise, the stern fact that Christianity has there met with its fiercest and most determined opponents, that it is the great seat of caste prejudice and priestly domination, that it is the chief and acknowledged bulwark of idolatry and superstition in all India, and that, in short, Hinduism has there sat enthroned in the midst of pomp and power, sustained by the learning and subtlety of the Brahmans, and by the wealth and authority of rajas and princes from all parts of the country, for a period stretching over many ages, it is most surprising that so much has been achieved. In appearance, Christianity has been more successful in many places in India than in Benares; yet, when the peculiar obstacles which exist in that city are taken into consideration, I believe it is not too much to say that it has, in the aggregate, accomplished as much there as in any city in the land. It has been proved, too, in Benares, as elsewhere, that, wherever idolatry has come into direct antagonism with the Gospel, it has, together with other acknowledged evils, such as caste, superstition, and false philosophy, in association therewith, fallen before it.

To extend these observations, so as to include within their scope the entire peninsula of Hindustan, and, at the same time, to bring them to a conclusion, I would remark, that the results of missions in India are not surpassed by anything that has been accomplished, of a religious character, in modern times, either in England, or in America, or in any quarter of the globe. These results are both *direct* and *indirect;* direct, in the way of conversions from the heathen; indirect, in regard to the general enlightenment and progress of the people, incident to the operation of Christian Truth and European Civilization upon their minds. It is progress in sound knowledge, in thought, in the quickening of conscience, and in true religion. Christianity is now a power in India, a felt and acknowledged power, which men of all castes and ranks, including Hindus of the strictest sects, respect and fear. What is the great prominent question at this moment agitating no small portion of the millions of India? Not the increased social happiness and prosperity of the people, nor the augmentation of commerce and trade, nor the vast improvements in the country,—visible on every hand, wonderful as they all are,—but this, What is Truth? What constitutes religion? What is the destiny of Idolatry, and what that of Christianity, in the coming ages? The people are thinking, comparing, arguing,—not knowing exactly what to do. India is much in the condition of Rome previously to the baptism of the Emperor Constantine. Idolatry, here as there, now as then, is falling into disgrace. Men are becoming wiser. Truth, in its clearness and power, is gradually entering their minds, and changing their habits and lives.

India is undergoing an intellectual and also a moral and religious revolution. The Past is slowly losing its bewitching influence over the public mind. The Hindu dares to think, and has ever dared,—though he lacks the courage to act up to new convictions;—yet the inspiration of earnestness has entered his breast; and, as his convictions become fixed and definite, he will, I doubt not, fling away from him the weight of prejudice and custom, which has oppressed him so cruelly and so long.

Let us not forget what the grace of God can do, and what it has already done. It can change the heart of the polite, metaphysical, idol-loving Hindu, just as it has changed the heart of the savage African and New Zealander. It can bring him, humble, self-abased, stripped of pride and vain-glory, to the foot of the Cross, to crave there meekly the forgiveness of his sins.

Religious controversies and excitements are always the most momentous, and, perhaps, in the end, most productive of beneficial results. The violent mental commotions of the Middle Ages, the extraordinary religious awakening at their close, produced the most stupendous consequences for good. And who shall say what the intellectual and religious awakening of India, which has just commenced, will not produce? No prophet is needed to tell the issue. It will infallibly produce, for India, all that the Reformation has produced for England and the world. It must extinguish idolatry, must break in pieces its images, must wipe out its distinguishing symbols and signs, must destroy its temples, must cleanse the land of its foulness; so that, perhaps, in many places, as in some of the islands of the South Seas, no traces of its previous existence will be discoverable. It will annihilate caste; it will clear the atmosphere of superstitious and impure rites; and the praises of the Great Creator, the One Living and True God, will be sung, in His sanctuaries, from one end of the land to the other.

India, converted to the Lord, is a subject which the Indian missionary delights to think on. The day is approaching, and may come when many least expect it.

And, when the warm feeling and poetic imagination of the Hindus are directed to our common Christianity; when their hearts have been vitalized by its influence; when they have, as a people, risen into the region of holy thought, and of earnest prayer to their Father above; then may it be expected that they will make sudden and rapid progress in civilization, and in whatever contributes to a nation's greatness, and will share with us in the exalted privilege and honour of extending the kingdom of Christ, and of hastening His universal reign.

I venture, therefore, to predict a Future for India, of unparalleled glory and lustre. And why should not Benares still hold a foremost place in her history? Why should not she take the lead of all Indian cities, as she ever has done, and show, by her own example, and for their imitation, how she can abolish useless social burthens, can abandon exploded errors, and can accept the Truth in all its forms; how she can strive after and attain to the highest and purest happiness, and can bring herself, with God's help, to hate whatever He hates, and to love whatever He loves?

I will sum up these remarks on the religious and social condition and future prospects of India, by an extract from an article in an American Quarterly Review, from the pen of the Rev. Dr. Thomson, a Bishop of the Methodist Episcopal Church of the United States, who lately journeyed in India, on a tour of visitation to the missions of that body, situated chiefly in Rohilkhand and Oudh. Speaking of British ascendancy in India, Dr. Thomson writes:—"What will this power effect? Judge by what it has already effected. It has reduced anarchy to order, given law, established justice, protected the land from invasion, and prevented it from being ravaged by intestine wars. It has suppressed suttee and dacoity, forbidden human sacrifices, repressed infanticide, and made slavery illegal. It has woven a network of telegraphs around the empire, from Galle to Peshawur, and from Peshawur to Rangoon. It has established a regular system of postage for letters, papers, and books, at low charges and uniform rates. It has improved old roads, and made new ones, sent steamers up the principal streams, constructed a canal nine hundred miles long, and will, probably, soon construct others in the valleys of the Mahanaddy, the Kistna, and the Godavery. It has commenced a system of railways, embracing about five thousand miles of trunk lines, at a cost of nearly three thousand millions of dollars, which, when completed, will unite the extremes of the Peninsula, open hitherto inaccessible tracts, and bring all parts close to each other and to the civilized world. Already the steam-horse traverses the Gangetic valley from Calcutta to Delhi, crosses the Peninsula from Madras to the western shore, and prances from Bombay to Nagpore.

"It has steadily increased the trade of the country,—which, before the days of Clive, could be conveyed in a single Venetian frigate,—until it now reaches nearly five hundred millions of dollars annually. It has raised the revenues of the government to two hundred and fifteen millions. It has given India the newspaper, that great educator; so that there are twenty-eight newspapers published weekly in Bengal,—three of them in English, by the natives,—thirty native presses in Madras, and I know not how many in Bombay and Ceylon, and twenty-five presses among the missions alone. It has established schools in all parts of the land, in which those sciences are taught that undermine the prevailing systems of superstition and error. It has made the English language classical in the country; and, by this means, it is furnishing the native mind with the rich and Christian stores of which that noble tongue is the medium. It has protected missionaries of Christ, and their converts.

"Look, then, at this great Peninsula, linked to the continent and the world by its languages, commerce, and religions; source of the false faiths which, together, ensnare six hundred millions of the human race, and the stronghold of a delusion that blinds a hundred and eighty millions more . . . . There are more Mohammedans under Victoria's sceptre than under any other on earth. The Sultan has but twenty-one millions; she has twenty-five millions, at least. There are more heathen under the same Christian Queen than under any sovereign except the Emperor of China. And this mass is, all through and through, and more and more, subjected to Christian influences. The telegraphs are so many ganglia in a great nervous system, diffusing new sensations; the railways are so many iron arteries, pumping Christian blood through the native veins; the newspapers are so many digestive powers, preparing healthful moral food; the schools are so many batteries, thundering at the crumbling battlements of error; the missions are many brains, thinking new and better thoughts.

"Knowledge must be diffused through the earth. We know two things more, namely, that our religion can withstand modern science, and make it tributary to itself, and that no other religion can; for every other faith has linked its science with its doctrines, so that they must both fall together. As to take Paris is to take France, and to take Sebastopol is to shake Russia to the Arctic seas, and to take Richmond is to shake out the rebels of the United States from the Potomac to the Rio Grande, so to Christianize India, owing to its key position in heathendom, is to shake out the idols from the face of the whole earth."

APPENDIX A.

Narrative of Fă Hian, concerning his visit to Benares and Sárnáth. Extracted[1] *from the Foĕ Kouĕ Ki, by MM. Rémusat, Klaproth, and Landresse.* Paris, 1836. Ch. xxxiv., pp. 304, 305.

Fă Hian, on his way back to Pa lian foĕ (Páṭaliputra),[2] followed[3] the river Heng (Ganges) westward. After ten *yeou yans* (about seventy miles), he came to a temple entitled Vast Solitude. It is one of the stations of Foĕ (Buddha). There are devotees there at this day. Still following, for twelve *yeou yans*, the course of the river Heng, towards the west, he reached the city of Pho lo naï (Benares), in the kingdom of Kia chi (Káśí). Ten *lis* to the north-east of the city, one comes to the temple located in the Park of the Immortal's Deer. This Park was, of yore, the abode of a Pў tchi foĕ (Pratyeka-Buddha): deer constantly repose in it. When the Honourable of the Age was on the point of accomplishing the Law, the gods sang, in the midst of the enclosure: "The son of King Pĕ tsing (S'uddhodana) has embraced a religious life; he has studied the doctrine; and, in seven days, he will become Foĕ." The Pў tchi foĕ, having heard this, assumed *Ni houan* (*Nirváṇa*). It is on this account that this place is called the Garden of the Plain of the

[1] At page 231 *supra*, I have promised Mr. Laidlay's translation of the passage in question; but it has seemed preferable, on some accounts, to substitute that here given.

[2] His point of departure was Buḍdha-Gayá.

[3] The French is "descended." Perhaps this word was chosen to denote, that, in passing along the Ganges from Buddha-Gayá to Benares, one's direction is rather southerly than northerly.

Immortal's Deer. Since the time when the Honourable of the Age accomplished the Law, the men of later ages have constructed a chapel in this place.

Foĕ, desiring to convert, from among the five men, Keou lin (Kauṇḍinya), these five men said among themselves: "For six years this Cha men (S'ramaṇa) Kiu tan (Gautama) has practised austerities; eating, daily, only one hemp-seed and one grain of rice; and he has not yet been able to obtain the law. *À fortiori,* when one lives in the society of men, and gives one's self up to one's body, mouth, and thoughts, how could one accomplish the doctrine? When he comes to-day, let us be careful not to speak to him." When Foĕ drew near, the five men rose, and did homage to him.

Sixty paces to the north of this spot, Foĕ, facing the east, sate down, and began to turn the Wheel of the Law. From among the five men he converted Keou lin (Kauṇḍinya), Twenty paces to the north is the spot where Foĕ recounted his history to Mi lĕ (Maitreya). Fifty paces thence, to the south, is the place where the dragon I lo pŏ asked Foĕ: "In what space of time shall I be able to obtain deliverance from this dragon's body?" At all these spots they have raised towers, among which are two *seng kia len* (*sanghárâma,* or monasteries), in which are devotees.

APPENDIX B.

Narrative of Hiouen Thsang. Translated by myself, from the "Mémoires sur les Contrées Occidentales de Hiouen Thsang" of M. Stanislas Julien, translator of the original Chinese work. Vol. i., pp. 353–376.

KINGDOM OF P'O-LO-NI-SSE.

(*Váráṇasí*).

The kingdom of *P'o-lo-ni-sse* (Váráṇasí, Benares) is about four thousand *lis* (667 miles)[1] in circuit. To the west, near the Ganges, is the capital, which is from eighteen to nineteen *lis* (three miles and upwards) long, and from five to six *lis* (about one mile) broad. The villages lie very near together, and contain a numerous population. Families of very great wealth, whose houses are stored with rare and precious things, are to be seen. The people are gentle and polished, and esteem most highly men given to study. The greater portion of them believe in the heretical doctrines [Hinduism]; and few revere the Law [religion] of Buddha. The climate is temperate, grain is abundant, the fruit-trees are luxuriant, and the earth is covered with tufted vegetation. There are thirty [Buddhist] monasteries, containing about three thousand devotees, who, all, study the principles of the school *Tching-liang-pou* (the school of the Sammatíyas), which holds to the *Minor Vehicle.*[2] There

[1] Taking the common reckoning of six *lis* to the mile. M. St. Martin assigns only five *lis* to the mile.

[2] According to M. Julien, whose explanation is based on a Chinese Dictionary, the Buddhists recognize Five Vehicles, that is to say, five means, used by as many classes of eminent men, for the attainment of beatification.

are a hundred temples of the [Hindu] gods, and about ten thousand heretics [Hindus], who, for the most part, worship the god *Ta-tseu-thsaï* (*Maheśwara Deva*). Some cut off the hair, others reserve a tuft upon the crown of the head, go naked, and are destitute of any kind of clothing (the *Nirgranthas*). Some besmear their bodies with ashes (the *Páśupatas*), and zealously practise severe austerities, in order to obtain release from life and death, [that is, from transmigration].

In the capital there are twenty temples of the [Hindu] gods.[1] Towers of many storeys are seen there; and magnificent chapels, constructed of stone, skilfully carved, and of richly painted wood. Umbrageous trees cover them with their shade; and streams of clear water flow in all directions. The statue of the god (*Maheśwara Deva*), in *Teou-chi* (brass), is little less than a hundred feet in height. Its aspect is grave and majestic; and, at sight of it, one is filled with respectful awe, as if it were, indeed, alive.

To the north-east of the capital, and to the west of the river of *Po'-lo-ni-sse* (Váráṇasí, that is, the Ganges), is a *Stúpa* [or sacred tower], built by king *Wou-yeou* (Aśoka), about one hundred feet high. A stone column stands over against it, of blue colour, bright as a mirror, and of a highly polished surface, in which one may always discover the shadow of *Jou-laï* (the Tathágata).

Passing on about ten *lis* north-east from the river of *Po'-lo-ni-sse* (Váráṇasí), he reached the Monastery of the Deer Park (Mṛigadáva), which is divided into eight sections, and is entirely surrounded by walls. There you see balustrades and two-storeyed pavilions, of admirable construction. The devotees—of whom there are as many as fifteen hundred—study the doctrine of the school *Tching-liang-pou,* holding to the *Minor Vehicle.* In the midst of the walled enclosure is a *Vihára,* two hundred feet in height, surmounted by an *'An-mo-lo* (Amra, or mango), wrought in embossed gold. The foundations and stairs are of stone. All round the monument there are a hundred rows of niches, made of brick, arranged one above another,

[1] This shows that the 'hundred temples,' with the 'ten thousand heretics' attached to them, comprised the number in the entire kingdom of Benares. In like manner, the 'thirty (Buddhist) monasteries,' with their three thousand occupants, refer not merely to the city, but to the whole kingdom, the city included.

each of them containing a statue of Buddha, in embossed gold. In the centre of this *Vihára* stands a statue of Buddha, in *Teou-chi* (brass). It has exactly the height of *Jou-laï* (the Tathágata), who is represented turning the Wheel of the Law [*i.e.*, preaching].

To the south-west of the *Vihára* is a stone *Stúpa*, erected by king *Wou-yeou* (Aśoka). Although its base is embedded in the earth, it has about a hundred feet of elevation. In front of this monument, a stone column has been set up, some seventy feet high. The stone is smooth as jade, and shines like a mirror. Those who pray fervently discern in it a multitude of figures; on all occasions, every one sees there images that answer to his virtues or his vices. It was at this spot that *Jou-laï* (the Tathágata), after having attained to perfect knowledge, began to turn the Wheel of the Law.

The *Stúpa* on the side of the aforesaid marks the place where *'O-jo-kiao-tch'in-jou* ('Ajnáta Kauṇḍinya), etc. [the other companions of Buddha], having seen the *Pou-sa* (the Bodhisattwa) relinquish his austerities, suddenly desisted from following him and from watching over his safety. Having arrived at this place, they gave themselves up to meditation.

The *Stúpa* on the side of that last-mentioned occupies the site where five hundred Pratyeka-Buddhas (*To-kio*) entered *Nie-pan* (Nirváṇa) together. There are, also, three other *Stúpas*. The three last Buddhas reposed on that spot, and there walked for exercise.

To the side of the place where the three Buddhas walked for exercise there is a *Stúpa*. It was there that *Meï-ta-li-ye-pou-sa* (Maitreya Bodhisattwa) received a prediction announcing that he should attain to Buddhahood. Of yore, when *Jou-laï* (the Tathágata) was at Rájagṛiha (*Wang-che-tching*), on [Mount] Vulture-Peak (Gṛidhrakúṭa), he addressed the *Pi-tsou* (Bhikhshus) as follows: "In coming ages, when the inhabitants of this island of *Tchen-pou* shall have become just and upright, and when men shall attain a longevity of eighty thousand years, a *Po-lo-men* (Bráhman) child named *T'se-chi* (Maitreya) will be born there. His body will be of the colour of the purest gold, and will shed abroad a lustrous radiance. He will renounce his family, will attain to superior knowledge (Paramabodhi), and, at three great synods, will expound the Law for the behoof of all men. Those whom he will convert and save are the numerous mortals to whom I have bequeathed my Law, in order to conduct them to happiness. To the Three Jewels[1] they will, with their whole heart, pay profound reverence. Whether they remain with their families or quit them, whether they observe the precepts or transgress them, all will have the happiness of being converted and guided to good; all will obtain the fruit of *Bodhi*, and final deliverance. By explaining the Law in the three great Synods, he will save the disciples to whom I have bequeathed my Law. Subsequently, he will convert their virtuous friends who have the same vocation.

"At that moment, *T'se-chi-pou-sa* (Maitreya Bodhisattwa), having heard these words of Buddha, rose from his seat, and said to Buddha: 'I desire to become this Honourable of the Age, under the name of *T'se-chi* (Maitreya).' Then *Jou-laï* (the Tathágata) spoke to him as follows: 'Agreeably to the wish you have just expressed, you shall see this fruit, face to face, [that is, you shall become that Buddha]. What I have just declared will be owing to the influence of your instructions.'"

To the west of the place where *T'se-chi-pou-sa* (Maitreya Bodhisattwa) received this prediction, there is a *Stúpa*. It was there that *Chi-kia-pou-sa* (Śákya Bodhisattwa) received, likewise, a prediction. In the Age of the Wise (Bhadrakalpa), when the life of man lasted for twenty thousand years, *Kia-ye-po-fo* (Káśyapa Buddha) appeared in the world. He turned the Wheel of the excellent Law, converted mortals, and received from *Hou-ming-pou-sa* (Prabhápála (?) Bodhisattwa) the following prediction: "This *Pou-sa* (Bodhisattwa), in the ages to come, at the time when the life of man shall last for a hundred years, will obtain the dignity of Buddha, under the name of *Chikia-meou-ni* (Śákya Muni).

A short distance from the place where *Chi-kia-pou-sa* (Śákya Bodhisattwa) received this prediction, to the south, are ancient stone seats, erected on the spot where the four last Buddhas walked for exercise. They are about fifty paces in length, and seven feet in height, and consist of blue stones. A statue of *Jou-laï* (the Tathágata), in the attitude of walking, is placed there. Its body surpasses

[1] In Sanskrit, *triratna* or *ratnatraya*. These, on the authority of M. Julien, are Buddha, the Visible Communion of Saints, and the Law.

human stature; and its entire appearance exhibits an imposing majesty. From the top of the fleshy cone which projects from the head, flows a mass of waving hair. Celestial prodigies are seen there, and the divine power displays itself with effulgence.

Within the enclosure of the monastery-walls is a multitude of sacred monuments. There are several hundred *Viháras* and *Stúpas.* We notice only two or three; for it would be difficult to describe them in detail.

West of the walls of the *Seng-kia-lan* (Sanghuáráma, monastery), is a reservoir of pure and limpid water, about two hundred paces in circuit. Here *Jou-laï* (the Tathágata) formerly bathed.

A little further to the west is a great reservoir, one hundred and eighty paces in circuit. Here *Jou-laï* (the Tathágata) washed his devotee's water-pot.

A little further to the north is another reservoir, one hundred and fifty paces in circuit. Here *Jou-laï* (the Tathágata) washed his garment. These three reservoirs are haunted by dragons. The water is deep, sweet to the taste, pure, and transparent. It never either increases or diminishes. When men of proud hearts come to bathe in these reservoirs, the *Kin-pi-lo* (Kumbhíras, alligators) destroy a great number of them; but, should a pious person come, he may draw water without any fear.

On the side of the reservoir where the Buddha washed his garments is a large square stone, on which may be seen the marks of the *Kia-cha* (Káshâya, brown vestment) of *Jou-laï* (the Tathágata). The threads of the cloth have a brilliant hue, and stand out distinctly, as if they were carved. Men animated with a sincere faith come here, daily, to offer their adoration. But, should heretics or evil-doers trample on this stone contemptuously, the king-dragon, who lives in this reservoir, at once unchains the winds and the rain.

A short distance from these reservoirs is a *Stúpa.* In ancient times, when *Jou-laï* (the Tathágata) was leading the life of a *Pou-sa* (Bodhisattwa), and was a king of elephants, armed with six tusks, a hunter, wishing to carry off these valuable ivories, clothed himself, craftily, with a *Kia-cha* (Káshâya, or devotee's brown garment), bent his bow, and awaited his prey. The king of the elephants, out of respect for the *Kia-cha* (Kásháya), forthwith tore out his tusks, and presented them to him.

A short distance from the place where the king of the elephants tore out his tusks is a *Stúpa.* At the time when *Jou-laï* (the Tathágata) was leading the life of a *Pou-sa* (Bodhisattwa), being moved with pity, on perceiving that the people of the period did not observe the rules [of civility], he took the form of a bird, and, having approached an ape and a white elephant, asked them, at this very spot: "Which of you first saw this tree *Ni-keou-lia* (Nyagrodha, sacred fig-tree)?" Each having given a reply, they immediately placed themselves according to their ages. The good effects of such conduct spread abroad, gradually, on all sides; men learned to distinguish between superiors and inferiors; and both the devotees and the laity followed their example.

Not far from this place, in the midst of a large forest, is a *Stúpa.* It was on this spot that, of old, *Jou-laï* (the Tathágata) cut short a great controversy with *Ti-p'o-ta-to* (Devadatta), when they were both kings of the deer. In ancient times, at this place, in the midst of a vast forest, were two herds of deer, each numbering a hundred head. In those days, the king of this kingdom (Benares) hunted in the low and humid plains. The *Pou-sa* (Bodhisattwa), king of the deer, advanced to the king, and proffered this request: "Great king, you hunt in the midst of the plains, you burn (the herbage), and you shower arrows: our companions and our subjects (*i.e.*, deer) are about to perish this very morning; and soon their bodies will fall into decay, so that you will find nothing more to eat. We wish, in turn, to supply the king with a deer day and day about. The king will be able to nourish himself with fresh meat; and we ourselves, thus, prolong our frail existence." The king was delighted with this proposal. He ordered his charioteer to drive back; and he returned to his palace. Thenceforward, the deer of both herds were sacrificed in turn.

Now, in the herd of *Ti-p'o-ta-to* (Devadatta) there was a hind, great with young, whose turn had come to die. Addressing her master, she said to him: "Although I ought to die to-day, yet the turn of my little one has not yet arrived."

The king of the deer, waxing angry, said to her: "Who is there that does not value his life?"

The hind, sighing, replied: "Our king has no tenderness. I am to die on the first day." She went and told her distress to the Bodhisattwa, king of the deer. The king of the deer said to her: "What a matter for grief! As an affectionate mother, you extend your kindness even to a being not yet born. Very well! I will take your place to-day."

He repaired, at once, to the gate of the king. The people along the road carried the news, saying, in a loud voice: "This great king of the deer is on his way, at this moment, to the city." The inhabitants of the capital—alike magistrates and common people—hastened, emulously, to see him.

The king was loth to credit this news; but, when the warder of the palace-gate announced it to him, at last he believed it. Then, addressing the king of the deer, he asked him: "Why have you come here all of a sudden?"

The deer answered: "There is a hind who ought to die; but she carries a little one that has not yet seen the light of day. As I cannot permit this evil, I venture to offer myself to die in her stead."

At these words the king sighed, and said: "I am a deer, with a human body; and you are a man, with the body of a deer." Thereupon, he gave all the deer their freedom, and no longer wished that they should sacrifice their lives for him. In consequence of this circumstance, he gave up that forest to the deer, and called it *the forest given to the deer,* from which came the name of the Deer-Forest (Mṛigadáva).

From two to three *lis* [about half a mile] to the south-west of the monastery is a *Stúpa,* about three hundred feet in height. It is a large and lofty monument, resplendent with the most rare and precious materials. As it has no storeyed niches, there has been placed (on its summit) a kind of devotee's water-pot, inverted. Although this *Stúpa* is surmounted by an arrow, it is not crowned by a bell-shaped cupola.

At its side is a small *Stúpa.* It was at this place that *'O-jo-kiao-tch'in-jou* (Ajnáta Kauṇḍinya) and others, to the number of five, departed from their compact,[1] and advanced to meet Buddha."

Originally, the prince royal *So-p'o-ho-la-tha-si-tho* (Sarvártha-

[1] The compact was, not to accost Buddha.

siddha), after departing from the city, went and established himself on the mountains, and concealed himself in the valleys: he neglected his person, to devote himself to the Law. Thereupon, King *Tsing-fan* (Śuddhodana Raja) gave the following orders to three persons of his family, and to the (two) maternal uncles (of the prince royal): "My son, *I-tsie-i-tch'ing* (Sarvárthasiddha), has left his family, in order to give himself to study. He wanders alone upon the mountains and in the plains, and lives apart in the midst of the forests. On this account I order you to follow his steps, and ascertain where he dwells. Within the palace, you are his paternal and maternal uncles; abroad, you are at once princes and ministers. It is absolutely necessary that you find out what he does and where he lives."

On receiving these commands from the king, these five men departed, one after another, to shield him with their protection. Subsequently, they sought, themselves, after the means of escape from life and death [*i.e.*, from transmigration]. Then they said to one another: "When any one aspires after knowledge, is it obtained by austerities, or in the bosom of joy?"

Two of them answered: "It is in tranquillity and joy that knowledge is obtained." But the other three maintained, that it was by severe austerities that knowledge could be attained. The two first and the other three were still disputing the point, without having cleared up the matter, when the prince royal, reflecting on the sublime verities, imitated the conduct of those heretics who submit to hard privations, and who eat (daily) only a few grains of hemp-seed and uncooked rice, to sustain life. The two first, beholding him, said to one another: "That which the prince royal does is not conformable to the true way. Knowledge ought to be obtained by pleasant means; but he has recourse, to-day, to painful austerities. He cannot be our companion. Let us leave him, and go away. Let us think on the means of acquiring the fruit (of knowledge). For six years the prince royal has devoted himself to penance, and has not yet seen the fruit of *Pou-ti* (Bodhi). If we examine into his austerities, we shall perceive, that they do not constitute the true method. But, when he shall have received a dish of rice and milk, he will obtain knowledge."

On hearing these words, the other three, sighing, exclaimed: "He was on the point of putting the seal to his merits; but now he holds back. For six years he devoted himself to penance; and in one day he has lost the fruit of it."

Thereupon, one after the other, they made quest for him. The two first, on seeing them, sate down in a suitable place, and conversed together in a grave and loud tone. Then, resuming their discourse, they spoke as follows: "Some time ago, we saw *I-tsie-i-tch'ing* (Sarvárthasiddha) leave the palace of the king, and betake himself to a desert valley; strip off his costly garments, and cover himself with a deer's skin; exhibit burning zeal, and put forth energetic efforts; lead a chaste life, and torment himself in spirit, in search of the sublime Law, and for the acquisition of the supreme recompense. But, behold, he has already to-day accepted, from the hand of a young cowherdess, a dish of rice and milk. He has destroyed the germ of knowledge, and frustrated his project. We see, now, that he will succeed in nothing.

The two others said to them: "How is it, sirs, that you have been so slow in perceiving this? He behaves like a fool. Formerly, he dwelt in the recesses of the palace, and lived happily in the most honourable and glorious rank. Unable to subdue his will, he went and concealed himself far away, upon the mountains and in the woods. He renounced the throne of King Chakravartin (*Tch'ouen-lun-wang*), to lead the life of a vile and abject man. Is he worthy to be thought of more? In speaking about him, the heart is wrung with sadness."

In the meantime, the *Pou-sa* (the Bodhisattwa), having bathed in the river *Ni-lien* (Nairanjaná), and having sate down under the *Pou-ti* (Bodhidruna) tree, arrived at perfect knowledge, and was surnamed *Master of gods and men.* He remained immovable and taciturn, thinking only of discovering those who deserved to be saved. "This son of *'Yo-t'eou-lan*,"[1] said he, "has devoted himself to meditation which excludes all thought (Naivasanjná samádhi). He is worthy of receiving the excellent Law."

The Devas who traverse the air announced to him this intelli-

[1] This word is incorrect. It should be *Yo-to-lo-mo-tseu* (Udra, son of Ráma).

gence: "It is already seven days since the son of *Yo-t'eou-lan* (Udra Rámaputra) has abandoned life."

Jou-laï (the Tathágata), sighing deeply, (said): "Why did not he meet with me? When he was on the point of understanding the excellent Law, why did he suddenly change existence?"

He then reflected anew attentively, and searched in the midst of the world. "There is still" (said he) *'O-lan-kia-lan* (Áráḍa Kálâma), who has arrived at the condition of being detached from all (Akinchavyáyatana). To him I must communicate the sublime principles (of my doctrine).

The Devas resumed: "It is five days since he died." *Jou-laï* (the Tathágata), sighed again, lamenting his scant good fortune. Once more reflecting, he said: "To whom ought I still to teach the Law? In the Deer-Park (Mṛigadáva) are five men whom, in preference to others, I ought to instruct and guide."

At this moment, *Jou-laï* (the Tathágata) rose up from under the tree of *Pou-ti* (Bodhidruma, the tree of knowledge), and repaired to the Deer-Park (Mṛigadáva). Tranquillity breathed in his whole person, and diffused afar a divine light. His hair had the lustre of jade; and his body was as yellow as pure gold. He advanced, with a calm step, to give directions to those five personages. They, perceiving *Jou-laï* (the Tathágata) in the distance, said to one another: "He who comes there is *I-tsie-i-tch'ing* (Sarvárthasiddha). Months and years pass away without his being able to obtain the fruit of sanctity (Bodhi). The end of his ambition has already eluded him. This is why he seeks us as disciples. We must, each of us, remain mute before him. Let us be careful not to rise to go meet and salute him."

Jou-laï approached them with slow steps, moving all beings by his divine majesty. These five men, forgetting their compact, advanced towards him, saluting him; and, having questioned him, they followed him respectfully. *Jou-laï* drew them gradually to himself, and taught them the sublime principles (of the Law). When they had done living in fixed habitations during the rainy season, they acquired the fruit of *Bodhi*.

When he had gone two or three *lis* [about half a mile] to the east of the Deer-Park (Mṛigadáva), he came to a *Stúpa*. By its side is a dry reservoir, eighty paces in circuit, called both the *Saviour-Reservoir* (Jívakahrada?) and the *Hero's-Reservoir* (Tyágihrada?). Here is what is read on this subject, in the ancient descriptions (of this kingdom):—

"Several hundred years ago, a recluse abode near this reservoir. He had built a hut, that he might live apart from the world. He had studied magic, and fathomed the science of the gods. He was able to transform small pieces of brick into precious stone, and to metamorphose animals; but, nevertheless, he was not able to cause himself to be conveyed by the winds and clouds, and to follow, through the air, the chariot of the immortals. He pored over mysterious diagrams, and explored the secrets of the ancients, to discover, withal, the science of the *Ṛishis*. Their books informed him, that 'the *Ṛishis*, endowed with a divine power, possess the art of living eternally. If you wish to acquire this science, it is necessary, first of all, to form an immovable resolution, to erect an altar six feet in circuit, and to cause that a hero, renowned for his fidelity and courage, should arm himself with a long sabre, and stand guard at the corner of the altar, to suppress his breathing, and to remain speechless from evening till morning. He who seeks to become a *Ṛishi* must seat himself on the middle of the altar, must hold in his hand a long sabre, must recite magical prayers, and must concentrate within himself his faculties of seeing and hearing. On the approach of morning, he will rise to the rank of a *Ṛishi*. The sharp sabre which he holds in his hand will be changed into a valuable sword; he will dart up into the heavens, and pass through the air; he will become the king of the company of *Ṛishis*. Brandishing his sword, he will issue his orders; and he will be gratified in all his desires. He will never more be liable to feebleness, to old age, to sickness, or to death.'

"When the recluse had learned the secret of becoming a *Ṛishi*, he undertook a journey, with the object of discovering a man of heroic character, and spent long years in active search, without finding the object of his desire. In the course of time, he met with a man, in a certain city, who walked along uttering plaintive cries. The recluse, observing his appearance, experienced a lively feeling of joy. Then, drawing near, he questioned him softly, and said; 'What has reduced you to utter these rending moans?'

" 'Being poor and needy,' he replied, 'I was working for wages, for the relief of my necessities. My master, seeing my sad condition, employed me with entire confidence, promising, at the end of five years, to reward me most liberally. On this, I laboured diligently, forgetting pain and fatigue. But, when the fifth year had almost expired, having one day committed an offence, I was shamefully beaten, and could obtain nothing. Thinking on this misfortune, I am consumed with chagrin, (and I ask myself) who will take pity on me?'

" The recluse directed him to accompany him. On their arriving at his hut, by the aid of a metamorphosis, wrought by his magical power, he obtained for him, in an instant, an excellent repast. Then he made him bathe in the reservoir, clothed him with new garments, and gave him five hundred pieces of gold, adding: 'When you shall have spent them, you must come and ask me for more. I beg it of you not to scorn me.'

" From that time, he often gave him valuable presents, secretly lavished great kindness upon him, and filled his heart with gratitude. The valiant champion asked that he might sacrifice his life to repay all these favours.

" 'I was seeking for a brave champion,' said the recluse to him, 'and now, after a great number of years, I have had the good fortune to find him in you; and your remarkable aspect answers to the image of him which I had pictured to myself. I have only one thing to ask of you, which is, simply not to utter a word during an entire night.'

" 'Why do you speak,' answered the champion, 'of merely keeping silence? I would not refuse even to die for you.'

" On this, he constructed an altar; and, in order to acquire the divine art of the *Ṛishis,* he did everything according to the prescribed formula. He sat down, waiting for the setting of the sun. As night drew on, each acquitted himself of his respective duty. The recluse recited magical prayers; and the brave champion held his sharp sabre in his hand. But, a little before dawn, suddenly he uttered piercing cries. At this moment, a mass of fire descended from heaven, and volumes of flame and smoke rose like clouds. The recluse forthwith carried away the man, and made him enter the reservoir, that he might escape death; and then he questioned him thus: 'I admonished you to maintain silence. Why did you utter cries of terror?'

"The champion replied: 'After I had received your orders, and the middle of the night had arrived, my spirit was troubled, as though in a dream; and wondrous portents appeared, one after another, to my eyes. I saw my old master, who came and accosted me with kind words. Although I cherished lively gratitude for his kindnesses, yet I controlled myself, without answering him a single word. The man became angry. I was immediately put to death, and remained, for some time, in that sad condition. On beholding my own corpse, I heaved deep sighs; and I also resolved not to speak for ages, in acknowledgement of your generosity. Shortly after, I was born again, in the house of a Bráhman, in Central India. When my new mother had conceived me, and brought me into the world, I endured all sorts of pains and hardships. Always impressed with a sense of your goodness, I never uttered a single word. When I had finished my studies, put on the cap of manhood, and contracted marriage, I lost my father and mother, and my wife presented me with a son. On thinking, day by day, of your bygone kindnesses, I still controlled myself, and refrained from speaking. All my relations and neighbours were astonished at my silence. When I had passed the age of sixty-five years, my wife said to me: "You must speak; and, if you persist in your silence, I will kill your son."

"'I then said to myself: "I am well advanced in years, and I already see myself broken by old age; this infant is my only child." If I uttered those cries, it was only to disarm my wife, and to prevent her from killing it.'

"'It is my fault,' replied the recluse. 'All this perturbation was only the work of Mára (the demon).'

"The brave champion testified his gratitude to him. He groaned bitterly at the failure of his design, and died of indignation and anger. As he had escaped the disaster of the fire, the reservoir was called the *Saviour-Reservoir* (Jívakahrada?); and,—inasmuch as this man perished for wishing to display his gratitude,—also, the *Reservoir of the Hero* (Tyágihrada?)."

To the west of the "Reservoir of the Hero" (Tyágihrada?), is the *Stúpa* of the three quadrupeds. In the age when *Jou-laï* (the Tathágata) was leading the life of a *Pou-sa* (Bodhisattwa), it was at this place that he burnt his body. In the beginning of the *kalpas* (ages) there were, in this forest, a fox, a hare, and a monkey, who, although of different species, were united by a close friendship. At that time, *Chi* (S'akra), the master of the gods, wished to make proof of those who were leading the life of a Bodhisattwa. He descended upon the earth, and, assuming the appearance of an old man, spoke thus to these three animals: "My children, do you take pleasure in this peaceful and retired spot? Do you feel no fear?"

"We tread upon the tufted herbage," they replied; "we roam in a thick forest; and, although we are of different species, we take pleasure together; we are tranquil and happy."

"Having learned," rejoined the old man, "that you were bound in a close friendship, forgetting the burthen of age, I have come from a great distance expressly to find you out. To-day I am oppressed with hunger. What will you give me to eat?"

"Be so good," said they, "as to remain here a little, while we run and make search."

On this, forgetting their own interests, and animated with a common spirit, they went away, each apart from the rest, in quest of food. The fox, having skirted a river, brought between his teeth a fresh carp; the monkey gathered fruits and flowers, of great rarity, from the depth of the forest. Then they reassembled at the place where the old man had halted, and presented them to him. But the hare returned empty-handed, and began to gambol from right to left.

"From what I see," remarked the old man to him, "you have not shared in the sentiments of the monkey and the fox. Each of them has given me proof of his devotion; but the hare has returned empty, and he alone has not given me food. These words suffice for making him understood."

The hare, on hearing these severe reproaches, spoke thus to the fox and the monkey: "Gather together a quantity of wood and grass; and I will then do something."

At these words, the fox and monkey ran, emulously, and brought grass and branches. When they had made a high heap of them, and a strong fire was about to be kindled, the hare said: "O man, full of humanity, I am small and feeble; and, as I was unable to find what I sought after, I venture to offer my humble body to furnish a repast for you."

Scarcely had he ceased speaking, when he cast himself into the fire, and there died immediately.

At that instant, the old man resumed his form of king of the gods (S'akra), collected the bones of the hare, and, having for a long time heaved sorrowful sighs, said to the fox and the monkey: "How is it that he was the only one able to make such a sacrifice? I am powerfully affected by his devotion; and, not to let the memory of it perish, I will place him in the disk of the moon, so that his name may go down to posterity."

Hence, all the natives of India say, that it is since this event occurred that a hare has been seen in the moon.

In after times, a *Stúpa* was erected at this spot.

APPENDIX C.

Respecting Divodás, Professor Wilson says:—"Some rather curious legends are connected with this prince, in the Váyu and Brahma Puráṇas, and Hari Vaṁśa, and, especially, in the Káśí Khaṇḍa of the Skanda Puráṇa. According to these authorities, S'iva and Párvatí, desirous of occupying Káśi, which Divodása possessed, sent Nikumbha, one of the Gaṇas of the former, to lead the prince to the adoption of Buddhist doctrines; in consequence of which, he was expelled from the sacred city, and, according to the Váyu, founded another on the banks of the Gomatí.

"Some further illustration is derivable from the Mahábhárata, S'anti-Parvan, Dána-dharma. Haryaśwa, the king of the Káśis, reigning between the Ganges and the Yamuná (or in the Doab), was invaded and slain by the Haihayas, a race descended, according to this authority, from S'aryáti, the son of Manu. Sudeva, the son of Haryaśwa, was also attacked and defeated by the same enemies. Divodása, his son, built and fortified Benares, as a defence against the Haihayas; but in vain; for they took it, and compelled him to fly. He sought refuge with Bharadwája, by whose favour he had a son born to him, Pratardana, who destroyed the Haihayas, under their king Vítahavya, and re-established the kingdom of Káśi."

Professor Wilson's Translation of the *Vishṇu Puráṇa* (Hall's edition), vol. iv., pp. 33, 40.

INDEX.

Ádampura Mahalla, 299
Ád-Bisheśwar, 55, 318–321
Áditya, 127
Ádkesav, or Vishṇu, 185
Ád-Mahádeva, 104, 105
Agni, 160, 170
Agwán, 90
Ahalyá Bai, Rani, 167
Ahmad Ḳhán, Saiyid, 339
Ahyabar Galí, 154
Aiśwarya Náráyaṇ Siṅh, Babu, Secretary of the Benares Institute, 339
Ájnáta Kauṇḍinya, 372
Ajunta Caves, 20
Álamgírí Mosque, 312–314
Aláuddín, 31
Alipore Mahalla, 274
Alpmṛiteśwar, 80
Ambheri, Rajas of, 131
Amṛit Kuṇḍ, 219
Amrit Rao, 168
Anant Chaudas Melá, 222
Anark Chaudas Melá, 224
Ancient Remains, Benares :—
  Bakaríyá Kuṇḍ, 273–287
  No. I. Ráj Ghát Fort, 292–297
  No. II. Near Ráj Ghát Fort, 297, 298
  No. III. Small Mosque in Budáoṅ Mahalla, 298, 299
  Ancient Mound or Ridge, 299–302
  No. IV. Tiliyá Nálá and Maqdam Sáhib, 302–305
  No. V. Láṭ Bhairo, 305–308
  No. VI. Battís Khambhá, 308–310
  No. VII. Arhái Kangúra Mosque, 310–312
  Hindu Temple of Kírtti Bisheśwar, Álamgírí Mosque, 312–314
  No. VIII. Chaukhambhá Mosque, 314, 315
  No. IX. Aurungzeb's Mosque, near Bisheśwar Temple, 316–318, 320
  No. X. Ád-Bisheśwar Temple and neighbouring Mosque, 318–321
  No. XI. Stone Pillar, Sone ká Táláo, 321, 322
Annpúṛná, 43, 57, 150, 214
Apsarases, 162
Áráḍa Káláma, 375
Archæological Report, Major-General Cunningham's, 236–243, 250–254, 256–260, 261, 262
Arhái Kangúra Mosque, 310–312
Arjuna, 170
Aryan race, 1, 24
Ashṭang-Bhairo, 128
Ashṭa Śakti, 257
Ashṭbhují, 153
Así, 34, 326
Asiatic Researches, 219, 250
Asiatic Society of Bengal, 236, 242, 245, 248, 251, 252, 257, 260, 264, 269, 270, 273, 286
Así Sangam and Ghát, 139, 177, 178, 184, 217, 218, 221
Asnán Játrá Melá, 217
Aśoka, 19, 21, 85, 233, 234, 244, 265, 266, 290, 306, 367, 368
Assyrian Architecture, 22
Asuf-ud-Daulah, Nawab, 198
Atri, 151
Aurangzeb or Álamgír, 28, 32, 39, 51, 55, 110, 112, 128, 153, 156, 191, 192, 306, 312, 313
Aurangzeb's Mosque, 316–318, 323
Ausán Ganj Mahalla, 87, 116, 117, 120, 151, 197

Baber, Emperor, 255
Bágeśwarí, 89, 90, 164, 214
Baijnáth, 227
Bakaríyá Kuṇḍ, Ancient Remains at, 25, 27, 93, 215, 216, 273–287, 292, 293, 308, 309, 310, 323
Balbhadra, 120
Baldeo, 170
Bálkṛishṇa, 151
Ballantyne, Dr., late Principal of the Government College, Benares, 331
Balwant Singh, 198, 202, 212
Banár-así, 326
Banár, Raja, 35, 100, 292

Baptist Mission, Benares, 333, 334, 337
Bápú Deva S'ástrí, Pandit, Professor of Astronomy, Government College, Benares, 137, 339
Bará Ganes', 120, 121, 215, 221, 227
Baráhan Deví, 131
Barhiyá Tank, 226
Barná Piyála Melá, 225
Bárnarasí Deví, 100
Barná Sangam and Ghát, 33, 139, 178, 184, 186, 187, 221
Batasparíkhshá Melá, 218
Battís Khambhá, 308-310
Báwan Avatár, 222
Báwan-dwádasí Melá, 221
Benares,—Courts of Law, 337; Government or Queen's College, 236, 259, 307, 331, 332, 337, 347; Government Normal School, 332; Public Buildings, 337; Ward's Institution, 337
Benares Institute, 336, 337
Benares, Insurrection at, 197-212
Benares, Maharaja of, 118, 169, 212, 222, 227, 337, 338
Benares Proper, 74, 93, 94, 95, 97
Benares, Secrole, 337
Bengali Tolá, 146, 147, 155
Bengali Tolá Preparatory School, 335
Beni Rám, Pandit, 218
Bhadaini Mahalla or Ward, 167, 224
Bhadrakalpa, 369
Bhadres'war, Temple of, 168
Bhagavad Gítá, 347
Bhairo or Bhaironáth, 47, 61, 64, 74, 119, 124, 128, 150, 170
Bhairo ká Táláo, 190
Bhantá, 226
Bharadwája, 381
Bhatt Brahmans, 347
Bhawání, Rani, 158, 164, 167, 175, 180
Bhikshus, The Five, 5, 6, 11, 365, 368, 372
Bhilsa, 29, 244
Bhilsa Topes, 20, 245, 267, 268
Bhím, 217
Bhímchandí, 179
Bhittiyantra, 136
Bhobanes'war, Temple of, 29
Bhút, 119
Bhút-Bhairo, 119
Bijai Dasamí Melá, 223
Bijaigarh, Fort of, 202
Bindhyáchalá, 90
Bírbhadra, 78, 153
Bird, Mr., former Resident of Benares, 194
Bísbáhuka, 84
Bishes'war, 47, 147, 156, 175, 227
Bishes'war, Temple of, 28, 50, 52, 61, 316, 317.
Bodhi, Fruit of 369, 373, 375
Bodhidruma, 374, 375
Bodhisattwa, 368-372, 374, 379
Brahma, 69, 99
Brahmá, 43, 78, 82, 140-143, 170, 185
Brahmadatta, King of Benares, 11
Brahmá-ís'war, 185
Brahmes'war, 142
Bráhman, 14, 40, 48, 69, 84, 102, 126, 135, 148, 152, 191, 193, 194, 267, 346, 354, 378
Brahma Purána, 381
Brahmávarta, 266
Brahmaloka, 143
Brahmo Samáj, 336, 344, 345, 354
Brambanan, temple of, 260
Briddhkál, 73, 75, 80, 94, 156, 312
Briddhkál Melá, 218
Budáoṅ Mahalla, 298
Buddha, or Gautama, 5, 6, 85, 153, 232-234, 238, 248, 251, 259, 261, 301, 364, 369, 370, 372; The Tathágata, 242, 367, 368, 369, 370, 371, 375, 379; The Great S'ramana, 242, 365; S'rí Dharmarás'i, 251; his Life, 264, 265
Buddhas, four last, 369
Buddha Gayá, 259
Buddhi, 72
Buddha, Law of, 5, 256, 266, 364-366, 368, 369, 374, 375
Buddhism, Decline and Fall of, 267, 268-270
Buddhist Confession of Faith, 242, 262, 263
Buddhist Missionaries, 12, 301
Buddhist Supremacy in India, 12, 30, 265, 266
Buddhist Triad, 259
Burnouf, M. 242
Búrwá-Mangal Melá, 228, 229
Buyers, Rev. W., 192, 193

Carnac, Lieutenant-Colonel, 200
Chakravartin, King, 374
Chakrayantra, 137
Chakr-pushkarni, 69
Cha men (S'ramana), 365
Chandan Ekádasí Melá, 217
Chandra, 144
Chandra Gupta, 265
Chandrakánta, 107
Chandra-kúp, 143, 144
Chandramá, 170
Charana-páduká, 70
Chaturbhuj, 130, 151
Chaukhá Ghát, 218, 223, 225, 226
Chaukhambhá, 223, 224
Chaukhambhá Mosque, 314, 315
Chaukí Ghát, 154

Chausaṭhí Deví, 90, 228
Cheit Singh, Raja, 34, 169, 172, 197, 198–212, 228, 250
Cherry, Mr., formerly Political Resident of Benares, 338
Chi-kia-meou-ni (S'ákya Muni), 369
Chi-kia-pou-sa (S'ákya Bodhisattwa), 369
Chi (S'akra), 379
Chitraghaṇṭá, 251
Chitrkoṭ, 221, 222
Christianity, 38, 40
Church of England Mission, Benares, 333, 334, 337
Clive, Lord, 361
Cunningham, Major-General, late Government Archæologist in India, 235, 236, 244, 250, 255, 256, 260, 265, 268

Dafálí, 216
Daitya, 114
Daksh, Raja, 77, 79, 80
Dakshes'war, 76, 80
Dálbhyes'war, 129, 130
Dána-dharma, 381
Daṇḍpán, 62, 65, 66
Dangal Melá, 229
Dasahrá Melá 217, 222
Das'ás'amedh Ghát and Temple, 43, 95, 139, 140, 142, 153, 223, 228, 333
Das'áswamedhes'war, 142
Dattátreya, 151
Davidson, Mr., 261
Deer Park of the Immortal, 232, 233, 234, 235, 364, 367, 372, 375
Deo Narain Singh, Raja, K.C.S.I., President of the Benares Institute, 183, 339
Devadatta, 371
Dhamnár, caves of, 259
Dhan, worship of, 223
Dhan Teras Melá, 223
Dhanwantari, 219
Dharaddí Melá, 228
Dharma, 5, 85
Dharmanada, 107
Dharmes'war, 86
Dharm-kúp, 35, 86
Dharmsálá, or hostel, 179
Ḍhelá Chauth Melá, 221
Dhruv, Dhruves'war, Dhruves'wara, 128
Dhúpchaṇḍí, 177
Dhútapápá, 107
Digaṅsayantra, 137
Divodás, 47, 82, 84, 140, 141, 143, 381
Divodáses'war, 84
Díwálí Melá, 224
Duláres'war, 154
Duncan, Mr. Jonathan, former Resident of Benares, 250, 252
Durg, 159–162
Durgá, 47, 144, 155, 157–159, 162, 163, 166, 170–172, 214, 223, 228.
Durgá-kuṇḍ, 33, 90, 166, 219
Durgá Melá, 219, 223
Durgbijay Singh, Babu, 212
Durvásas Ṛishi, 114, 151
Dwáraká-tírth, 218
Dwárpáles'war, 64

Egyptian Architecture, 22
Ellora, cave at, 20
Equinoctial Circle, 137

Fa Hian, 35, 231, 232, 234, 235, 256, 266, 267, 364
Fa Hian's Narrative concerning Benares, 364, 365
Faiz-ulla-Ḳhán, Nawab, 201
Fátimá Melá, 219
Fergusson's Handbook of Architecture, 19, 29, 283, 294
Foe (Buddha), 364, 365
Foe Koue Ki, 231, 364
Fouceaux, M., 261
Fowke, Mr., formerly Resident of Benares, 201
Futteh Narain Singh, Babu, Vice-President of the Benares Institute, 339

Gáe Ghát, 104
Gajendramoksh, 170
Gandharvas, 162
Gaṇes' or Siddha-vináyak, 47, 49, 59, 65, 71, 74, 76, 83, 90, 100, 106, 122, 144, 150, 152, 163, 166, 168
Gaṇes' Chauth Melá, 227
Gangá (the Ganges), 57, 98, 107, 142, 147, 170, 174, 194, 217, 356
Gangá-putras, or Sons of the Ganges, 16, 46, 352
Gangá-Saptamí Melá, 216
Garuḍ, 171
Gau-gaur Melá, 214
Gaurí, 98, 140, 160–162
Gaurí-kuṇḍ, 150
Gaurí S'ankar, 59
Gayá, 5, 124, 139
Gází Miyáṅ Dargáh, 215, 216
Gází Miyáṅ Melá, 215
Gází Sultán, 216
Ghaṇṭákarṇa, 118
Gor Jí, Pandit, 90, 105
Govardhan, 171
Gṛidhrakúṭa, 368
Griffith, Mr. R. T. H., Principal of the Government College, Benares, 331
Gulzár Mahalla, 305
Gunahrí, 220, 221
Gupta era, 28, 55, 286, 290, 306, 326

Guru-púrṇimá, 218.
Gyan-Bápí or Gyán-Kúp, 53, 73

Haihayas, race of, 381
Hall, Dr. Fitzedward, Librarian of the India Office, 35, 236, 331, 381
Hanumán, or Mahábír, 59, 73–76, 89, 91, 100, 126, 129, 170, 224
Hardwár, 139
Hardy, Rev. R. Spence, 5
Hari Gupta, 261
Harináth, Temple of, 149
Hari Vaṁs'a, 381
Haryas'wa, King of the Kás'is, 381
Heng (Ganges), 35, 364
Himáchal, Mount, 149
Hindu Temples in Benares, number of, 41, 42
Hindu Triad, 185
Hiouen Thsang, 8, 231, 232, 234, 235, 255, 256, 259, 262, 267, 268, 272, 286, 366
Hiouen Thsang's Narrative concerning Benares, 366–380
Hipparchus, 134
Hiraṇyakas'ipu, 215
Hodgson, Mr. B. H., late Political Resident in Nepál, 242, 262
Holí Melá, 192, 227, 228
Holiká, 228
Hom, 127
Horne, Mr. C., late Judge of Benares, 273, 296, 297
Hou-ming-pou-sa (Prabhápála ? Bodhisattwa), 369
Humáyún, Emperor, 255

Indian Architecture, 22, 24, 28, 52
Indra, 160, 161, 170, 171
I's'ána, 251
I's'ipattana Vihára, 5, 6, 11, 256
I's'war, 69, 128
I's'war-Gangí, 116, 220
I-tsie-i-tch'ing (Sarvárthasiddha), 373–375

Jagannáth, 120, 139, 177, 217, 218, 229
Jagat Ganj, 26, 250
Jagat Singh, Babu, 25, 250–253, 260
Jáges'war, 116, 151
Jahnu Ṛishi, 216
Jaina, 289, 294, 317, 318
Jaiṭpurá Mahalla, 89
Jala, 160
Jamanes'war, 98
Jámbavatí, 127
Jamditíyá Melá, 225
Jam Ghát, 225
Jamná, 98, 142, 170, 225
Jánakí, 90
Jarṇanada, 107
Játakas, 11
Jaunpore, Atállah Mosque, 282, 283
Jaunpore, Jama Mosque, 282, 283
Jay Náráyaṇ Ghosál, Raja, 333
Jay Siṅh, Raja, 129, 132
Jewels, The Three, 369
Jogí-bír, 277
Jou-laï (the Tathágata), 367–371, 375, 379
Julien, M. Stanislas, 231, 366, 369
Jwaraharés'war, 91

Kailás, 79, 83
Kajrí, 220
Kajrí Melá, 220, 221
Kálí, 74
Kálí S'ankar Ghosál, Raja, 338
Kalká, 225
Kál-Kúp, 66
Kámes'war, Kámanánáth, 113, 114
Kandhawa, 177
Kánheri, caves at, 259
Kantit, Raja of, 220
Kapila, Raja of, 264
Kapildhárá, 178, 180
Kapilmochan Tank, 190, 195
Kardames'war, 178, 179
Kárkotak Nág Tírth, 220
Kárleṅ Cave, 20
Karṇghaṇṭa, 118
Kártavírya, 170
Kártik Púrṇimá Melá, 225
Káshaya, or Brown Vestment of Buddha, 234, 262, 370, 371
Kás'í-deví, 118, 119
Kás'í Karwaṭ, 55
Kás'í Khaṇḍa, 68, 76, 82, 88, 96, 98, 106, 149, 159, 218, 381
Kás'í, Kingdom of, 35, 36, 364, 381
Kásí-máhátmya, 96
Kásípurá Mahalla, 117
Kásí-rahasya, 96
Kás'yapa Buddha, 369
Kauṇḍinya, 365, 368
Kedár, 93, 95, 149, 156
Kedáres'war, Kedárnáth, 147, 149, 150, 153
Keou lin (Kauṇḍinya), 365
Kern, Dr., late Anglo-Sanskrit Professor, Benares, 332
Ketu, 66
Kewal Galí, 155
Kiachi (Kás'í), 35, 364
Kia-ye-po-fo (Kás'yapa Buddha), 369
Kinnaras, 162
Kiraṇanadí, 107
Kírtti Bishes'war, 312–314
Kittoe, Major, late Government Archæologist in India, 25, 235, 250, 251, 254, 268, 269, 331, 334
Kiu tan (Buddha), 365
Klaproth, M., 231, 364
Koṭ-Linges'war, 100
Koṭwál, 124

Kṛishṇa, 8, 87, 127, 170–172, 345
Kṛishṇa Lílá, 227
Kuber, 170
Kurukshetr Táláo, 167

Ladak, 259
Lakshmaṇ, 90, 91, 150
Lakshmaṇbála, 109
Lakshmí, 74, 102, 113, 126, 222, 224
Lakshmí Kuṇḍ or Tank, 222
Lakshmínáráyaṇ, 74, 150
Lál Khán, 188
Landresse, M., 231, 364
Lanká, 223
Láṭ Bhairo, 305–308
Latífpúr, Fort of, 202, 208, 209
Layard, Mr., 22
Lingam Lakshmají, Pandit, 354
Linges'war, 103
Lolárik Chhaṭh Melá, 221
Lolárik Kúáṅ, 167, 221
Lomas'a Ṛishi, 20
London Mission, Benares, 333, 334, 337
Loṭá-Bhaṇṭá, 125, 126
Loṭá-Bhaṇṭá Melá, 226

Macaulay on Warren Hastings, 9
Machaudarí, 114, 115
Mádhodás ká Dewhrá, 110
Mádhodás's Garden, 197, 208, 209, 210, [211
Maga, 173
Mahábhárata, 4, 67, 167, 217, 381
Mahábír: see Hanumán
Mahádeva: see S'iva
Mahákál, 67
Mahákálí, 160, 161, 170
Mahendra, son of As'oka, 266
Mahes'wara, 9, 233, 367
Mahi Pála, 251
Mahmúd Sultan, 215, 289
Mahommad Sháh, Emperor, 132, 133
Mahomet, 13
Maitreya, 365, 368, 369
Mandaráchal, 140
Mangalgaurí, 107
Maṇikarniká Temple and Ghát, 67, 69, 72, 104, 139, 177, 178, 186
Mán-Mandil Ghát, 129, 137, 139
Mán-Mandil Observatory, 43, 129, 131, 135, 136, 137, 273, 300
Mánsarwar, 150, 151.
Mán Siṅh, Raja, 42, 151
Manu, 381
Maqdam Sáhib, 302–305
Mára, 378
Marhiyá Ghát, 216
Márkaṇḍa, Márkaṇḍes'war, 76
Markham, Mr., formerly Resident of Benares, 201, 204
Maṭh, 145
Mathurá-prasád, Babu, 340
Martin Luther, 351
Mémoires de Hiouen Thsang, 231, 366–380
Mi le (Maitreya), 365, 368
Mill, Rev. Dr., 242
Minarets, The, 111, 112
Minor Vehicle, 366, 367
Mír Ghát, 84, 86, 224
Míra Sáhib, Tomb of, 302
Mogaliputra, 244
Mohammadan Mosques in Benares, number of, 41, 42
Mohurram, Festival of the, 191, 214
Moon, The, 109, 151
Mount Himálaya, Raja, 80
Mṛigadáva (The Deer Park), 367, 372, 375
Muktikshetra, 68
Mullens, Rev. Dr., 39
Müller's (Professor Max) History of Ancient Sanskrit Literature, 4
Mural Quadrant, 136, 137
Muskábád, 324
Mutiny, The Sepoy, 294

Nága, Nages'war, 75, 89, 220, 262
Nagarpradakshṇá Melá, 226
Nág Kúáṅ, 87, 88, 220
Nág Panchamí Melá, 220
Nairanjaná, 374
Nálanda, 259
Nának Sháh, 102
Nárad Muni, 77, 78, 170
Náráyaṇa, 102
Narsiṅh, 113, 114, 215
Narsiṅh Chaudas Melá, 215
Naubat-Khána, 163
Naugrah, Nava-graha, 65, 91, 154, 257
Navarátri Melá, 214
Nepalese Temple, 137
Nie-pan (Nirváṇa), 368
Ni-houan (Nirváṇa), 364
Nikumbha, 381
Ni-lien (Nairanjaná), 374
Nirbuddhes'war, 98, 104, 105
Nirgranthas, The, 367
Nirjalá Ekádas'í Melá, 217
Nirváṇa, Nirvṛitti, 5, 257, 261, 263, 364, 368
O-jo-kiao-tch'in-jou (A'jnáta Kauṇḍinya) 368, 372
O-lan-kia-lan (A'ráḍa Káláma) 375

Pa lian foĕ (Páṭaliputra), 364
Panchgangá Ghát, 104, 107, 109, 110, 139, 225
Panchgangá Melá, 214
Panch-kosí Road, 47, 61, 123, 174, 179, 180, 181, 184, 321, 327
Panch-kosí Melá, 226
Panchmukhi, 84

Pánch Pâṇḍav, 67, 177, 217
Panch-Tírth, 140
Pâṇini, 3
Paramabodhi, 368
Paras'urâma, 170
Párvatí, 47, 68, 74, 80, 86, 381
Párvatyes'warí, 105
Pás'upatas, 367
Pâṭaliputra, 364
Patharaká Siwán, 324
Pavana, 160
Persian Architects, 23
Pĕ tsing, or S'uddhodana, 364
Pho lo naï (Benares), 35, 364
Pilgrimage of Fa Hian, 231, 364
Pilpilla Tírth and Ghât, 103, 104
Pír A'lim, 216
Pis'ách-Mochan, 123, 124, 126, 226
Pi-tsou (Bhikshus), 368
Pole Star, Temple of the, 128
Po-lo-men (Brahman), 368
P'o-lo-ni-sse (Benares), 366, 367
Popham, Major, 206
Pou-sa (Bodhisattwa), 368, 369, 370, 371, 374, 379
Pou-ti (Bodhi), 373–375
Pralâdh Ghât, 190
Pratardana, 381
Pratyeka-Buddha, 364, 368
Prayâg, 142
Prinsep, Mr. James, 21, 24, 41, 42, 69, 71, 89, 108, 115, 219, 299, 317
Ptolemy, 134
Pújá, 125
Purâṇas, 37, 95, 347
Púrṇas'ubhakaraṇí, 68
Pў tchi foĕ (Pratyeka-Buddha), 364

Rádhá Krishṇa, 87, 172
Raffles, Sir Stamford, 260
Ráhu, 65
Rájagṛiha, 368
Ráj Ghât, 190
Ráj Ghât Fort, 28, 292, 297–301, 309, 323
Rájmandira Ghât, 214
Rám, 90, 91, 113, 150, 170, 215, 222, 223, 345
Rámâyaṇa, 222, 347
Rámes'war, 177
Rám Ghât, 145, 215
Rám Lílâ, 222
Rám Lílâ Melá, 222
Rámnagar, 34, 118, 169, 173, 199, 205, 208, 209, 222, 227, 229
Rám-naumí Melá, 215
Rath-Jâtrá Melâ, 218
Ratnatraya, 369
Ratnes'war, 81, 312
Rávaṇa, 223
Remusat, M., 231, 364
River of Death, 102
Roṭá-bhanṭá, 226
Rudrsar, 143
Rukmes'war, Temple of, 154
Runjeet Singh, Maharaja, 51
Ruru, a Demon, 159

Sadânand, Lálá, 199, 200
Sahjá, 225
Sákhí-Binâyaka (Gaṇes') 59, 178
S'akra, 379, 380
S'akya Muni, 5, 6, 12, 256, 261, 264, 301, 369
Sálár-i-Mualla, 215
Sálâr Masâúd, 215
Sálâr Sáhu, 215
Sámba, 127
Sámbâdit, 128
Sami, a kind of tree, 223
Sâmkâtik, 152
Sammatíyas, School of the, 366, 367
Sánchí, 244, 294
Sangames'war, 185, 186
Sangamitrá, 266
Sangkar, 252, 253, 260
Saníchar, 56, 59
Sankaṭá Deví, 143, 144, 214
Sankaṭá Ghât, 145
Sankudhárá, 220
Sankudhárá Melâ, 218
S'anti-Parvan, 381
Saraswates'war, 98
Saraswatí, 107, 170, 185
Sárnáth, 5, 25, 35, 180, 231, 232, 235, 236, 244, 255, 262, 267, 271, 272, 286, 309–311, 321, 323, 325, 364:—
  Buddhist Stúpa, Dhamek, 236–243, 256
  Carving (No. I.) on Buddhist Stúpa, 240
  Carving (No. II.) on Buddhist Stúpa, 241
  Foundation of Ancient Stúpa, 248–254
  Chaukandí Stúpa, 255, 256
  Remains of Buddhist Monastery, 245–248, 256
  Chaityas, small Seal, 262–264
  Statues and Bass-reliefs, 248, 260, 268
Sarvárthasiddha, 372–375
S'aryáti, son of Manu, 381
Satdhárá, 244
Satí, 77, 79, 80, 121, 186
Satjug, 73
Scindia, Maharaja, 185
Seng-kia-lan (Buddhist Monastery) 365, 370
Shachi, 267
Shewei, 267
Shuhadá, Sultán-us, 215
Shujáh-ud-Daulah, Nawab, 198

Siddhes'war, 91
Siddhes'warí, 143, 144
Siddhi, 72
Siddhimátá Deví, 90
Sikh Religion, 102
Sindhia Ghát, 72
Sítá, 113, 170
S'ítalá, 65, 85, 100, 130
S'iva or Mahádeva, 47, 50, 53, 60, 65, 68, 76, 97, 108, 114, 126, 140, 143, 145, 149, 152, 157, 160, 163, 170, 172, 178, 185, 227, 251, 345, 355, 381
S'iválá Ghát, 34, 197, 204
S'iválaya, 145
S'iva Prasád, Babu, Joint Inspector of Schools Benares Division, 312, 339
S'ivapur, 177, 225, 226
S'iva-rátri Melá, 227
S'iva's Láṭ or Pillar, 190, 192, 193, 305–308
Skaṇḍa Puráṇa, 96, 381
Soma, 130
Somes'war, Temple of, 130
Sone ká Táláo, 321, 322
So-p'o-ho-la-tha-si-tho (Sarvárthasiddha), 372, 373
S'ramaṇa (Buddha), 242, 365
S'rí Maut Baija Bai, 54
S'rí Sthira Pála, 251, 254, 255
S'rí Vasanta Pála, 251, 254
Stone Pillar, Sone ká Táláo, 321, 322
Subhadra, 120
S'uddhodana, Raja, 364, 373
Sudeva, son of Haryas'wa, 381
S'ukres'war, 59
Súraj-Kuṇḍ, 127, 128
Súrajnáráyaṇ, the Sun, 47, 59, 65, 74, 100, 109, 113, 126, 127, 174, 185, 221
Surayá Melá, 222
Súrya, 170
Súrya Puráṇa, 127

Tárakes'war, 70
Ta-tseu-thsaï (Mahes'wara), 9, 367
Tching-liang-pou (Sammatíyas), 366, 367
Tch'ouen-lun-wang (King Chakravartin), 374
Thaṭherí Bazar, 223, 224
Thomas, Mr. E., late Judge of Benares, 25, 236, 245, 246, 254, 263, 268, 269
Thomason, Mr., late Lieutenant-Governor of the North-Western Provinces, India, 332
Thomson, Rev. Dr., 360
Tiliyá Nálá, 28, 300, 302–305
Tilubhaṇḍes'war, 151–153, 155
Ti-p'o-ta-to (Devadatta), 371
To kio (Prateyeka-Buddha), 368
Tresham, Mr. D., Head Master, Government Normal School, Benares, 297, 332
Trilochan, 96, 98, 100, 102, 104, 156
Triratna, 369
T'se-chi-pou-sa (Maitreya Bodhisattwa), 369
Tsing-fan (S'uddhodana, Raja), 373

Udra, son of Ráma, 374, 375

Váhan, 172
Varaṇá, 34
Váráṇasí (Benares), 34, 35, 232, 366, 367
Váráṇasí, Kingdom of, 35, 36, 233, 366
Vasishṭha, Muni, 149
Vast Solitude, Temple of the, 364
Váyu, 170
Váyu Puráṇa, 381
Vedantism, 37, 355
Vedas, The, 118, 173, 227, 347
Vedavyás, 118, 173, 174, 227
Vedavyás Melá, 227
Vináyakapála, Raja, 36
Vis'álákshí, 86
Vishama-Bhairava, 119
Vishṇu, 68, 97, 102, 114, 126, 130, 152, 170, 185, 215, 222
Vishṇu-Puráṇa, 381
Vis'wakarman Cave, 20
Vítahavya, 381
Vizianagram, Maharaja of, K.C.S.I., 182, 339, 354
Vyás, 105
Vyáses'war, 118

Wang-che-tching (Rájagṛiha), 368
Warren Hastings, 197–211
Wazír Alí, Nawab, 338
Well of Immortality, 219
Wilford, Col., 250, 251
Wilson, Professor H. H., 242, 381
Wou-yeou (As'oka), 367, 368

Yájes'wara, 116
Yamadwitíyá Melá, 225
Yantra Samráṭ, 136, 137
Yas'u, son of Sujáta, 11
Yava-vináyak, 178
Yoganí, 47
Yo-to-lo-mo-tseu (Udra, son of Ráma), 374